D0108492

A WARREN BENNIS BOOK

This collection of books is devoted exclusively to new and exemplary contributions to management thought and practice. The books in this series are addressed to thoughtful leaders, executives, and managers of all organizations who are struggling with and committed to responsible change. My hope and goal is to spark new intellectual capital by sharing ideas positioned at an angle to conventional thought—in short, to publish books that disturb the present in the service of a better future.

BOOKS IN THE WARREN BENNIS SIGNATURE SERIES

Branden	*Self-Esteem at Work*
Mitroff, Denton	*A Spiritual Audit of Corporate America*
Schein	*The Corporate Culture Survival Guide*
Sample	*The Contrarian's Guide to Leadership*
Lawrence, Nohria	*Driven*
Cloke, Goldsmith	*The End of Management and the Rise of Organizational Democracy*
Glen	*Leading Geeks*
Cloke, Goldsmith	*The Art of Waking People Up*
George	*Authentic Leadership*
Kohlrieser	*Hostage at the Table*

HOSTAGE AT THE TABLE

HOSTAGE AT THE TABLE

How Leaders Can Overcome Conflict, Influence Others, and Raise Performance

George Kohlrieser

Foreword by Joe W. Forehand, Chairman, Accenture

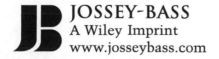

JOSSEY-BASS
A Wiley Imprint
www.josseybass.com

Published by Jossey-Bass
A Wiley Imprint
989 Market Street, San Francisco, CA 94103-1741   www.josseybass.com

Jossey-Bass books and products are available through most bookstores. To contact Jossey-Bass directly
call our Customer Care Department within the U.S. at 800-956-7739, outside the U.S. at 317-572-3986,
or fax 317-572-4002.

Jossey-Bass also publishes its books in a variety of electronic formats. Some content that appears in
print may not be available in electronic books.

Library of Congress Cataloging-in-Publication Data

Kohlrieser, George, 1944-
    Hostage at the table : how leaders can overcome conflict, influence others, and raise
performance / George Kohlrieser ; foreword by Joe W. Forehand.—1st ed.
      p. cm.
    Includes bibliographical references and index.
    ISBN-13: 978-0-7879-8384-0 (cloth)
    ISBN-10: 0-7879-8384-5 (cloth)
    1. Conflict management. 2. Leadership. 3. Management—Psychological aspects. I. Title.
HD42.K64 2006
658.4'092—dc22   2006005268

Printed in the United States of America
FIRST EDITION
HB Printing   10 9 8 7

CONTENTS

Foreword   ix
Joe W. Forehand

Preface   xiii

1   Are You Being Held Hostage Without Knowing It?   1

2   Finding Freedom Through Your Mind's Eye   19

3   The Potential of the Bonding Cycle   37

4   The Strength of a Secure Base   66

5   The Art of Conflict Management   99

6   Effective Dialogue   123

7   The Power of Negotiation   149

8   Mastering Our Emotions   176

9   Living with a Hostage-Free State of Mind   204

Notes   225

Acknowledgments   235

The Author   239

Index   241

FOREWORD

Hostage at the Table is different from other leadership books you will read. George Kohlrieser has created a powerful metaphor born out of years of personal experience and insight as a hostage negotiator. He takes an original approach, drawing on emotional, and at times frightening, situations to underscore his thesis. The result is powerful, and the themes he presents—which guide the reader on a journey to a "hostage-free" state of mind—are relevant in both business and life.

I met George for the first time many years ago. He has been a core contributor to the Accenture Leadership Development Program, which has helped develop more than three thousand of Accenture's future leaders.

Through our program, I have had the privilege of seeing George in action. Over the years, I have realized the power of his hostage negotiation framework—which emphasizes areas such as conflict resolution, bonding, and dialogue—in helping people break through many of the roadblocks to effective leadership.

There are two things our people always remember from their time with George. The first is what he calls the "mind's eye"—that our state of mind can propel us or limit us; it is an entirely individual choice. As George points out, in life, as in business, if we set the stage in our mind's eye with the outcome we want to achieve, we set the stage for success.

In my more than thirty years in business—working directly with hundreds of different enterprises—I have become a firm believer that the highest performers (whether individuals or organizations) see possibilities, not limitations. That said, everyone experiences some very high points and some very low ones. In my view, the low points tend to separate the best leaders from the rest. Those who emerge from tough times are winners who make no excuses. They refuse to be seen as victims.

In fact, this way of thinking has had a profound impact on my own experience. Leaders have the power to influence, motivate, and inspire people to achieve extraordinary things. If there is one quality that defines an exceptional leader it is optimism and a "can do" spirit. To me that is a key element of living "hostage free."

The second thing our people remember so vividly is how George approaches conflict resolution. As he demonstrates in our courses, leaders need to "put the fish on the table": instead of dancing around a tough issue, one should acknowledge it, communicate honestly, and show mutual respect.

Perhaps not surprisingly, many leaders struggle to develop this behavior. George offers help by encouraging leaders to view dialogue as a means to a greater truth. Most of us would agree that leaders need to excel at listening and at dialogue. However, George shows that leaders actually can block dialogue without even realizing it or become a hostage when others block the dialogue. This is a critical point because when managed well, dialogue and conflict resolution can build stronger teams and help people feel a much greater sense of engagement.

Overall, the themes in this book echo a constant theme at Accenture about what it takes to achieve and sustain high performance. We believe that the highest-performing organizations have exceptional leaders who know how to get the best from their teams. They also have a "secret sauce" that is the essence of the organization and its people that cannot be copied by competitors.

I believe George would agree. He also recognizes that the ongoing challenge for organizations of all sizes is how to get people to feel empowered, see beyond obstacles, and act like winners—not be held hostage. George offers an answer: leaders can infuse their workforces with powerful mind-sets. They can help people step up and "will" themselves to what and where they want to be.

George's stories remind us that we are not victims of circumstance—we have the power to react. Our actions will always determine the outcome. That makes all the difference.

This book is certain to make a positive difference in leadership and business, and I want to thank George for making his experiences available to all of us. His insights are truly relevant to anyone or any organization seeking to perform at the highest level. This book will inspire you to raise your game.

April 2006   JOE W. FOREHAND
                                                            CHAIRMAN, ACCENTURE

To my wife, Cinzia, and our four children—
Doug (deceased), Paul, Giulia, and Andrew—
for their energy, their inspiration, and the great
learning opportunities they have provided me with
over the years

PREFACE

The seeds of this book were sown after a defining moment in my life in a hospital emergency room in Dayton, Ohio. As a young psychologist working for the Dayton Police Department, I accompanied the police to the hospital to deal with an agitated, violent man who was brought to the hospital with injuries resulting from a stabbing wound inflicted by a girlfriend. While I talked with this man in a treatment room, he suddenly grabbed a large pair of scissors and took a nurse and me hostage, saying he would kill both of us. For two hours we pursued a dialogue focused on him, his life-threatening injuries, and the care required to keep him alive. The turning point in the crisis came when I asked, "Do you want to live, or do you want to die?" "I don't care," was his answer. I then asked, "What about your children losing their father?" He visibly changed mental states and began to talk about his children rather than his anger at his girlfriend and the police. In the end, he agreed to put the scissors down voluntarily and allowed the nurse and a surgical team to treat him. In an even more surprising moment after putting the scissors down, this very "violent" man then approached me, with tears in his eyes, gave me a hug, and said, "Thank you, George. I forgot how much I love my kids." His words of gratitude wired my brain forever to believe in the power of emotional bonding, dialogue, and negotiation with even the most dangerous person. I also surprised myself with the power I had to regulate my own emotion from sudden terror to calm, focused resolve.

The lessons I learned on that evening in 1968 are just as valuable to me now as a professor of leadership and organizational behavior as they were in my earlier careers as a clinical psychologist, a police psychologist, a hostage negotiator, an organizational psychologist, and radio talk-show host. I discovered that

my learnings as a hostage negotiator could be applied successfully to situations of powerlessness and entrapment in which a
person is a metaphorical hostage rather than a physical hostage.
In fact such potential "hostage" situations occur everyday professionally and personally.

My goal in this book is to offer what I have learned as a hostage
negotiator for you to apply to situations in which you may be a
metaphorical "hostage" in your life. Any time you feel entrapped,
powerless, and helpless, you are, in fact, a "hostage." While this
book especially addresses leaders in organizations, it can be helpful
to everyone in all walks of life.

Throughout my life, working with individuals, leaders, teams,
and organizations, I have found many people held hostage by others, by situations, or even by their own emotions. They responded
similarly to someone physically held hostage when there was no
real "gun to their head." They behaved like hostages even though
they didn't realize it and, in fact, had the power to do something
about it. I also discovered people who could easily have been held
"hostage" by a person or situation and yet were not. In fact, the
hostage metaphor is a powerful model to understand behavior,
and the hostage negotiation framework can help anyone who is a
metaphorical hostage.

The story of my life is closely entwined with how this thinking
came together. I was born into a family of five brothers and sisters
on a farm in Ohio. My parents owned and worked the land as
farmers as well as running a poultry business. As the eldest male
child, it was a great honor for me to enter a Catholic seminary at
age thirteen with the goal of becoming a priest. This experience
brought with it many benefits: learning to live in a community;
periods of intense study, education, and play; the forming of values and character; and learning about meditation and spirituality.
One negative aspect was the loss of a "normal" adolescence. After
some eight years, what had been a positive experience slowly
became a negative ordeal when I could not face the truth that I
wanted to leave. I had, in fact, become what I now understand to
be a hostage to my own conflicting emotions about being in the
seminary. I was fortunate enough to know a wise, extraordinary
man, Father Edward Maziarz, who became a confidant. During one
earthshaking dialogue, he looked right into my eyes and, with the

wisdom of ages, calmly said, "George, you are free. You have the right to choose to do whatever you want." It was like a lightning bolt coming out of the sky that forever changed my destiny. His words and his authenticity touched the depths of my soul. The ensuing silence was sweet as my mind reorganized itself to accept that as a fundamental truth. As I burst into tears of relief, I asked him to repeat those beautiful words. They unlocked a prison door that I myself had created. At that moment, I understood one of the basic truths of life—what Warren Bennis calls the "crucibles of leadership"—those defining moments in one's life that are a severe test of patience and beliefs, a trial that influences, shapes, and changes one's life forever. I was twenty-one at the time. It took another year to complete the process for me to actually leave the seminary.

In thinking back to that time, I realized that in becoming a hostage to my emotions, I had stayed in that situation long after it was time to leave. I was hostage to my grief about leaving what was familiar and all the benefits and security it brought. I also felt sad about not meeting the expectations of myself and others. I am eternally grateful to Father Ed, whose words rewired my brain and influenced my mind's eye (a concept you will read more about), thus reshaping my focus. Father Ed also represents another concept you will learn about in this book—that of secure bases, which are the anchors and supports you have in life in the form of people or goals that become major sources of empowerment. You will have the opportunity to see how important secure bases are for all of us.

While finishing my psychology degree, I worked on a federal-government-sponsored program, the first to place psychologists side-by-side on the street with police. The purpose of the program was to reduce homicides in domestic violence situations by offering immediate help. It was crisis intervention aimed at helping the most violent people and most vulnerable victims and then linking them to the community mental health system. I became involved thanks to the trust of a wonderful psychologist, Dr. John Davis, who asked me if I was interested in the project. After saying yes, I asked him why he had asked me. He responded, "You are one of a few people I know who like challenge to this degree, and you have the caring and skill to deal with violent people and the resilience to survive whatever happens on the street." I was honored by his confidence in me. For my part, I never carried a gun, despite being advised and encouraged to do so. I knew that my best weapon was words: talking, listening, dialogue, and negotiating.

During the time I worked with that project, I personally was taken hostage four times—once in a hospital emergency room, and three times in homes during domestic violence disputes. It was those experiences that convinced me so deeply of the power of the hostage metaphor. You have the power never to be a metaphorical hostage and the power to influence and persuade others to make constructive choices even in extreme emotional states.

In 1972 I was asked by the chief of police to teach in the Dayton Police Academy in programs for police leadership development and to help establish two hostage negotiation teams—one for the Dayton, Ohio, Police Department and one for the Montgomery County, Ohio, Sheriff's Department. Since then, and for the past thirty-five years, I have been involved in hostage negotiations in many forms, including direct negotiating, and training and debriefing hostage interventions throughout the world.

At the same time, I worked in a psychiatric hospital teaching mental health specialists to work with chronic schizophrenics. I witnessed horribly inhumane treatment of patients and became a part of a change initiative to transform the way the psychiatric hospital staff dealt with patients, moving from use of force and seclusion to the concept of creating bonds with people held hostage by the most severe psychiatric disorders. I already knew from working with the police what emotional bonding could accomplish. I now discovered that the same was possible with individuals who had extreme mental disorders. I will always be grateful to Dr. Carl Rogers, who personally helped me understand the power of "unconditional positive regard"—a fundamental aspect of authentic bonding. He was convinced of the importance of this concept for every human being, regardless of circumstances. That idea remains a fundamental part of how hostage negotiators create the bond to convince the hostage taker to release his hostages.

Over time, I expanded from the world of clinical psychology to the world of executive education with business leaders. In the clinical world, dialogue and conflict resolution were a central focus of my work. Simultaneously, my work in organizations involved a similar focus in a different context. Dialogue and conflict resolution build strong teams, and great leaders must be able to deal effectively with people. In my work, the hostage metaphor was a recurring theme for both individuals, teams, and organizations that were blocked, lacking empowerment, or trapped in internal or external conflicts. The resolution always came when personal power, team power, and organizational power brought an escape from the hostage mentality and the establishing of a mind-set of choice and freedom.

For many years I have taught workshops, made presentations, and given speeches to leaders across many organizations, industries, and businesses in some eighty-five countries. Time and again, I have found that even "high potential" leaders and chief executives can make enormous strides when they understand the fundamental need in humans to create attachments, to bond, and to grieve losses. This is the same understanding every hostage negotiator uses to be successful.

In this book, I have chosen powerful hostage scenarios and other violent encounters in my effort to demonstrate the ideas presented. I have found that the emotional immediacy of such stories can provide great insight into why individuals create positive or negative outcomes in business or life. I think you will find you can easily apply these ideas to your own work and life.

All the stories in this book are from real people facing real-life situations. They are taken from my own experiences: when I was a hostage negotiator or when I worked with senior business executives in companies and consulted with organizations, or from colleagues, or from the media. With the exception of the news stories, names have been changed to protect people's identities.

Can we understand what it means to be taken hostage? And how does it feel to be a hostage in a metaphorical sense—the hostage in our heads? If we understand how the mind works, and the incredible power we all possess to determine how we feel about our own lives, we can learn how to free ourselves from the limitations and mental "chains" that may stop us from reaching our full potential. We can all become better leaders, managers, employees—and better people—by doing this.

The chapters in this book are designed to take you on a journey that leads to a place where you can live and work in a hostage-free state of mind. First, it is important to understand what I mean when I use terminology related to hostage situations. The word *hostage* was taken from Old French (circa 1275) and used in relation to a person being given as security. For example, a landlord might hold a lodger as security for payment of rent or for services. The use of the word *hostage* in relation to acts of terrorism is as recent as the 1970s. Finally, in a metaphorical sense, every day we allow ourselves to be taken hostage by ourselves or others.

To overcome this metaphorical hostage mind-set, it is important to understand the concept of the "mind's eye" and how that determines the way we think, focus, and achieve results. We also need to look at the tremendous power of the bonding cycle—forming attachments, bonding, separating, grieving, and rebonding—and discover the ways the mind's eye is formed. We must appreciate how critical it is to go through the grief that results from broken and lost bonds because unresolved grief can block people from moving on in life.

Special forms of attachment and bonding are the secure bases in our lives. Secure bases are the most influential sources of what shapes our mind's eye, teaching us how to deal with the painful side of life.

In the course of this book, we will explore skills and techniques that can help resolve conflicts, even though most people naturally fear dealing with conflict. Through understanding the mind's eye and secure bases, we can learn to apply the skills for managing conflict, and to reach greater truth through a powerful dialogue. The richness of discovery when two people, or a group, enter into a true dialogue with open hearts and minds should not be underestimated in its ability to build bonds and resolve conflicts. An extension of dialogue is negotiation. We will examine the power of negotiation, encompassing influence and persuasion, and the ability it has to change the destiny of destructive processes. Recently, the Dalai Lama was quoted as saying that war is an outdated idea. Imagine using the power of talking, dialogue, and negotiation as a primary way of solving disputes.

Understanding how our emotions work is a vital aspect of self-awareness that enables us never to be a metaphorical hostage. How we master our emotions affects the amount of pain or joy we feel. There are many people who suffer deep losses and yet come back to finding joy in their life. By being master of our own selves, we increase the likelihood that we will never be held hostage by ourselves or anyone else. If we can understand the beliefs and values that shape our thinking, and recognize and respect the intrinsic dignity of the individual, we can act in ways that ensure we stay empowered even if we are a physical hostage.

The essence of these ideas is based on what I know to be true about being a person, including how to be a husband, a father, a friend, a leader, a teacher. The core concepts described here are like pieces of a puzzle. If one or more pieces are missing, then a person can easily start acting like a hostage, finding himself or herself powerless and trapped. The result is a state in which a person is not living up to his or her full potential. When all the puzzle pieces fit together, they create a beautiful picture of a place where the person has a sense of real freedom and satisfaction and can learn to live an empowered life. This is something every leader must do and model.

The twenty-first century has begun with a number of disturbing trends, including the upsurge in terrorism; the swing toward political and religious fundamentalism; widespread natural disasters, possibly caused or exacerbated by global climate change; and the phenomenon of globalization. To handle these and the stresses they cause, we need to be able to manage our emotions so that we can still find joy in life over and over again. It is my personal vision and mission that, one day, every woman, man, and child in every country around the world can live their lives with a hostage-free state of mind and appreciate the greatest gift of all—experiencing the joy of being alive. It is my hope that reading this book will be much more than an intellectual exercise for you. Through engaging in a dialogue with me and yourself, I hope that you will have an emotional experience that will stimulate your heart, mind, and spirit to take you to new places in your personal and professional life.

> To see a World in a Grain of Sand
> And a Heaven in a wild Flower
> Hold Infinity in the palm of your hand
> And Eternity in an hour
>
> *Excerpt from Auguries of Innocence,*
> *William Blake*

CHAPTER ONE

ARE YOU BEING HELD HOSTAGE WITHOUT KNOWING IT?

A nine-year-old girl was spending time with her grandparents in Kansas. The grandfather was away, so she was sleeping with her grandmother. Suddenly, she awoke in the middle of the night to see her elderly grandmother sitting up in bed and a man standing over her, dripping with rain and with a wooden club in his hand, ready to strike. The little girl felt a scream rising, and then her grandmother touched her hand and she felt a flood of calm wash over her. The grandmother said to the man, "I am glad you found our house. You've come to the right place. You are welcome here. It is a bad night to be out. You are cold, wet, and hungry. Take the firewood you have there and go stir up the kitchen stove. Let me put some clothes on, and I will find you some dry clothes, fix you a good hot meal, and make a place for you to sleep behind the stove where it is good and warm." She said no more but waited calmly. After a long pause, the man lowered the club and said, "I won't hurt you." She then met him in the kitchen and cooked him a meal, gave him the dry clothes, and made a bed up for him behind the stove. The grandmother then went back to her bed and she and her granddaughter went back to sleep. They awoke in the morning to find the man gone.

At about 10 A.M., the police arrived with a canine unit that had followed the man's scent to the house. They were shocked to find the grandmother and granddaughter still alive. The man was a psychopathic murderer who had escaped from prison the night before and had brutally slaughtered the family who were the nearest neighbors.

This amazing grandmother had created so much emotional bonding with the intruder that he could not kill her. She had treated him with a kindness and respect that had disarmed him both literally and figuratively. The fact is people do not kill people; they kill things or objects.

This remarkable story is summarized from Joseph Chilton Pearce's book *Magical Child*.[1] Think for a moment. What would you do if you were taken hostage? Imagine that you suddenly found yourself in a hostage situation where you are held with a gun against your will. How would you react? How would you feel? What would you do? What would you say to the hostage taker(s)?

Fortunately, the likelihood of physically being taken hostage is slim. However, all of us can be taken hostage metaphorically—that is, made to feel threatened, manipulated, and victimized—every day by bosses, colleagues, customers, family members, or virtually anyone with whom we interact. We can also become hostage to events or circumstances happening in our lives. We can even become hostages to ourselves, our own mind-sets, our emotions, and our habits.

Consider the following everyday situations in which people allow themselves to be taken hostage.

- While you are in your car on your way to work, another driver cuts you off. Immediately you feel angry and hostile toward the "jerk" in the other vehicle. This feeling can linger, keeping you in a negative frame of mind for a good part of the day.
- Your boss criticizes you, and in response, you defend yourself or even attack her, causing the situation to escalate. The conflict stays in your mind, resulting in a feeling of distrust between the two of you.
- You are going on a business trip and, because you are leaving, your child cries. You then rush out the door feeling guilty and telling yourself that you are a terrible parent. For the remainder of the trip, you feel down and even depressed.
- You say hello to a colleague as you walk by, but he does not respond. You begin complaining to others about your colleague, your work, and the company. Soon you start thinking, "Nobody cares about people around here."

People enraged by another person, a traffic jam, missing luggage, a lost job, a delayed flight, or even the weather—any set of external circumstances beyond their control—are allowing themselves to be taken hostage. Without realizing it, how many of us let an external event control our lives? Have you ever been upset because your holiday was ruined by bad weather? Have you ever been put into a bad mood by someone else's negative attitude? Have you ever said to someone, "You make me so upset!" If so, you have allowed yourself to be taken hostage.

Many business people I work with have high intellectual intelligence (IQ) and yet have an underdeveloped sense of emotional intelligence (EQ). They concern themselves with facts, figures, and details at the expense of the emotions, feelings, and motivations of their coworkers. Even the terms *hard facts* and *the soft stuff* used in business imply that data are somehow real and strong while emotions are weak and less important. I have seen examples of over-domineering leaders inflicting untold pain and misery on employees through their need to control both people and situations. Employees can also take their bosses hostage, minimizing success and making work a misery.

The competitive nature of many business leaders can lead to situations in which they compete with their own people and other teams rather than collaborate. Issues may then be driven under the table, and conflicts can go unresolved, creating an atmosphere of discomfort, hostility, or even fear.

I meet many business leaders who misunderstand the role of power in leadership. Through an inability to face their own personal fears or concerns, they are driven to use power, control, and formal authority as the ways to manage their people. It is easy either to take others hostage or to take yourself hostage in the work environment to avoid those difficult conversations. In contrast, open and honest dialogue is necessary to build a sustainable and high-performing team environment. By identifying a common agenda, using ongoing dialogue, and creating a climate of trust, leaders can empower their people to perform at their full potential. Harnessing the competitive instincts of the individual into a drive toward a common goal can bring out the best in every team.

Authentic leaders learn to manage their competitive nature and find that, ironically, through helping others to grow and develop, they actually have greater success than if they concentrate only on themselves.

The *American Heritage Dictionary* (4th ed.) definition of a hostage is "one that is manipulated by the demands of another." In the workplace, managers and/or staff can sometimes feel like hostages caught in the cross fire between the boss, the customers, and colleagues. Entrepreneurs who must, for example, fire twenty-five employees can be held hostage to their own emotions and feelings of pain at the action they know they must take. In today's business world, the global accessibility created by technology can intrude on family and personal lives to the extent that people feel hostage to their jobs, causing profound pain to others and themselves. Bosses who face employees who are not motivated or colleagues who are cynical may begin to feel their work has no value. The result is they become hostage to their staff's low motivation and the cynicism of colleagues.

While the likelihood of literally having a gun to our heads is thankfully small, the real concern is the endless number of situations in which we feel controlled, attacked, and compelled to respond. These situations can lead to an escalation and a sense of helplessness and feeling like a hostage.

The feeling of being held hostage is particularly apparent in interpersonal relationships when power, authority, or position are abused or unduly feared. On the one hand, the person in authority may misuse power while, on the other, the person subject to that authority may be unduly afraid. The question is, Why do so many people endure unhappy situations? Why do they stay in abusive relationships, either with a partner, at work, or with a friend? The reasons are complex, but, essentially, they have lost the ability to control their brain to focus on other options and to use personal power to act on those options.

CONTROLLING OUR BRAIN IS ESSENTIAL

According to neurologist Paul MacLean, the human brain consists of three separate, though interconnected, brains.[2] They are the reptilian brain, the limbic system (sometimes referred to as the "Paleomammalian brain"), and the neocortex.

At the most basic level, the human brain is hardwired for attack or defense. This fight-or-flight mechanism is controlled by our reptilian brain rather than by the rational part of the brain. The reptilian brain has a single focus: survival. It does not think in abstract terms or feel complex emotions. It is responsible for basic urges such as fight, flight, hunger, or fear. It is also nonverbal, operating purely at the level of visceral stimulus response. It is filled with programmed responses and will repeat the same behaviors over and over again, never learning from past mistakes. It remains active, even in deep sleep, and is the part of the brain always on the lookout for danger. It is called the reptilian brain because its basic anatomy is also found in reptiles.

The limbic system is the brain we share with other mammals, and it handles emotions and feelings. Everything in this emotional system is either agreeable or disagreeable, and survival depends on the avoidance of pain and repetition of pleasure. It appears that the limbic system is the primary seat of emotion, attention, and emotionally charged memories. It acts as a judge in relation to the neocortex, deciding whether the ideas there are good or bad. The limbic system expresses itself exclusively in the form of emotions.

The neocortex is the part of the brain that we share with the higher apes (for example, chimpanzees, gorillas, and orangutans), although ours is more sophisticated. It is in the neocortex that we process abstract thought, words, symbols, logic, and time. MacLean refers to this brain as "the mother of invention and the father of abstract thought."[3] Although all animals also have a neocortex, theirs are comparatively small. For example, a rat without a neocortex can act in a relatively normal way, whereas a human without a neocortex would be in a vegetative state. The neocortex is divided into left and right hemispheres, known as the left brain and the right brain. The left half of the cortex controls the right side of the body and vice versa. The left brain is more rational and verbal, while the right side of the brain is more spatial and artistic.

We can be taken hostage by the fight-or-flight mechanism in the reptilian brain or by the emotions in the limbic system. When taken hostage in this way, we succumb to what Daniel Goleman calls an "amygdala hijack."[4] (The amygdala is a small brain structure that is part of the limbic system; see also Chapter Eight of this book.) This occurs when someone overreacts in an impulsive, instinctive way, producing a negative outcome. The neocortex can override the emotions from the other two brains and make it possible for us to choose whether or not we become hostage to automatic emotional reactions.

The phrase "going postal" refers to one kind of situation in which the limbic system takes over and leads to serious consequences. The term was coined in the United States after a postal worker who was fired returned to the post office with a gun and shot some colleagues. Today the phrase is used in general when someone goes into a rage. Such incidents of rage happen all over the world, though more typically with words and emotions rather than physical violence. When operating at the level of primitive brain responses, people can get themselves into situations in which they repeat the same pattern and experience the same problems over and over. However, by using the neocortex, people can overcome the emotions that are hijacking them and choose to give a different meaning to a circumstance rather than complying with a set pattern that repeats a negative situation. We can learn to manage emotions and to regulate their discharge. For example, when you lose your luggage at the airport, rather than yelling at the person behind the lost luggage counter, it is better to control your anger and work with that person to find your luggage.

POWERLESSNESS IS POISON

Feeling powerless is one of the first signs of being taken hostage. Powerlessness poisons the person through feelings of helplessness or entrapment. The poison creates a cycle that provokes continuous negative interpretations of reality.

What are the words or phrases that accompany this feeling of being a hostage?

- "I have no choice."
- "I am trapped."
- "I feel terrible."
- "I just hate this."
- "It's going to be another one of those days!"

Such phrases are negative self-talk that comes from our inner worlds. The dialogue we have with ourselves inside our heads can either keep us in a hostage state or help us to control it. The hostage feeling starts with the mind-set of being forced to do something we do not want to do and then continues with a negative attitude. We can understand the poison in our state of mind by listening to the words we use. The hostage mentality focuses on the negative by repeatedly telling us what we cannot do, how helpless we are, and that we will never get what we want. Interestingly, research by Robert Schrauf, an applied linguistics expert, shows that regardless of culture or age, we have far more words that express negative emotions than positive ones. In studies of thirty-seven languages, researchers found seven words related to emotions that have similar meanings in all these languages: joy, fear, anger, sadness, disgust, shame, and guilt. Of these seven words, only one is positive—joy.[5] This research is significant because it helps us to understand the importance of finding positive ways of describing emotional experiences. It is a combination of self-talk and the management of our emotions that determines whether or not we are a hostage.

Mary confronts her manager, James, because of a strong exchange between the two of them in a meeting during which Mary felt embarrassed in front of her colleagues. Mary says, "I think you were really over the top attacking me like that." James responds, "Look, I was just telling the truth, and if you don't like it you can always leave the team."

James reveals he has been taken hostage because of his defensive-aggressive response. What is the alternative? Ask a question. Engage in a dialogue to clarify intentions. Make a concession or even an apology. For example, he could say, "Mary, help me to understand what you did not like about what I said" or "Would you like to know what my intentions were?" or "I apologize for saying you can always leave the team; that was over the top."

In this kind of situation, a true leader will work to keep the relationship intact and manage any desire to retaliate by focusing on the needs of the employee, the team, and him- or herself. Successful leaders are able to take this approach instinctively and automatically. Others lack the knowledge or the skill to deal effectively with such situations, and they can learn a great deal from hostage negotiation techniques.

As we saw with James and Mary, if someone provokes a reaction from us when we are not in control, we can easily become metaphorical hostages. This is a problem because it creates a block in the bond in the social relationship and drags us into a negative emotional reaction that can lead to a state of cynicism and detachment. Ultimately, negative states are a problem because they may interrupt social bonding and affect a person's physical health in many ways.

The goal is to maintain a sense of control through the mind-sets we have and the words we use. This is how hostage negotiators succeed. The challenge is to remain both authentic and spontaneous at the same time. The following example shows how our mind-sets are critical in controlling focus and attention.

If you are walking down the street and someone comes up behind you, puts a gun to your head, and says, "I am going to kill you," you do not have to feel like a hostage. While it is true that physically you are indeed a hostage, you do not have to feel like one because you still have the power to think, feel, breathe, and speak. You can ask the hostage taker a question. "Will you please put the gun down and let me help you get what you want?" If the response is, "No, I am going to kill you right now," change the goal, and with another question you can say, "Please, will you just give me five minutes so you can tell me what you want? I am George and I have four children." The gunman says, "No, I am going to kill you right now." Ask again. "Will you give me just four minutes, then? I really want to help you get what you want." The gunman says, "No, I am going to kill you right now!"

Now, when I share this story I ask if this is a good negotiation, and most people say no. Actually, it is a good negotiation. You are still alive! Controlling one's state, managing one's feelings, and using words—to ask questions and seek a solution—is what hostage negotiation is all about. "Will you give me three minutes?" "No." "Will you at least give me two minutes?" "Okay, Buddy, you've got thirty seconds." In those thirty seconds, you had better bond and engage in dialogue as you have never done before in your life! In a subtle way, the no's are a concession and must be seen with a positive mind-set. As we will see later (in Chapter Seven), concessions are part of the fundamental process of creating and maintaining bonds. If we could measure the blood pressure and state of arousal of the man holding the gun, it would be lowering with each concession. Of course, if you have the opportunity to escape safely, you should take it. If you cannot escape, your best bet is to talk. Hostage negotiators use questions to find out what is motivating the other person and to lead the focus of the dialogue.

Over twenty-five-hundred years ago, the Chinese philosopher Lao Tzu wrote that the biggest problem in the world was that individuals experienced themselves as powerless.[6] A hostage mind-set makes people feel negative, trapped, powerless, disconnected, and unable to influence and persuade. That negative state can easily persist, poisoning their minds, emotions, bodies, and souls. The hostage mentality can lead to an embittered or resentful attitude over major losses such as death, divorce, or loss of a job, and even over relatively "small" things such as the loss of an office, an argument with a neighbor over noise, or a disagreement between husband and wife over household chores.

Sadly, much of everyday life for many people is built around negative states. When this happens, the negativity takes root, festers, and poisons the mind so that reactions tend to be out of proportion to the actual event itself.

According to psychologists Martin Seligman and Steven Sauter, the less control a person feels he or she has over a stressful situation, the more traumatic it will become.[7] The person who feels like a hostage may be displaying what Seligman calls "an attitude of learned helplessness." This is characteristic of people who have no sense of "controllability," or, in other words, those who lack a feeling of control over persons, things, and events.[8]

In his studies of the relationship between fear and learning, Seligman accidentally discovered an unexpected phenomenon while doing experiments on dogs using Pavlovian techniques (classical conditioning). The Russian physiologist Ivan Pavlov had discovered that when dogs are presented with food, they will salivate. He then found that if a ringing bell is repeatedly paired with the presentation of food, the dog salivates. Then, if the bell is rung and there is no food present, the dog still salivates. The dog has learned to associate the bell with food.[9]

In Seligman's experiment, instead of pairing the bell with food, he paired the bell with a harmless shock, restraining the dog in a hammock during the learning phase. The idea was that after the dog had learned the association, it would then feel fear when it heard the bell and run away or display some other avoidant behavior. Seligman then put the conditioned dog into a cage that consisted of a low fence dividing the box into two compartments. The dog could easily see the fence and jump over it if it wished. When the bell rang, Seligman was amazed when the dog did nothing. He then decided to shock the conditioned dog another time and, again, nothing happened. The dog just lay in the box. Then, when Seligman put an unconditioned dog into the box, as expected, it immediately jumped to the other side. What the conditioned dog learned during the period it was in the hammock was that escape was futile, and therefore it did not try to escape even when the circumstances made it possible to do so. The dog had learned to be helpless and passive—in other words, to be a hostage.[10]

The theory of learned helplessness was then extended to human behavior and provided a model to explain depression, a state characterized by a lack of control over one's life, a state of indifference, and a lack of feeling. It was discovered that depressed people learned to be helpless and believed that, whatever they did, any action was futile. Researchers have discovered a great deal about depression from learned helplessness. They have also found exceptions—people who do not get depressed even after many difficult life experiences. Seligman's research revealed that a depressed person thinks about negative events in more pessimistic ways than does a nondepressed person.

Those people who allow their thoughts to drift toward the negative are more likely to feel that their situation is hopeless than are those people who have a positive mind-set. Unfortunately, many of us can become hostages through our own passivity, enduring pain, like Seligman's dogs, and failing to understand that we do have the power to do something about it, even if there is a real gun at our head. There are people who are held hostage with a gun to their head who do speak, think, and act. And yet, there are people with no gun to their head who spend their lives feeling like a hostage to their boss, colleague, spouse, friend, or anyone who has power over them.

The Stockholm Syndrome and Hostage Mentality

The term *hostage* is often associated with an extreme act when one person or group, often viewed as terrorists, takes control away from an individual or group and keeps them captive against their will with the goal of getting something. An unusual event that can occur is when the hostage forms an emotional bond to the hostage taker, as illustrated by the following story.

In April 2005, police arrested convicted murderer Randolf Dial, who had kidnapped Bobbi Parker during his escape from an Oklahoma jail in 1994 and then lived with her for some eleven years. Her two daughters were eight and ten when she was taken hostage, and her husband was the assistant warden at the prison. Dial was quoted as saying, "I had worked on her for a year trying to get her mind right. I convinced her that the friend was the enemy and the enemy was the friend." Investigators believe that Dial kept Parker from escaping all those years by threatening to hurt her family. Bobbi Parker was not held by handcuffs or ropes. In fact, sometimes she was able to drive alone. She was held by her own fears and the feeling of powerlessness to act with the goal of protecting her family. This unusual bonding can happen when there is a deep emotional shock such as fear of being killed or fear of someone else being killed.

These positive feelings toward the hostage taker can develop spontaneously and without conscious control; this is called the Stockholm Syndrome, a condition in which hostages become sympathetic toward their captors and begin to identify with them and defend them against the authorities. It is the ultimate attempt by a hostage to survive.

On August 23, 1973, two bank robbers carrying machine guns entered a bank in Stockholm, Sweden. After being trapped, they took four terrified hostages, three women and one man, for 131 hours. The hostages were strapped with dynamite and held in a bank vault until they were rescued on August 28. Authorities were alarmed at the growing hostility of the hostages to the police during the siege. The hostages had begun to feel the captors were actually protecting them from the police. After their rescue, the hostages continued to show a shockingly hostile attitude toward the authorities, considering that their captors had threatened and abused them and they had feared for their lives. In the interviews following their release it was clear they supported their captors and actually feared the authorities who came to their rescue. One woman later became engaged to one of the hostage takers, and another developed a defense fund. Clearly, the hostages had bonded emotionally with their captors.[11]

Perhaps the most famous example of someone exhibiting the Stockholm Syndrome was Patty Hearst. She was a millionaire heiress who was kidnapped by the Symbionese Liberation Army in February 1974, and she went so far as to assist the group with armed bank robberies. She was later released from prison as authorities gained a deeper understanding of this phenomenon.

The Stockholm Syndrome is one of the most interesting phenomena of attachment and bonding behavior. It is a survival mechanism whereby the hostage, in a severe emotional shock of fearing death, begins to feel gratitude for still being allowed to live. In addition, when food and water are given, more gratitude emerges, which further deepens the bond. "Gifts" such as being allowed to go to the bathroom with dignity or being allowed to move around continue to deepen the bond. The former enemy is now becoming an ally. Further exchanges and dialogue can lead to the hostage identifying with the cause of the hostage taker. In fact, he or she may then act on behalf of the hostage taker, as we saw in the Patty Hearst example.

A similar thing may happen when a person forms a bond to someone who uses ongoing verbal abuse, negative behavior, or punishment as a form of control. The person becomes a hostage to the abuser after failing to understand his or her own power to draw a boundary or to leave. This is the classic victim-persecutor relationship based on a bond that discounts the pain because of the fear of leaving.[12]

However, the Stockholm Syndrome does not develop in all hostages, due to the failure to bond by either the hostages or the hostage takers. As was mentioned earlier, bonding with a hostage taker is a good survival strategy up to the point when it is appropriate to break the bond, that is, after being rescued or escaping. However, for some former hostages this is easier said than done, which can cause great pain and confusion in their lives.

Recently, another bank robber who took hostages was shot by the police sharpshooter. After he fell to the floor, two women hostages picked him up and physically held him at the door for another bullet. Some people are essentially immune to feeling like a hostage as they have strong identities and they choose not to surrender their personal power to the hostage taker, or may immediately take their power back when it is safe to do so. The important point to remember in these situations is, What is your goal? Be clear about what you want and then act in the way that is most likely to help you achieve the goal. In a hostage situation the goal usually is to survive, and the best strategy for that is bonding.

In some situations, resistance to an event or situation can stimulate an almost automatic reaction that may increase the force against the opposition. The events at Waco, Texas, are an example of when an extreme reaction led to a tragedy.

In February 1993, more than seventy agents from the Bureau of Alcohol, Tobacco and Firearms (ATF) raided the Branch Davidians, a religious cult led by David Koresh. The ATF suspected the group of having a large cache of high-powered weapons, as well as explosives. According to reports, when the team arrived to enforce warrants for arrest at the cult's compound in Waco, shooting started almost immediately, leaving four ATF agents and six Branch Davidians dead. The FBI moved in, and a lengthy standoff ensued. For more than fifty days, the FBI tried to persuade the Davidians to give themselves up. The standoff ended on the morning of April 19 when a tank and other FBI armored vehicles moved in. The FBI then spent several hours shooting tear gas into the compound. Shortly after noon, the building was engulfed in flames. By the end of the day, more than seventy men, women, and children were dead.

We can learn much about being a hostage from this tragic story. Did the fact that the ATF lost four members in the initial gun battle, with all the accompanying grief, influence the later drive to attack the Waco headquarters? Or, by overriding the instinctive reaction to attack and the emotional feelings of anger and exhaustion, would it have been possible for the ATF and FBI to use further negotiation to reach a peaceful solution? The answers to these questions are still being discussed by congressional investigations.

County Sheriff Jack Harwell, who had a positive bond with David Koresh that had extended over many years, was quoted as saying, "I would have handled it differently. I think he [Koresh] would have come in to talk to me if I had asked him. Then I would have told him we needed to go back out to the compound to serve these warrants. They thought of that place out there as their country."[13] Sheriff Jack Harwell was sidelined and mostly excluded from any decision making from the start to the finish. Could his bond with David Koresh have made a difference to the eventual outcome?

There are lessons from this incident that we can also apply to the business world. When there are territorial disputes between departments or differences of opinion between colleagues, a stand-off position often can be avoided through the power of dialogue and by simply talking through the issues.

BONDING IS THE ANTIDOTE

What I have learned from my years as a hostage negotiator is that we, as individuals, do not have to feel powerless in our daily lives— and that bonding is the antidote to the hostage dilemma.

In the early morning hours of Saturday, March 12, 2005, in Atlanta, Georgia, Ashley Smith was taken hostage in her home by Brian Nichols, the day after he had killed four people at a courthouse. Nichols had shot a judge, a sheriff's deputy, a stenographer, and, later, a park ranger. Ashley managed to escape unharmed. How did she achieve this? She created a bond with Nichols. At first, Nichols tied Smith up, gagged her, and told her, "I don't want to hurt you. You know, somebody could have heard your scream already. And if they did, the police are on their way. And I'm going to have to hold you hostage. And I'm going to have to kill you and probably myself and lots of other people. And I don't want that." Later, in her book Unlikely Angel, *Smith revealed that she had given Nichols methamphetamine when he had asked for marijuana. This information does not alter the fact that bonding was at the heart of her survival success.*

During the ordeal, Smith said, she gently talked to Nichols, turning from hostage to confidant as they discussed God, family, pancakes, and the massive manhunt going on outside her door. They even watched television reports about him together. She had Rick Warren's book, The Purpose-Driven Life, *and began reading extracts from it to Nichols, helping him to determine what his purpose in life might be.*

In reports after the event, Smith explained that she had told Nichols about her daughter and bonded with him after he said that he had a son who had been born the night before. Her husband had died four years earlier, and she told him that if he hurt her, her child would not have a Mommy or Daddy.

At one stage, Nichols told her he was "already dead," but Smith urged him to consider the fact that he was alive "a miracle." As they talked through the night, some of the fear subsided and Nichols untied Smith. When morning came, Nichols was overwhelmed when Smith made him pancakes with real butter. He told her that he "just wanted some normalness to his life." They then continued a powerful dialogue and created such a strong bond that he chose not to hurt her and, in fact, released her to go to see her daughter. His last words to Ashley were, "Say hi to your daughter for me."

The police commented afterward that she had acted very cool and level-headed, something they do not normally see in their profession. "We were prepared for the worst and got the best," said Gwinnett County Police officer Darren Moloney.[14]

As discussed in detail in Chapter Three, bonding in a hostage context is the ability to create an emotional connection, even with the most difficult or dangerous person, for the purpose of finding resolution to a difference or a problem. It is the idea of forming a relationship in which we understand what the other person needs or wants and then maintaining the relationship despite our own inner emotions driving us to attack or run away.

For leaders, teams and organizations, bonding is particularly important. The heart of any healthy group lies in the intensity of the bonding between people and to the organization's goals. This can be measured by the degree of engagement and emotional involvement. Whether it is a family, a club, or a company, when members of a group are attached to each other and to common goals, a sense of well-being, high energy, and enjoyment in working together exists. This environment allows people to express ideas, to feel safe, and to resolve conflicts even when there are profound differences.

When people are thinking with a hostage mind-set, they believe that they have no options but to change the external situation. They must quit their job, move to a new house, or resign from the team. A mind-set of escape connects to how our brain works. As we are hardwired to survive, we are basically looking for danger and paying attention to those things that frighten or scare us. Bonding is often counterintuitive, requiring us to focus on what the other person needs as well as knowing what we want—it allows others to have an impact on us and, in turn, us to elicit a response from them.

Bonding is so powerful because it personalizes the relationship, thereby taking any toxicity and poison out of the process. This power is demonstrated in the story of Nelson Mandela.

At forty-six, Nelson Mandela was sentenced to life imprisonment and placed in a cell for almost twenty-six years. Imagine how easy it would have been for him to become embittered and angry. What would this have achieved? He did not have control over the situation, so all he could have done was to be taken hostage. Instead, he remained focused on the positive, even learning the language of the guards (Afrikaans) so he could communicate with them and create a dialogue. When Mandela was imprisoned, his mind-set was to view his incarceration as training and preparation to help bring South Africa out of apartheid. How many of us could spend twenty-six years in prison and see it as training? Mandela was a physical hostage but certainly not a psychological one.

While in prison, Mandela rejected offers made by his jailers for remission of sentence in exchange for accepting South Africa's ethnic homeland policy and recognizing the independence of the Transkei, his birthplace. In the 1980s, Mandela again rejected an offer of release on the condition that he renounce violence. "Prisoners cannot enter into contracts. Only free men can negotiate," said Mandela.

It is significant that, shortly after his release on Sunday, February 11, 1990, Mandela and his supporters agreed to the suspension of armed struggle. Reports have also revealed that some of the prison guards wept when he was released. Mandela was inaugurated as the first democratically elected state president of South Africa on May 10, 1994.[15]

SUMMARY

We can be taken hostage by ourselves or other people just about any time and any place. Thankfully, most of us are not taken hostage with a physical weapon. However, we can become hostages when we give away our personal power and allow ourselves to feel trapped or helpless. Whether it relates to a minor event such as being criticized by a colleague, or a major situation such as having an ongoing struggle with a boss or partner, allowing ourselves to be taken hostage means we will have difficulty resolving the issue in a way that is productive.

Negativity from powerlessness is poison to our mind. People can learn helplessness as a repetitive response to problems of any kind. They have learned that "nothing they do makes a difference," so they give up and feel like a hostage. The antidote to powerlessness is emotional bonding. By connecting to people or goals, we can create bonds that enable us to feel empowered. Bonding is a survival mechanism for all of us. Through bonding, we enrich our lives.

It is vital to remember that we always have a choice in how we think, feel, and act. Depending on our mental state, the world looks very different. Learning not to be taken hostage by ourselves or others enables us to manage our lives without necessarily changing external circumstances. If we only look externally for satisfaction, we will find only fleeting gratification. To truly change our lives, we have to look inside ourselves. When we make a choice to cooperate, to collaborate, or even to give in, we are not being a hostage. When we are aware that we have a choice in any given situation, it enables us to feel more positive about the circumstances.

We can choose to enjoy all our relationships in a hostage-free state of being. Does this mean we will not face challenges or frustrations? Absolutely not. Freedom does not mean becoming disconnected—a person still needs to make concessions to a boss, customer, spouse, or friend; however, it is done from a positive state rather than from a negative state with a feeling of powerlessness.

With practice, we can recognize when we are reacting in an aggressive or defensive way and thereby either being taken hostage or taking someone else hostage. We can then choose the way we react. We need to focus our mind on the words we use and the transactions we use with others.

If we are able to recognize instinctive emotional reactions that repeat themselves, we can then interrupt the lack of self-management. By understanding ourselves and the way our mind works, we can learn to set ourselves free from inner constraints and make real choices. The concepts are equally relevant to any organization, business, school, or group. By encouraging those around us to also live a hostage-free life, we can manage all aspects of our life more effectively.

Key Points to Remember

1. A hostage mind-set involves feeling trapped, helpless, powerless, disconnected, and unable to influence and persuade.
2. The brain is hardwired to survive by looking for danger and pain. We can override this instinctual aspect of the brain to look for the positive and for ways to act with personal power.
3. Learned helplessness and lack of control of our mind-set causes people to be powerless. Recovering our power to choose a reaction to the events in our lives is possible for anyone who has become a hostage.
4. Know what you want and maintain a mind-set of "everything is possible." If you do not get what you want, find the positive in not getting what you want. Either way you win and will never feel like a hostage.

CHAPTER TWO

FINDING FREEDOM THROUGH YOUR MIND'S EYE

In 1998, Ben Lecomte, a Frenchman who lived in America, swam the Atlantic Ocean. It took him eighty days to complete the 3,716-mile journey. What was his motivation? He wanted to honor his father, who had died of colon cancer in 1992. At the same time, he wished to raise money for and awareness of cancer research. Ben raised over $175,000.

Lecomte said, "The death of my father had left a growing space in my life. After a short battle with cancer, my father passed away at the young age of forty-nine. So I decided to use this project as the best vehicle within my means to create awareness to raise funds for the battle against cancer. My deep thirst for adventure joins my intense feeling of mission in this project. These traits drive my strong desire to achieve my dream of swimming across the Atlantic Ocean."

Lecomte trained for six years before undertaking the swim. He was reported as saying that he would often visualize in his mind playing home videos of his dad teaching him how to swim. Crossing the Atlantic, he was in the water for six hours a day beside a support boat that projected a twenty-five-foot electromagnetic field to protect him from sharks. He had to eat for four hours a day to replace the more than nine thousand calories burned while either swimming through force eight storms and up to sixty-knot winds and twenty-foot waves or dealing with sea turtles, dolphins, jellyfish, and incredibly cold water.

As he started his difficult journey, he also proposed to his girlfriend. She told him to ask her "on the other side."

Part way, when he was recovering from exhaustion induced by the epic swim, again he asked his girlfriend to marry him, but she declined to answer. After he had come ashore in France, he proposed a third time, and at last she said, "Yes."[1]

Was this man mad—swimming over a period of eighty days, 3,716 miles with unrelentingly harsh natural elements besetting him above and below the water? Absolutely not! In fact, he had the highest of all motivations, driven by love, attachment, and bonding: honoring his father, living his dream, and proposing to his girlfriend.

Could you swim across the Atlantic Ocean? I am serious about this question. Could you? I am not asking whether you want to do it, rather, could you do it? The answer is yes, you could! The possibility is there in all of us even if we have physical limitations. Lecomte was not a professional athlete but an airline employee. Unraveling what motivates us is key to performing at our best. Knowing our own motivations can immunize us against becoming hostages or allowing others to take us hostage.

While Ben's great swim is certainly amazing, the most important point of this story is how he kept himself motivated. If accomplishing things is important for you, then you must learn to use your mind's eye just as Ben did. What exactly did Ben do? He had to focus on the benefits of this swim and not on the pain or frustration he faced each day. If he woke up in the morning, completely exhausted from vomiting through the night, and said to himself, "I can't get out of bed," he would not have gotten out of bed. What did Ben do at that point? What do we all have to do? He had to manage his mind's eye by focusing on his father, his girlfriend, and his goal—any positive way to change his state to get out of bed and into the cold water for another day's swimming with the sharks. Ben had to stay focused on the benefits or, quite simply, he would have become a hostage to his own pain or to the avoidance of the pain. The moment Ben shifted his focus to the pain and the frustration, his swim would have been over.

Think of a challenging physical exercise. Jogging? Marathon running? Walking? Swimming? Hiking? Skiing? Playing tennis? What happens to us while we are doing this exercise if we focus on the pain? We will stop. What must we focus on to keep going, to override the pain we feel in our bodies? In asking marathon runners, I have heard a variety of answers: simply finishing the goal, watching the crowd, looking at the trees, focusing on the next four steps, reflecting on pleasant memories, or even thinking about the hot shower at the end.

All high performers have a secret—they use their mind's eye to focus on the benefits and not the pain. This positive focus determines the state they are in, which determines the result they achieve. The mind's eye directs whether we focus on the pain and frustration (the negative) or on the benefit (the positive). It filters reality and shapes our view of the world. The mind's eye is both a system of selective attention and a system of interpretation and is one of the most powerful mechanisms in our brain. It forms the way we view a particular situation and determines how we will act or react. Successful sports figures, inspiring leaders, great teachers, creative artists, and brilliant scientists all know that success requires a positive energetic state, and that starts in the mind's eye.

As Figure 2.1 illustrates, the positive or negative state we create determines the result of everything we do. Our mind's eye is shaped by our experiences, and the extraordinary workings of our inner mind determine the way we view the world and, ultimately, success or failure. For many people, the future is mostly a memory

FIGURE 2.1. THE MIND'S EYE DETERMINES RESULTS

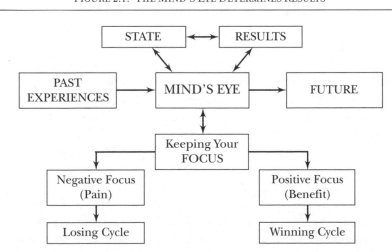

of the past as they repeat patterns of behavior that they have learned in the past and then project onto current or future events. However, no one needs to be a hostage to previous experience, no matter how negative.

Most people are driven by fear or by avoidance of pain. Only a few are driven by the benefits. The mind's eye controls what we focus on in life, and there is both a positive and a negative side to everything. Positive things such as winning the lottery, getting married, or starting a new job have a potential negative side, while negative things such as the loss of a job, a divorce, or even the death of a loved one, can lead to a positive aspect.

In the most devastating of circumstances, we can find our way back to the beauty of life by facing and dealing with whatever is in the way (loss, grief, anger, sadness, revenge, and so on). Not finding the joy of life after a loss means that we have been taken hostage. Life is bittersweet, filled with both joy and pain. Happiness is, however, a state of mind and a choice that is directed by the mind's eye.

FOCUSING WITH THE MIND'S EYE

Have you ever told yourself you were going to fail at something before you started? Presenting on a key issue to the boss? A critical exam? Asking someone for something? What we believe will happen generally does happen. The mind's eye makes it possible to achieve just about anything we want—the important element is to focus on the positive outcome. Focusing on a negative outcome will ensure that we will become a hostage.

If a child is told, "Don't spill the milk," he or she will probably spill the milk. Or, if he or she hears, "Don't fall off of your bike," the child will probably fall off the bike. Why does this happen? Research has demonstrated that the brain uses pictures as a primary way of getting the mind's eye to focus. So what is the picture a person gets? An image of spilling the milk. An image of falling off the bike.

Another interesting example has to do with car accidents. If a car is skidding on ice and the driver focuses on the tree ahead, hoping to avoid it, the chances are that the car will hit the very object the person wants to avoid. For this reason police officers, security drivers, and race-car drivers are all taught to focus on where they want to go—not on the objects in the way. Of course, there must be awareness of obstacles. However, they should not be the center of attention.

People can lose control of their lives and experience a sense of hopelessness and frustration because they are focusing on the wrong things—probably what they want to avoid or what they have lost. It is all too easy to "overfocus" on the "problems" or barriers—where they do not want to go. We take ourselves hostage when we do this, and it leads to the very outcome we want to avoid. Being a hostage to another person or being a hostage to our own inner reactions, thoughts, and emotions are strongly interconnected—both elements are usually present when we are taken hostage. The outcome is to become a victim—that state in which one feels negative, helpless, deprived, and out of control.

Joanne believed Brian had hijacked a business meeting she was leading by questioning her methodology. He had made a disparaging comment after her introduction, and from then on, he steered the other committee members away from the real focus of what she was there to present and onto the side issue of the actual approach she had used. His unexpected interruptions had unnerved her and spoiled what was a critical presentation for the project she and her team had spent the past six months working on.

Although Brian's actions may well have been disruptive, Joanne was the one who allowed the meeting to be derailed by losing sight of what she wanted to achieve. She simply lost control of the meeting by falling into the trap of seeing Brian as the problem. Her emotions allowed Brian to take her hostage. She let her mind's eye focus on how Brian was disrupting her rather than on what she wanted to accomplish with the presentation. How could she have handled this event differently? What would a hostage negotiator do to handle such a situation?

First, she could have made a concession to him by recognizing a "point of truth" and then redirecting the conversation to focus on her goal or the common goal. The moment she defended herself she became a hostage.

Next, she could have asked Brian questions to change his focus or used her role as leader to clarify the purpose of the meeting, thus allowing her to refocus on a positive goal.

Last, she could have negotiated for a discussion of methodology at a later point. By managing her own state and her mind's eye, thus avoiding being taken hostage by Brian and herself, Joanne could have gone a long way toward ensuring her success. The power to control our own destiny is always with us.

UNDERSTANDING THE MIND'S EYE OF ANOTHER PERSON

Hostage negotiators are trained to understand quickly what is in the mind's eye of a hostage taker. This is the secret to understanding the motivation behind why someone engages in constructive or destructive behavior. Without understanding someone else's motivation, we will not be effective in establishing a strong enough bond to influence the other person. Hostage negotiators listen carefully, ensuring that their questions, how they talk, and how they respond all take into account the motivation of the hostage taker. Refocusing the mind's eye of the hostage taker, from the negative to the positive, becomes the primary goal.

When Ashley Smith was taken hostage by Brian Nichols (see Chapter One), she focused on influencing his mind's eye away from the negative aspect of killing her and himself toward the positive aspects of what meaning his life could have in the future. Ashley told Brian that what he did was wrong and said, "You need to go to prison and you need to share the word of God with all the prisoners there."

Needless to say, hostage negotiators regularly deal with difficult characters. A simple technique used by hostage negotiators is to separate the person from the problem and maintain a measured state of control during the crisis. In the movie *The Negotiator,* Kevin Spacey plays the role of a hostage negotiator who is negotiating with another hostage negotiator turned hostage taker, played by Samuel L. Jackson. At one point, Spacey's character says, "My goal is not to determine guilt or innocence, it is to get all hostages, including you, out alive." Nothing could pull him from that focus. Hostage negotiators convince hostage takers to change their minds about what they are going to do, even with the probability that they will go to prison. In fact, using this approach, hostage negotiators achieve a 95 percent success rate.[2] Leaders do not come near this level of success in changing the mind-sets of employees.

The hostage negotiator will not allow himself to be taken a metaphorical hostage by the aggression, despair, negativity, or hopelessness of the hostage taker. If he can quickly see what is at stake, what is motivating the hostage taker, he is well on his way to resolving conflicts.

Remember, our state of mind is reflected in how we present ourselves, and it is an important part of how we appear to others. The way we talk shows what is in our mind's eye. Further information comes from our facial expressions, posture, and tone of voice. A good hostage negotiator uses all the senses to know what is motivating the hostage taker. When we learn to understand what motivates others, our ability to deal with people is improved beyond measure.

THE POWER OF A STATE OF MIND

What is a state? In 1963, Eric Berne, the founder of transactional analysis, defined what he called an ego state as "a coherent set of feelings, thinking and behavior."[3] I broadened that idea and think of state as how we are at any one moment in time. A state includes our physiology, attitude, emotions, mood, behavior, and beliefs all coming together in one stance. Do you know when you are in a positive state, an angry state, an enthused state, or a discouraged state? The heart of being successful rests in the state we create. In turn, the focus of our mind's eye determines our state.

Lance Armstrong, the renowned cyclist, has won the Tour de France seven times—even though he should be dead from cancer. In 1996, he was diagnosed with an advanced form of testicular cancer that then spread to his abdomen, lungs, and brain. "At one point, he had a minority chance of living another year," said Craig Nichols, Armstrong's principal oncologist at the time, when interviewed in The New Yorker. *"We cure at most a third of the people in situations like that."*

Miraculously, after a year of surgery combined with aggressive chemotherapy, Armstrong was declared cancer-free. Nichols described Armstrong as "the most willful person I have ever met. And he wasn't willing to die."

In his autobiography, It's Not About the Bike: My Journey Back to Life, *Armstrong writes, "Cycling is so hard, the suffering so intense, that it's absolutely cleansing. The pain is so deep and strong that a curtain descends over your brain."*

When he returned to cycling in 1998, he could not find a team other than the U.S. Postal Service to support him, for others regarded him as "damaged goods." What was Armstrong's reaction? He unequivocally stated, "That year was the greatest of my life."

Armstrong gained a perspective earned only after enduring a life-changing experience. He says that cancer was the best thing that ever happened to him. Before becoming ill, he did not care about strategy, tactics, or teamwork—but nobody becomes a great cyclist without mastering these aspects of the sport. He is now motivated not only to win bike races but to compete every day for the gift of life. His focus in his mind's eye has also spread to helping others who suffer with cancer. Through the sales of his LIVESTRONG yellow wristbands, more than $10 million has been raised for cancer research.[4]

Being in the right state determines the result. It is the secret formula of all success. Unfortunately, most people have difficulty in getting to that state. Or if they get into the right state, they cannot hold it. Anyone who has ever done sports training instinctively knows about "states." If we focus on the pain in our bodies when we are training, what happens? We stop. This is what the majority of people do; they focus on the pain, the frustration, the barrier, as opposed to the benefit, the goal, the outcome.

In 2002, in a California lottery, Jack Whittaker won the highest amount ever paid out in an undivided jackpot: $314.9 million. After taxes, he had $113 million. Two years later, his wife, Jewel, said, "I wish all of this never would have happened. I wish I would have torn up the ticket."

Since winning the lottery, Jack Whittaker has been arrested twice for drunk driving and was ordered into rehabilitation. He pleaded no contest to a charge of attacking a bar manager, and two lawsuits accused him of making trouble at a nightclub and at a racetrack. He and his wife separated. Whittaker, a wealthy man before the win, said he would lavish his winnings on his daughter and granddaughter. In September 2003, an eighteen-year-old friend of his granddaughter was found dead at the Whittaker's home. In December 2004, his granddaughter was found dead from a suspected drug overdose.[5]

In the cases of many lottery winners, unhappiness often follows the initial excitement of the win. Most people who win the lottery end up in a worse state five years later. When looking at why these lottery winners, in general, do not find happiness, we see that there is something about not being able to integrate the win into their minds and into their lives in a constructive way. The money changes them (their states) in such a way that destructive outcomes eventually beset most lottery winners.

How do we prevent ourselves from letting our own problems take us hostage? We must control our mind's eye and maintain the state required to get the result we want.

In managing the mind's eye, there is a basic rule to follow in any hostage-type situation: when verbally attacked, do not attack back. Disarm the person by asking a question. I recommend that people practice switching states on a regular basis. When someone or something is irritating or annoying, switch to another state with a more positive frame of mind. The more practice we have in switching states, the easier it will become. According to Daniel Goleman, Richard Boyatzis, and Annie McKee, in their book *Primal Leadership,* "Self awareness facilitates both empathy and self-management, and these two, in combination, allow effective relationship management."[6]

INFLUENCING INNER STATES AND OUTER STATES

We can all talk ourselves into either a positive or a negative state through the power of our own internal dialogue. Understanding the mind's eye not only helps us influence ourselves, but when we understand what is in the mind's eye of another person, we can then influence that person for a mutual benefit.

When my son, Andrew, was four, he was stuck in an elevator with his mother. My wife pushed the alarm button, and it took about five minutes for them both to get out of the dark elevator.

The next day, I was going out with him, and as we left the front door he said with terror in his voice, "Dad, I am not going on that elevator. It will get stuck again." How did I help him to refocus his mind's eye? Holding out my hand, I gently said, "Andrew, let's take the elevator."

He replied, "No, it will get stuck." I continued warmly, "Andrew, that's not true. The elevator is your 'friend.' Trust me—it won't get stuck." Changing states, he firmly took my hand and we entered the elevator. As we descended, Andrew started talking to the elevator, saying, "Friend, would you like a cookie?" I then played the role of the elevator saying, "No thanks, I'm busy getting you down safely. You can offer a cookie to Helen downstairs when you get out." As we walked out, Andrew turned and with a big smile said, "Goodbye, friend." To this day, he still sometimes refers to the elevator as his friend.

When I tell this story in my workshops, I ask participants, "Did I lie to my son when I said the elevator would not get stuck again?" A significant number say yes. A majority say no. In fact, I do not believe I lied. I was talking from the state of certainty that any leader must have to create a sense of security. If I had said to my son, "There's only one chance in two billion that the elevator will get stuck," he would have focused on that one possibility. Remember, the brain is hardwired to search for danger and the negative in order to survive. As Andrew's father, I was what is known as a "secure base," a person who provides a sense of comfort and support to an individual and who enables him or her to explore and take risks. With me as his secure base, Andrew was able to rewire his brain to believe that elevators are safe. However, the next question may well be, What would I have done if the elevator became stuck again? Simple—I would have maintained a sense of calm and focused on how darkness is his friend.

Similarly, the Senoi tribes of Malaysia teach children how to use their mind's eye to turn nightmares into pleasant dreams by changing threatening and dangerous images into allies.[7] This kind of strategy was also useful during bombing raids in the Second World War and in the Balkan War. Mothers who remained calm could hold their small children and, in a state of protection, these children would continue to sleep. Other parents were so terrified that they could not offer their children a sense of protection, and it was these children who were traumatized by the bombs. When a person has a sense of calm in his or her mind's eye, this feeling can spread to others, just as when people are in a state of distress, they often make those around them feel anxious, afraid, or upset. This can easily be applied to relationships in organizations.

According to Goleman, Boyatzis, and McKee, in their book *Primal Leadership*, "Leadership begins with the leader managing their own inner life so that the right emotional and behavioral chain reactions occur. For many of us, it is our most difficult challenge."[8] How many of us know the feeling of being scattered? We are pulled in so many different directions: too many requests, too many e-mails, too many calls. One of the secrets of high performers is their ability to tune out unnecessary clutter so that they can stay focused on what they need to do to maintain a positive state.

THE SELF-FULFILLING PROPHECY AND THE MIND'S EYE

A self-fulfilling prophecy results when people talk themselves into failure or success. The power of both success and failure starts inside our minds. Our inner world can either interfere in our lives or give us an advantage. We all have the power, through the choice and focus directed by the mind's eye, to create either a winning cycle or a losing cycle. However, many people are not aware that they have a choice and, therefore, are hostages to their emotions, which can extend into fear and negativity about the future.

Athletes know that they cannot afford to let their mind drift to the negative during a performance. For example, tennis players need to be able to maintain a positive state throughout the game, no matter what happens. If they miss a point at a crucial stage of the game, they must go through a grief reaction and clear their mind in seconds, ready for the next volley. If players allow negative feelings to linger in their mind, they put themselves into a loser's cycle that then perpetuates itself. The same is true in business. Leaders must be able to deal with a disappointment or setback in a split second and continue to lead so as not to destroy the morale and motivation of those around them.

How does authority relate to a self-fulfilling prophecy? If we have a negative view of authority, there will be negative consequences in our lives. When there is a lack of trust in authority, there tends to be a lack of trust in ourselves. Since we have all had experiences with authority, the question is, How have those experiences affected our mind's eye and, in turn, our view of ourselves? Positive experiences in dealing with authority are important in creating a sense of belonging, in finding meaning in loss and failure, and in building self-confidence.

How many parents poison children's minds? Can a teacher poison a student's mind? Can a manager poison an employee's mind? An authority figure of any type can poison a mind. For example, if someone has cancer and the doctor says, "I'm really sorry, this is a tragedy, most people only live two months with this," then the patient most likely will die close to the given date. If the doctor says, "Well, this is very serious, but there are people who have lived for many years with this condition," then that person may well live for an extended period. In a study by Sardell and Trierweiler on how patients perceive disclosure of a cancer diagnosis by a physician, they concluded, "Maximizing hope during the disclosure of a diagnosis is one way clinicians can contribute to psychological adjustment early in the treatment process."[9]

Physician Hippocrates, 460–400 B.C., wrote "Some patients, though conscious that their condition is perilous, recover their health simply through their contentment with the goodness of the physician."[10] The positive focus of the mind's eye and the belief in the authority figure leads to a self-fulfilling prophecy.

As mentioned earlier, the relationship to authority figures from the past strongly affects our self-fulfilling tendencies in a way that the future may be influenced by memories from the past. By living a memory, and repeating the behaviors and actions that we engaged in previously, we determine what is going to happen in the future. If the memories from the past are positive, then the result will likely be positive. However, if the memories from the past are negative, then the result will likely be negative.

Unless we actively intervene in this process, these past experiences that filter through the brain will become a prediction of the future. A good example is a person who fails in a job interview and then walks into another interview already thinking deep in her mind that she is not going to get the job. Without deliberate interference, she becomes a hostage to her own negative self-fulfilling prophecy. Awareness and self-mastery are the key elements to avoiding becoming a hostage.

Scott found himself a hostage to his own self-limiting beliefs. Traveling frequently and spending at least five days a week away from his family, this thirty-six-year-old man was being groomed for upper management at his company. He came to me quite distraught during a workshop.

"I have to leave my job," he told me.

"Why?" I asked, genuinely curious about what had triggered this statement.

"It's killing my five-year-old daughter. When I go away, she cries and cries and cries. So now I leave the house early in the morning before she's awake."

I asked him if he called his daughter while he was away.

"No. She just cries into the phone."

"What happens when you come home?"

"Well, she just continues to play and essentially ignores me."

"What do you do?"

"I don't want to interrupt and force myself on her, so I let her play and do whatever she's doing. I don't want to be a bad father."

Scott allowed his fear of being a bad father to take him hostage. As the father, it was his responsibility to initiate a change in the self-fulfilling prophecies that both he and his daughter were living.

My suggestion to Scott was to talk about and agree on the things they would do together on his return and to engage her in his travels by leaving notes around the house for his daughter along with pictures of where he had gone. I also encouraged him to ask her to give him a note or picture to take with him. In a short time, he had created a focus that took the pain out of the separation for both of them. In addition, I suggested that he call her at least once a day while he was away, and when he returned from a trip, he was to pick her up and hold her. It is possible to keep the bonding even when physically away. Scott had to manage the focus in his mind's eye and help his daughter do the same by focusing on what they would do on his return.

Within two weeks, a negative, self-fulfilling prophecy was eliminated and the bond renewed between them. The mother, who had felt helpless, became an active part of the problem-solving process as well.

Why did Scott think he was a bad father? The stimulus for the whole sequence of events began when Scott had to miss his daughter's first piano recital because of a business meeting. When he went away, his daughter's distress reinforced this opinion of being a negligent and uncaring father. Once Scott changed the focus in his mind's eye to look for a solution and ways to be a good father, he was able to help himself and his family change their situation.

Another interesting aspect to this story that sheds light on Scott's behavior is the knowledge that Scott's father had traveled a lot, and Scott had painful recollections of his own father's absence. Scott's memory of his father and himself became a self-fulfilling picture of the future, and in that sense, he was a hostage to both his past and present pain. The fact is Scott is a wonderful father, and he trusted me to help him understand that.

How many people continue to exist in a state of misery and unhappiness and seemingly do nothing to change it? How many people go to their deaths with unfulfilled dreams? Alternatively, how many people are willing to take risks in their lives, willing to do things and seek out new challenges time after time? Either way, a self-fulfilling prophecy is actively at play, whether it is a negative one or a positive one. Our goal is to understand the power to create a future we want. People who feel like hostages must understand and then act on their own power to be able to influence their destinies as much as possible.

Transactional analysis founder Eric Berne described the self-fulfilling prophecy as a life script: for many reasons, people make choices throughout their lives that become a kind of "script" and, unfortunately for many people, because the mind drifts to the negative, that script turns into an ongoing, unfulfilling outcome—a negative self-fulfilling prophecy.[11]

SEEING WITH THE MIND'S EYE

The human eye captures incredible amounts of information with a single glance and passes it all to the brain. The brain then translates this information into a form we "see." It would be more accurate to say that we see with our brain rather than with our eyes. However, the more interesting point is that the brain does not always need to receive information through the eyes in order to "see." It can recall sights, sounds, and feelings from memory and run the whole sequence like a movie, all inside our head, in the mind's eye.

The power of imagination is incredible. Often we see athletes achieving unbelievable results and wonder how they did it. One of the tools they use is visualization or mental imagery. A successful athlete will have won the race, or title, or medal many times in his own mind's eye before setting foot on the track. A diver will have climbed the ladder to the board, felt her toes springing off the edge, seen her body arc in a perfect dive, felt her fingertips touch the water and then her whole body immersed before coming up for air, heard the cheering crowd yelling her name, felt the trophy in her hands, and perhaps even imagined the phone call home to tell her loved ones about the victory—all of this in her mind long before the "real" event.

Visualization is a method practiced by many successful people, and it remains an untapped resource for most of us. To practice visualizing in our mind's eye, we must focus on what we want to accomplish and picture achieving that goal in every possible detail. Envision where the action takes place and what is happening. Visualize all the details of the event. Imagine dreaming of a promotion at the office. Picture sitting at a new desk. Picture answering the phone and talking with people. Imagine the comfort of the chair, and the view from the desk. Imagine the feeling of success in the new job. Plan the details until there is a feeling of comfort, confidence, and success. When practicing visualization, the more detail the better. Replay this mental movie as often as possible. Make "wishes" and "dreams" become paramount in the mind.

Place visual pictures and reminders where they can be constantly seen. The process of visualization has been repeatedly proven to work. I am always moved by stories of ordinary people who have triumphed and accomplished extraordinary results because they made the choice to create their destinies and visualized their achievements before they ultimately succeeded.

Marilyn was preparing for a presentation at which, for the first time in her life, she had the opportunity to stand in front of a crowd of fifty people, including the president and CEO of the company. Initially, she was quite nervous about the opportunity. What if she forgot her speech? What if the laptop broke down? What if the audience was not interested? Her brain was working perfectly well by searching for all the potential dangers. However, she was coached to use visualization techniques to help her prepare. She imagined standing in the room, even visiting the location beforehand so what she saw in her mind matched the reality. She imagined what she would be wearing. She imagined the audience responding positively to her speech. She imagined herself enjoying the presentation. She did all these things many times, over and over, in the weeks before the actual event. When the time came, Marilyn gave the best presentation of her life. The CEO approached her afterward and said how much he had enjoyed her presentation. She had learned a simple technique to rewire her brain and guarantee success.

Mental imagery and visualization techniques are the hallmarks of high-performing people, who see a clear picture in their minds of where they want to go. While artists and athletes do this regularly, it is only now that leaders in the business world are discovering the power of the mind's eye and visualization. In business, having a vision helps leaders stay focused on their goals. Leaders also understand the importance of helping others see the vision; they know that the road traveled alone will not get them to their chosen destination.

Peter Senge writes: "If any one idea about leadership has inspired organizations for thousands of years, it's the capacity to hold a shared picture of the future we seek to create. One is hard pressed to think of any organization that has sustained some measure of greatness in the absence of goals, values, and missions that become deeply shared throughout the organization. IBM had 'service'; Polaroid had instant photography; Ford had public transportation for the masses and Apple had computer power for the masses. Though radically different in content and kind, all these organizations managed to bind people together around a common identity and sense of destiny."[12]

Being able to articulate their vision consistently and persuasively so that people buy in and become eager followers, or even better, eager partners, is crucial for reaching the highest levels of success. The clearer the picture in one's mind's eye, the easier it will be to communicate it to others. This mental blueprint of what we want to build, this inner picture of something that has not yet happened, will ultimately guide the strategies and actions that will make our visions a reality.

It is now considered standard practice for organizations to have a vision that employees can understand and feel emotionally connected to. In this sense, we can view this process as a collective mind's eye, bringing everyone together to work toward a common outcome. Inspiring leaders always create inspiring visions.

SUMMARY

The mind's eye is an important part of the brain. For many people, the surprising discovery is that our brain is hardwired to look for danger and potential pain. This is how we have survived as a species for thousands of years. However, every event that happens in our lives has both a negative and a positive aspect. Using the mind's eye, we can make the choice to focus on the positive or negative aspects of any event. In that sense, being negative is a choice, being positive is a choice, and being happy is a choice.

High-performing people in sports, arts, and business do not allow their mind to focus on the negative. They are able to maintain a positive state of mind. When they have a setback, they are able to go through the disappointment, frustration, and grief reaction to clear their mind quickly so that they can continue in a renewed positive state. Those who allow negative feelings to linger put themselves into a losing cycle, which may then perpetuate itself.

Athletes and inspiring leaders learn to master both inner and outer states. If we can put ourselves in a positive mental state, we are more likely to get the result we want. To get in this kind of state, we need to be able to override the natural tendency to focus on the pain in any endeavor, and instead focus on the benefit or the pleasure that will be the result of our actions.

Anyone can exhibit leadership at any level in any organization or any aspect of life. Scholar Warren Bennis writes in *On Becoming a Leader* that the essence of leadership is full self-expression. "The key to full self-expression is understanding one's self and the world, and the key to understanding is learning—from one's own life and experience. The process of becoming a leader is much the same as the process of becoming an integrated human being."[13]

This means understanding our own motivation and that of others. It also means knowing the roots of what affects us—being aware of past experiences, positive or negative, that can distort perception. Using the mind's eye demands the ability to stay focused throughout our interactions with others. It means managing our emotions and positively influencing the emotions of others. This behavior will ensure that a person avoids being taken "hostage," metaphorically speaking, and instead maintains an inner authority that can "move mountains." Leaders who can positively influence the states of followers will achieve the highest levels of success. Great leaders deliver even criticism and tough feedback from a positive state.

What is in the mind's eye becomes reality. Every transaction (words, gestures, posture) reflects what is in the mind's eye, and experiences of the heart, mind, and soul feed the mind's eye. We simply remember the future from past conditioning if we do not actively intervene to focus and refocus the mind's eye.

When we can find meaning and purpose through the mind's eye, we are likely to find the greatest personal power to achieve our goals. When people drift toward negative thoughts, this thinking will affect what happens in their mind's eye. Negative states shrink the mind's eye while joy and satisfaction grow and nourish it.

Key Points to Remember

1. Our mind's eye determines our possibilities and our limits, and our state determines the result we will achieve. The ability to get into the right state is the secret of every high-performing leader.

2. Understanding what motivates us and others is the key to performing at our best. The highest motivation is selling to ourselves and others the benefits of discomfort or even pain in the service of accomplishing something we truly believe in.

3. A self-fulfilling prophecy is when people talk themselves into success or failure. Success in life is determined by the beliefs, the meaning, and the interpretation given to life events and experiences in our mind's eye.

4. Bringing inner and outer states together allows full use of personal energy to accomplish outstanding results. This integration gives us the foundation for being truly authentic.

CHAPTER THREE

THE POTENTIAL OF THE BONDING CYCLE

I first met Frank when he was ninety. From the moment we shook hands, I knew this gentle soul was a special human being. He had the spirit of a young man plus the laugh and smile of a truly happy person. What struck me most was his appreciation of the beauty and joy of life and his interest and curiosity about everything around him. On first impression, Frank showed such a lack of victimization and such profound joy in living that he seemed not to have suffered any loss or pain in his life.

As I got to know Frank, I discovered the immensity of the loss and pain he actually had overcome. When he was only ten, his mother had died, a factor that put him at high risk for later problems. As a young adult, he fought in World War I; as an elderly man, he still cried over friends lost in that horrible conflict.

Although he was too old to fight in World War II, he again suffered the loss of friends to armed conflict. Then, after fifty-four years of marriage, his beloved wife, Caroline, died; another loss that in itself put him at high risk for premature death. And there were many other less dramatic but stressful losses, all of which Frank bore with grace and determination to stay bonded to life and "enjoy the party."

In the autumn of 1993, approximately three months after the accidental death of my twenty-three-year-old son Doug, I was at the home of our mutual friend, Alice. As Frank entered the room where I was, he came tearfully toward me with open arms. We embraced, and after recovering enough to speak, he looked me in the eyes. What followed is etched forever in my heart and mind.

Quietly, he spoke: "George, I understand what you are going through. I never told you, but I also lost my son." We two fathers held each other in an embrace for life as the grief uncontrollably poured from our hearts. No words were necessary to convey what we both knew and understood about each other.

Frank's life was not complex. Born in 1896 to a working-class family in England, he was educated privately by the Quakers after his mother's death. When grown, he worked as a carpenter, a surveyor, and a member of the Royal Engineers until starting his own construction business at forty-nine. His willingness to take risks and his pride in his work made him successful. Involved in village life, he participated in the community theater group and ran for a local political office, but he did not garner any particular recognition or fame until after his hundredth birthday.

At that point, he was honored with a flight on the Concorde for his service to his country. Frank also began connecting with young people as he visited primary schools to teach youngsters what life was like at the beginning of the twentieth century. He also appeared in several BBC television shows about centenarians, gave speeches for veterans, delivered prayers on memorial days in Europe, and acted as the ceremonial leader in laying many memorial wreaths. He even visited 10 Downing Street and met Cherie Blair. Frank did not seek celebrity status, but when the world came to him, he was ready to share his story and his enthusiasm for life.

This synopsis of Frank's story does not reveal what made him special, however; nor does it indicate the substance that gave his life resilience, meaning, and joy.

One way Frank made his life meaningful was that he always lived with goals. For example, he was eager to reach his 104th birthday so that he would have lived in three centuries. Unfortunately, on the way to that goal, Frank suffered a stroke in the summer of 1999. This stroke left him unable either to speak or see. Despite the stroke, however, and with the support of many family members and friends, he achieved his goal of living into the twenty-first century.

In a conversation with me after he had regained his ability to speak, he wept as he spoke of the losses he had experienced since his stroke: his eyesight, his home, his ability to live independently and to watch TV. Yet

Frank's zest for living continued, as revealed in something he said to me: "I am rediscovering how wonderful it is just to listen to music or to the songs of birds."

This is another of the lessons Frank can teach us, another of the ways he had to make life consequential and fulfilling: he remained determined to reconnect continually to the joy of life, no matter how deep the pain and grief he suffered. His intention was to find new attachments and the emotional connection that drives a neverending search for the joy beneath the pain. Frank's motto for life remained "The party isn't over yet."

When I last spoke to him, I asked him if he felt that life was finally over.

"Oh my goodness, George, no!" he responded. "I enjoy living and life so much that 104 just isn't going to be long enough. Besides, I have so many recorded books to listen to. I have so many friends around me and so much to enjoy. After all, I am blessed with such good health; I have nothing to complain about." And with a spirited laugh he continued, "The party is over only when the band stops playing—and the band is still going strong!"

Frank died peacefully in his sleep in 2001 at the age of 105.

Frank's life is a model of the power of the bonding cycle and the ability to turn sorrow back into joy. I speak about Frank in almost every workshop or training that I conduct. With so much pain and suffering in life, people often use Frank's inspiring story as an anchor to hold onto in times of trouble in their own lives.

Frank's story has some important lessons for all of us. He provides us, as individuals, with a model of how to avoid victimization by living in a healthy, vibrant, energetic way. Rather than using our energy longing for the past, we need to find the will and determination to create new goals for the future and to "keep the party going," as Frank would say.

It is up to us to honor our own legacies, even to grieve for some of what we have lost, and then to reconnect with what is ultimately important. It is up to us to hear the band still playing, to respond by sharing what we have and what we know, to connect with others. Just like Frank, we can try to live our lives with the motto, "The party's not over!"

THE BONDING CYCLE

The bonding cycle is a powerful and fundamental concept that explains much about human motivation. Every relationship we have follows the pattern of the bonding cycle. Even in business, our interactions with others follow the stages of attachment, bonding, separation, and grieving. A person who is not bonded remains detached, and this can then manifest itself into physical and psychological problems for an individual and, ultimately, through this have a negative impact on the person's professional life as well.

Andreas was a senior vice president responsible for a substantial business with two thousand employees around the world. One day, his boss called him in and told him that even though he was getting good business results, he had a problem. People felt intimidated by him and he had created too many enemies.

Andreas responded: "Isn't that what I'm paid for—to get results, not to have people like me?"

His boss gave him six weeks to change his behavior. Sadly, Andreas was not successful in altering his conduct, so six weeks later he lost his job.

Now here was a man targeted to be on the short list as the next CEO of the company, a man with dreams of succeeding, a man who had never encountered failure. Andreas collapsed in total disbelief and went into a deep depression.

I spoke to him about creating bonds with those with whom he dealt. At that time, he ridiculed the idea, saying, "Doesn't bonding only happen in a chemistry lab?"

Eventually, however, he came to understand how his whole personality had been built on avoiding bonding and on avoiding grief. His mother had been very anxious; his father had been totally focused on work. Andreas had become an independent loner who did not know how to create bonds, and he now found himself in a situation in which he was out of a job.

Over the next eighteen months, Andreas grew to understand the importance of bonding and the methods of creating positive relationships. He was shocked and hurt, though, not to get a job immediately. In fact, he did not find another for eighteen months. He eventually became the CEO of a much smaller company.

Because of this experience, Andreas made a profound change to his identity. He came to terms with the fact he had never learned how to bond and had avoided grief his whole life—just like his father. The turning point came when he had a heart-to-heart discussion with his father. They talked about what had happened in their lives and the implications of what had happened to each of them and with each other. It was the first time the father had shared his pain about leaving his motherland and his family of origin along with the deep loneliness of being in a new country. Even after some thirty years, Andreas's father always felt a longing in his heart to return to his homeland. For the first time, they could cry together. Andreas never remembered his father hugging him or saying, "I love you." After that discussion, Andreas's father did just that.

Now Andreas feels that losing his job was one of the best events he has ever endured, despite all the pain. He was on the way to a heart attack, a divorce, and the loss of contact with his three children. He views being fired as a blessing, because he discovered another aspect of life: how to create bonds with people. He developed a renewed and profoundly different relationship with his wife, his children, his father, and all his friends, and he now has a job he loves. Further, both in and out of the workplace, he is dealing with people in a constructive way. Andreas has become a true high-performing leader creating a genuinely high-performing organization by how he builds bonds to people and goals.

Bill George in his book *Authentic Leadership* has this to say: "The capacity to develop close and enduring relationships is one mark of a leader. Unfortunately, many leaders of major companies believe their job is to create the strategy, organization structure and organizational processes. Then they just delegate the work to be done, remaining aloof from the people doing the work."[1]

Leaders who understand and create bonding are able to establish trust and engage in highly productive behavior. When we know how to bond, we are better equipped to avoid being taken hostage.

Every relationship we have—to another human being, to a goal, to a pet, or even to an object—follows the bonding cycle. Joseph

Chilton Pearce, author of *Magical Child,* understood bonding as a psychobiological form of communication, beyond ordinary consciousness and fundamental to healthy human functioning. "Bonding is a vital physical link that coordinates and unifies the entire biological system. Bonding seals a primary knowing that it is the basis for rational thought. We are never conscious of being bonded; we are conscious only of our acute *dis*-ease when we are not bonded or when we are bonded to compulsion and material things. The un-bonded person (and bonding to objects is to be very much un-bonded in a functional sense) will spend his life in a search for what bonding was designed to give."[2]

As Figure 3.1 illustrates, the bonding cycle is composed of four stages: attachment, bonding, separation, and grieving:

Attachment is a process of creating nearness and making a connection. This is what John Bowlby, founder of modern attachment theory, terms the "drive for proximity."[3] When there is proximity, we have the potential to experience a sense of comfort.

Bonding is the emotional exchange that follows proximity and attachment. Bonding creates a synergy whereby a mutual impact on emotions is created. It is an exchange of energy. Bonding has endurance, a depth that involves the emotions. It is possible to be attached without being bonded. Successful people are able to make attachments, bond, and rebond, and in doing so, they are able to inspire and motivate others. All things pass and, at some stage, there will be a separation.

Separation is an interruption to bonding and the attachment process. It can come in the form of change, loss, disappointment, or frustration. Separation results from the natural evolution of a relationship (growing up, growing older, or graduating), or it can be unexpected (death, accident, or sudden loss). Separation can lead to powerful emotions and can be a fundamental driver of destructive behavior because it leads to the fourth stage, grieving.

Grieving involves going through the mental and emotional stages of letting go and saying goodbye. Whether over small things or profound things, grieving is essential if human beings are to be resilient, to go on, to recover, and to find their own personal power. Feeling our personal power, coming back to the joy of life, reflects that we have come through a grieving process.

FIGURE 3.1. THE BONDING CYCLE

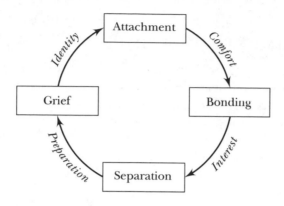

Many people experience the fullness of the bonding cycle in relation to a pet. A puppy is brought home, and everyone attaches to it because it is so cute. As the puppy grows and becomes a member of the household, bonding occurs. When the dog dies, separation occurs. To be able to bond to another puppy, the family must go through a grieving period. Those who cannot often say they could never own another dog. They are unable to live through the loss and reexperience the joy of owning another pet.

I think it is accurate to say that everyone in a hostage state is in some form of unresolved grief. The grief that follows loss and separation is for some people the most difficult part of life. Not facing it has profound consequences. The task of a hostage negotiator is to create a bond with the hostage taker. Through this bond, the conflict can be resolved in a peaceful manner. It is a myth that bonding occurs only with people we like. In fact, it is crucial that we learn to form and maintain bonds in ways that allow a relationship to exist even in the face of profound differences or serious conflict. Hostage negotiators are able to negotiate with desperate people because they are able to form bonds with them, irrespective of the acts that such individuals may have committed. Without a bond, there will not be a negotiation. Every act of violence involves a break or disruption in the bonding process. People who commit crimes or who act aggressively are in some state of detachment. Bonding interrupts the detachment process, and so the ability to bond and rebond is the key skill that all hostage negotiators need.

ATTACHMENT AND BONDING

Attachment behavior is considered a basic, inborn, biologically adaptive "motivational system" that drives an infant to create a few selective attachments in his or her early life.[4] Research shows that attachments provide a relationship in which infants will (1) seek proximity to the attachment figure; (2) have a sense of a safe haven—where their distress will be soothed by an attachment figure; and (3) develop an internal working model of a secure base that will provide them with the security that will enable them to explore the world, to have a sense of well-being, and to soothe themselves in times of distress in the future.[5]

All mammals have a basic need to seek proximity—that is, to be near or to be in the physical presence of another mammal. In addition, people's physical proximity to goals, homes, pets, or countries also can lead to attachment, and for some, attachments to these are stronger than their attachments to people.

A television news item told the story of a young boy who was in a coma for several months. When the boy's pet golden retriever was brought to him, the dog started to lick his face and make sounds in his ears. In a short time, the boy miraculously came out of his coma. Soon after, much to the surprise of all the doctors and nurses, he was able to go home. The doctors could only say that what happened was "unexplainable."

Attachment behavior biologically activates many hormones in the body and provides us with a sense of comfort. We are a walking pharmacy that is activated by proximity with other beings or things that are important to us. Bonding is all about how we hold the proximity and how we give and take emotional energy when we are in the state of attachment. The body, the emotions, the mind, and the spirit are all involved in the bonding process.

When attachment leads to the formation of a bond, our emotions are always involved. Expressing these emotions is part of the bonding process. People who are not aware of their emotions or who block their emotions are going to be limited in their ability to bond. Bonding requires having an open body, being flexible, and being able to express energy and warmth. A cold, detached person whose body is closed and who is rigid and inflexible, or who cannot look at or touch people will have difficulty in forming bonds. What is in our minds, what we think, and what we believe affect our ability to bond. A person who is not bonded remains detached. When people are either unable to bond or have unresolved broken bonds, they are more likely to be taken hostage by others.

In essence, the state of exclusion, of feeling isolated or disconnected, often results in people who look for what is wrong in themselves and others, as exemplified by the negative self-fulfilling prophecy. For example, a manager who stays in his office and refuses to engage in social bonding behavior is likely to drift toward a negative perception of others, and employees and colleagues, in turn, will perceive him as negative.

When people are detached they are not engaged in what they are doing. A lack of engagement can have serious consequences for a leader and an organization. A thirty-year international study by the Gallup organization on emotional engagement at work (released in 2004) showed that the majority of people do not feel emotionally attached to their jobs.[6] According to Gerald Wood, executive director of Gallup, Germany, "The level of emotional attachment to the job has a direct correlation to productivity, customer satisfaction, lost workdays, and turnover—key economic factors directly linked to state of mind."[7] A less engaged workforce results in reduced profitability for companies. This study demonstrates the level of broken bonding that exists in our work environments. The results included the engagement levels shown in Figure 3.2.

This means that in the best-scoring country, 70 percent of employees do *not* feel emotionally attached! Rather than being the work that puts employees off, the lack of attachment tends to be driven by the relationships with colleagues and, particularly, immediate managers. Says Wood, "What we have found is that the relationship with the direct managers is very important. That is where emotional attachment either happens or doesn't happen." Sadly, the research showed that "the majority of people who are unhappy with their jobs do not do anything to change the situation," according to Wood. People who feel powerless to change any situation in

FIGURE 3.2. INTERNATIONAL EMOTIONAL ENGAGEMENT LEVELS AT WORK

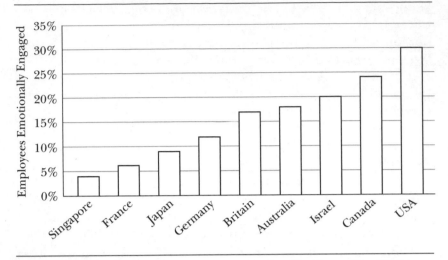

Source: Gallup Study, "Poll Reveals Germans Are Just Working to Live," 2004. Available at www.dw-world.de/dw/article/0,1564,1094681,00.html.

effect have become hostages. When we feel like hostages, we are more stressed and less positive and, therefore, we have less energy for what we are doing.

Bonding has the potential to produce tremendous energy. Mother Teresa could look at a flower, see God's presence, and be moved to tears. When she saw a child dying in the streets of Calcutta, she would be moved with deep compassion, taking the child to her orphanage knowing that he or she would die the next day. In her mind, no child should die alone. Most of us would burn out being around so much pain and suffering in children. However, Mother Theresa's work gave her great energy. She was able to achieve so much and give so much because of her ability to bond and rebond continuously.

The power of bonding should not be underestimated. Bonding can happen instantaneously or occur over time. It can include words or it can be nonverbal.

One of the most profound examples of bonding without words is the story of a man who was on an airplane leaving Denver airport. The wings were not de-iced correctly and, as a result, the plane crashed. During the forty-five seconds before the crash, the passenger never took his eyes off the flight attendant who was sitting at the front of the plane and looking into his eyes. After the crash, mud, snow, and rocks flew into the plane. The man suffered a punctured lung, a broken leg, and a concussion, but he was still able to pull one or two other people to safety before he drifted into a coma. A day or two later, when he awoke in the hospital, his first question was, "Where is the stewardess?" Told that she had died in the crash, he began to weep. What he said was that, next to his mother, he had never experienced having a person give him so much in such a short space of time. And he said, "You know, I felt no fear. I was prepared to die." Afterward, he suffered a deep grief reaction. For many years, he would take flowers to the stewardess's grave, explaining, "I never want her to be forgotten because she gave me so much in those few moments."

We know that, for many people, when they are bonded, they feel no fear. In fact, fear can be a manifestation of broken bonding at that moment.

SEPARATION AND GRIEF

Attachment and bonding always lead to separation. Separation is a transition or a change in attachment that can have a profound negative impact if not handled well. Separation can also be a positive experience at the right time and if dealt with in the right way. Separation opens the grieving process, which, in turn, opens the heart for new attachment. In some ways, separation is as natural as attachment. It can occur after one minute, one year, or even eighty years. Death itself—even if you believe in renewal after death—leads to a disruption of the physical level and the psychological level of bonding. When we go through separation, it leads us to the grieving process. Grieving is essential in all mammals in order for them to let go of an earlier bond and allow the heart to open and make a new attachment or, in some cases, to experience a renewal if it is to the same person or object. It is a continuous cycle.

In 1981, I was asked to present a workshop for pediatricians in a hospital in South Germany. One of the doctors approached me afterward to seek advice on one of her patients. Nine-year-old Hannah was unable to eat due to a large lump that had appeared in her throat. Doctors could find no medical reason for her condition. More than a month had passed since she had consumed any solid food.

The doctor wondered whether grief could be a factor. When I discussed the case with her, there were no obvious losses in Hannah's life. However, on going through the files, we found a note about her "pet pig." The doctor and I worked out a strategy together. She then spoke to the girl about her pet pig. Hannah's parents were farmers, and her father had given her one piglet, the runt, from a litter. She nurtured this animal and enabled it to survive and thrive. It was, in a sense, her "baby."

One day, she came home from school and discovered that her pig, "Squeaky," had been slaughtered. This was a profound shock for her. Furthermore, every day she had to pass the carcass hanging in the barn on her way to school. Five days later, her father tried to force her to eat the meat from Squeaky while her older brothers laughed and her mother sat passively. The next day, Hannah was hospitalized.

After the doctor discovered this trauma, the plan became to help Hannah grieve the loss of Squeaky. When the doctor first brought the subject up, Hannah turned away and refused to speak. With bonding and gentle persistence, the doctor continued to speak to Hannah, who responded with rage and anger, fists pounding her. The doctor kept the bond, and after some forty-five seconds, Hannah embraced the doctor and cried her heart out for nearly thirty minutes. Following this catharsis, she was able to eat some solid food for the first time in a month. The lump immediately reduced in size and vanished after two days. Her sobbing represented a major breakthrough, and, for the first time since her separation from the pig, she began the grieving process—her first step on the road to recovery. The support the doctor gave Hannah with the grieving process helped Hannah progress far more than medication did.

When people cannot deal with separation and grieving, they are unable to reattach and rebond. This unresolved separation and grief is at the root of victimization and feeling like a hostage. Sometimes guilt is a part of the situation. As long as people have guilt, they keep the bond in some destructive way, thus blocking the process of moving on to a new attachment. Despair is another possible outcome: it is the ultimate detachment. Despair takes root when people will only be comforted by that which they have lost:

the woman who has lost a child, the man who has lost a job, someone whose home burns down. If such individuals can only be comforted by that which they have lost, they are doomed to despair. That is why "I cannot live without you or without this" is a powerfully destructive statement. To avoid grief, some people go to the opposite extreme: they never attach or bond. Thus, there are two poles: people who are afraid to attach because they do not want to feel grief, and people who are grieving and are afraid of making a new attachment.

THE EIGHT STAGES OF GRIEF

Much excellent work has been done on grieving by scholars such as Elisabeth Kübler-Ross, Stephen Levine, and others.[8] Essentially, there are eight stages involved in the grieving process: denial; protest and anger; sadness, missing, or longing; fear or feeling of terror; mental and emotional acceptance; forming new attachments or making a renewal; forgiveness; and finally gratitude.

1. *Denial.* When people are in denial, they are experiencing grief and actually protecting themselves. There is a moment after certain losses in which denial is healthy, but it becomes destructive or a problem if it goes on for too long. Research into children sent to boarding schools at a young age shows that, for many of them, the pain of separating from their parents is great, and yet they feel unable to express it because they do not want their parents to feel bad. They thus suppress the emotion and "deny" their own feelings. By suppressing emotion they—and many people—"deny" their feelings and enter into a subconscious grief phase that results in them being unable to attach or make new bonds.

2. *Protest and anger.* After denial comes protest and anger. We see many acts of violence and aggression occurring as people act out their protests. Most people do not actually act out the violence, but they want to protest, and that is natural. People do not want to give up that which is comforting to them or to which they are biologically and psychologically anchored. It can feel like ripping your heart out when you face the loss of an attachment, whether it involves a person, pet, promotion, goal, or home.

I knew a grandmother who stood in front of her house as it burned to the ground. Tears ran down her face, and she begged the firefighters to put out the fire. She cried out, "I can build another house but it's the pictures, the pictures." She was referring to photos of her three-year-old child who had died over forty years earlier. As the house burned and she faced the loss of the pictures, it reactivated the whole grief process of losing her son again.

We can never be sure what people attach to as a source of comfort and bonding. I have grown to deeply respect why people form attachments to different things. What you find comforting, what I find comforting, those people or things become our anchors, our secure bases. Any one of us can lose our physical health, a person, a job, or a feeling of security when our house is robbed; if we lose too many attachments too fast, we may be unable to rebond and establish new ones.

Ken was a team member working closely with a colleague. The colleague was in an automobile accident and died. The shock was so deep that Ken began underperforming to the point that his job was threatened. Not only did he lose a good friend who was a secure base, but he also developed anxiety for the future related to the fact that he could die suddenly and leave his children without a father as his friend had. This is similar to what happens with firefighters and police officers who can have grief reactions to the loss of lives they encounter in the line of duty.

Protest is a natural and healthy part of expressing grief. Violence can emerge due to losses and can activate the grief. It is important that we are able to express our anger in a healthy way in order to ventilate it.

3. *Sadness, missing, or longing.* When people are truly grieving, the sadness comes from deep inside; they want to cry, to express their feelings with tears. It starts in the stomach and moves up, as a pain over the chest, then becomes a lump in the throat and pressure behind the eyes. The act of crying is essential in completing this process. One reason men die between seven and twelve years earlier than women do may be that many men are unable to cry, and to express their grief as part of the grieving process. As a

result, they detach and stay in a chronic state of loneliness, unable to form new bonds.

4. *Fear or feeling of terror.* When people feel fear it is a kind of contraction, and it means that they are retreating within themselves; they are facing the fact that they are separate and in danger. Attachment is not an escape from the fact that we are separate. However, although we are alone on this journey through life, we do not have to be lonely. Some people are hostages to loneliness because they fear grieving and rebonding. The fact that we are separate is brought to our attention every time we go through a grieving process. We actually see who we are at these times. Our identities actually build in the ability to handle a crisis, to handle separation, because the crisis brings us back to ourselves, the essence of who we are. Bonding itself does not build identity. In fact, if we use bonding as our primary form of identification, it becomes a form of codependency. When some people face a loss they feel a deep fear, which can be healed in many ways. When we are able to reach out, to take someone's hand, to speak about what we feel, we are able to use the bonding process to facilitate grief. We know that grieving cannot happen alone. It is a process that must occur with another person in a family, group, or tribe. One dramatic example of this phenomenon is war veterans who return from battle, often traumatized by the experience and suffering from posttraumatic stress disorders. The major problem for these veterans is the rebonding process. They must go through special grieving processes in order to be able to open their hearts again. Many veterans carry deep emotional scars because they never worked through their grief. In reality, unexpressed grief is likely to shorten your life.

5. *Mental and emotional acceptance.* This stage is the step of being able to accept the loss mentally and emotionally. This is important because it means that deep inside we have come to terms with the loss, accept it, and believe that we can continue to go on or even exist. To say we cannot live without somebody or something is an unhealthy and desperate statement, a kind of suicide. We must be willing to let go of everything—even our children, even those things we consider deeply important to us. That does not mean we want losses to happen, but if we can let go, go through the grieving process, and then rebond, we are more likely

to have fuller and even longer lives. In fact, we know that the same hormones that are involved in the longevity process are also connected to social bonding. George Burns, the famous comedian who died at one hundred years old and who always liked to bond with others, was deeply moved when his wife, Gracie, died. He visited her grave frequently and spoke to her every day. However, he did not stay detached, getting locked into despair or depression. He was able to maintain his connection with Gracie, but he also went through the grieving process, said goodbye, found new attachments, and eventually found the "joy of life" again.

6. *Forming new attachments or making a renewal.* When we can make new attachments, it brings comfort and anchoring and contributes to our physiological and psychological well-being. Many people remain stuck in the grief phase of the bonding cycle and cannot make new attachments after the loss of a job, or a divorce, or the change of a home. They want back that which they have lost. We know that second marriages have a higher divorce rate than first marriages. In part, it appears that people who marry on the rebound do not really marry the new person. They are marrying a substitute, and when there is a conflict, all the old grief is triggered and the grief process is activated. People who wait a year before they remarry have a far greater chance of not divorcing; in fact, only 35 percent get a divorce. In every new attachment, it is important to let go of the grief and accept the new person as he or she is rather than try to substitute for the loss.

Perhaps one of the most moving stories I have witnessed involves a couple who were married for over fifty years. Though they celebrated their golden wedding anniversary, their marriage suddenly fell apart. She became sick and they started fighting. Fifty-three years into a marriage, they wanted a divorce. They actually moved into separate living spaces. The daughter dragged them to my office, saying, "Please help. It doesn't make sense for people who have been married for this long to get a divorce." Here's the story: The couple had never really faced the fact that one day, the marriage would have to come to an end. They really thought they were going to live happily ever after. They got through both their twenty-fifth and fortieth wedding anniversaries. However the fiftieth anniversary brought home feelings of how long they had been together and thoughts that their time might be "running out," and they started discussing who was going to die first.

They argued so much about who should die first that they actually made suicide pacts and came within seconds of carrying them out. One time they tried carbon monoxide, another time with a gun, and yet another time with medication. That is how much they could not stand the thought of saying goodbye to each other.

The wife became so upset in the process that she had to be put into a hospital for treatment. They had not told anyone about this situation, which they carried like a secret burden, until they shared it with me and finally got some relief. As they started grieving, I asked the wife, "How many years do you think you need to say goodbye to your husband?" Tearfully, she responded, "At least another fifty-three years." So I said, "You better get started."

They were then able to reconcile the fact that one day they would be separated and that they were not going to live forever. The couple had been locked into anticipatory grief. If we cannot accept the separation that will eventually happen, then every moment becomes an anticipated loss and a constant stress. What happened with this couple was that they were able to change their mind's eye and their whole frame of reference when they were able to grieve. Each additional minute of their marriage then became a gift rather than a loss. They were then able to experience the joy of bonding again.

People who are afraid to die, to fail, or to go through a loss cannot really live. The moment we accept that we are going to die, then we can really live. The moment we can accept that, we can be separate, and then we can really attach because attachment becomes a true choice and we become grateful for every moment. The same process is true for our children. From the moment they are born, we have to watch them grow up and leave us. With each developmental stage, there is a grief reaction that some parents cannot handle. The child is not allowed to grow up individual and separate. As a result, the children leave home unable to handle the separation and grief and, often, there will be major conflicts and fights because one or both parents cannot really say goodbye to this stage of life. Therefore, the child has to fight or use aggression or anger as a way to become separate. Once we are able to say goodbye, form a new attachment, renew, and find a new source of comfort, then we are ready for the next stage, which is forgiveness.

7. *Forgiveness.* This stage is one of the deepest healing experiences. Forgiveness literally means being able to give again—in other words, it means that we put out our energy to be able to "give for" others. People who are not able to forgive tend to become victims or persecutors. They are unhappy and they suffer, and so they become hostages or take others hostage. The victim and the victim-turned-persecutor tend not to be able to experience real joy, real love, or real gratitude.

8. *Gratitude.* The final stage of grieving is gratitude, which is the signal that we really have completed the bonding cycle. Gratitude is what we experience when we are in a fully bonded state, to people, to pets, to places, to goals, to objects, to life itself. Some people have so many losses that they may actually break the bond to life and give up. Such individuals are either actively suicidal or—due to their despair, depression, lack of bonding, or loneliness—they are moved into feelings of being alone and suffer physiological and psychological consequences. Gratitude comes from the feeling of connectivity that we get from bonding. If we cannot bond, we cannot be connected and then we cannot experience the exchange of energy. The root of the word *happiness* is the word *happens*. Happiness can be found in things that happen. Happiness is not an elusive goal chased externally; rather, it is found in the part of the world that is happening now. Out of a sense of what happens—even if it is painful—there comes a "goodness." Moreover, in the goodness there is gratitude—a feeling of "thank you." Out of the sense of "thank you" comes the sense that we are not the center of the universe. There is something beyond us. We are not the cause. Victims, however, take themselves hostage because they block the process of gratitude. Victims feel sorry for themselves; they are passive and feel "helpless" to participate in getting what they want.

Loss of a job has caused a number of otherwise "normal" citizens to return to the workplace with a weapon and shoot innocent colleagues. These people exhibit an inability to get on with their lives; they are stuck in separation or grief. Yet loss and grief can be felt on a smaller scale, as, for example, when someone finds himself or herself in a reduced office space or loses special parking privileges or is angry with a neighbor who cut down a much loved tree. The inability to cope with these changes can lead people to feel resentful and then to act in ways that damage themselves personally and professionally.

After many years with the company, Mary had been hoping for a promotion. However, an outsider with general management skills but no specific expertise in her area was brought in, and she was demoted. Mary had a choice: to accept the situation but be bitter about what had happened, or to let go, move on, and find another job. Mary wisely chose to move on, landing a fabulous job at a more senior level and gaining the respect of her old colleagues at the same time.

It is often the fear and pain of loss that stops people from acting in a rational and healthy way. Research studies have shown that most people are motivated by the avoidance of pain, fear, and loss. However, by avoiding pain, people stop themselves from being able to go through the grief process and move on. This can even happen in positive situations, as when people experience a sense of loss caused by the end of a project. It is important that they recognize this, celebrate the project, acknowledge its end, and go through a debriefing process in helping employees move on.

For six months, four colleagues had been working together on a strategic project for the company. They were all different personalities but they were united behind a single goal—to lead the project to create a new slogan for their company.

During the process, they had their differences and did not always agree. However, as they deeply shared a common goal, they truly bonded as a team. When the project was successfully completed, the team was disbanded, and they each returned to their normal roles. However, for several weeks, they experienced a period of "grief" as they no longer needed to talk together on a regular basis. They kept in touch by e-mail, and whenever one was visiting the offices of another, both experienced an immediate sense of connection. This contact gradually declined over time, although the sense of bonding remained. This was an effective and powerful exercise both for the company (which got the best out of a high-performing team) and for the individuals (who were able to learn and develop through the experience as well as create lasting bonds with each other).

As already mentioned, all bonds will create a grief reaction when they end. Unfortunately, the grief reaction can stimulate the most violent force in the human being. If an individual cannot cope with the loss from a forced separation, then he or she may turn to violence or aggression as a coping mechanism to deal with the pain. There are numerous examples of people becoming violent after learning, for example, that their spouse wants a divorce or they have lost a job, or when they are facing arrest by the police, loss of custody of children, or being expelled from home.

Grieving is a necessary part of healthy development. The loss and pain we work through become part of our identities, and this is why being able to deal with separations in our lives is vital for our own growth. There is a kind of wound that is created during the grieving process—"the dark moments of the soul." Often, those individuals who make the deepest attachments to people or goals, who are the most successful or happy, are those who have known deep moments of struggle. When we bond, we merge our identities somewhat with the person or thing we are bonded to. During a separation, we again feel our own identities more strongly.

The Seven Manifestations of Broken Bonding

Bonding is often broken, and, as a result, many people become hostages to others or to themselves. They avoid or they refuse bonding, or they stay stuck in separation, or they stay blocked in the grieving process. Any break in the bonding cycle can lead to problems. The seven manifestations of broken bonding are psychosomatic illness, violence and aggression, addiction, depression, burnout, stress reaction, and organizational conflict.

1. *Psychosomatic illness.* Researchers are discovering that premature death has roots in broken bonding. In 1977, James Lynch published a book called *The Broken Heart: The Medical Consequences of Loneliness* describing that connection.[9] Since the 1977 book was released, literally thousands more research articles have been published demonstrating a strong link between our health and our social bonding systems.

That is why, for example, when people live with someone for several decades and then lose that companion, a high percentage of the survivors are dead within two months—some within hours or days after the loss. These people were in a deep state of grief and, even though their deaths may be attributed to a heart attack or some other cause, it is in fact a grief reaction to the disrupted bond. One study looked at people who have heart attacks and then go home and live alone. Eighty percent die within six months, while only 25 percent of those who live with someone else die.[10] Married people also live longer. If a person goes through open-heart surgery and has a pet at home, his or her chance of survival increases by 75 percent. Studies repeatedly show how important bonding is to our health.

Men are at greater risk than women. On average, men die seven to twelve years earlier than women, and the only variable that holds up in research is the social network. Men do not bond as deeply as women do, nor do they grieve as well. If you have a daughter, you live longer. If you have a lifelong friend, you live longer. In a ten-year study of death rates, there was a clear connection between the health of people's social networks and their physical health. Our relationships form one of the strongest buffers we have against stress and its negative impacts.

2. *Violence and aggression.* Violence begins when bonding ends. One of the most overlooked factors behind the violence and aggression we are experiencing every day, particularly in the Western world, is the number of people who are going through losses, have broken bonds, or remain unattached.

The rise in youth gang violence can be attributed to children who grow into adolescence in a high state of exclusion and loneliness and then turn to the gang as their source of social bonding. They will then commit any act of violence to remain a member of that gang, to continue to belong. This is driven by the need for attachment.

Violence, then, is a form of failed grieving or grief avoidance. It can be connected to present losses, to those from the past, or even to those of past generations that are carried into the present by way of resentment, a sense of injustice, or lack of forgiveness. Violence-prone people live on the edge of chronic loneliness or masked depression, lacking the power to get what they want in a constructive way. In the end, violence becomes an act of power to deal with whatever emotional volcano is inside. It gives temporary relief to the feeling of victimization and powerlessness. However, violence is not a solution. Healthy grieving has always been a social process occurring in a tribe, clan, or group in which other protecting, dependable persons help the individual who suffered the loss to fully rebond to life, whatever the loss or injustice might have been. Western culture, in many ways, has a grief aversion—we feel that after a loss, we should quickly move on. The cycle of bonding includes grieving. Those who are hostages to violence and aggression must learn to grieve and learn to bond, which includes feeling empathy and compassion.

3. *Addiction.* Arieti saw addiction as "a pathological attachment to a mood altering drug, person or experience."[11] A person who cannot effectively bond may substitute alcohol, food, drugs, gambling, sex, work, or shopping for the comfort that normally comes from interacting with people. At the root of addiction is the fact that other people are seen as a source of pain and frustration. Therefore, the desire to avoid pain in the mind's eye causes the person to seek comfort in something else. Ultimately, addictive behavior leads to a detachment from others that can inhibit effective bonding in relationships.

A study asked young adults, "When you are under stress or you need to change your mood, what do you do?" "Listen to music" was number one on the list of responses. It was not until number eight that "people" were mentioned. The inability to turn to people as a source of comfort is indicative of attachment problems and may lead to addiction problems. The absence of bonding is an increasing problem in today's culture. There was a time when families ate together, sat and talked together around the fireplace, and did other kinds of bonding activities together. In today's world, we see more and more children attaching to television or computers or being unattached completely, unable to turn to other people as a source of comfort. An addictive personality will often say "people are a pain" and then turn to something other than people as a substitute for human bonding. Alcoholics Anonymous remains one of the most effective systems for treating addiction of all kinds because it is fundamentally a grieving and rebonding process. When an addictive behavior is resolved, there is always one major change; the person begins to turn to other people as a source of comfort. Addiction is clearly a form of being a hostage. In the end, the resolution involves finding our own power.

4. *Depression.* Depression can be described as a biological and psychological mechanism in all mammals that often results when there is a disruption in attachment systems, past, present, or anticipated. Depression has physiological, metabolic, and genetic components that must be recognized. The social and psychological components of depression have to do with loss, unresolved grief, and not getting enough positive bonding from their present attachment system. It can be because they lost something in the past or because they are anticipating the loss of something in the future. The fact that there are many chemical changes in depression is connected to the fact that when we come out of the social bond, or we remain outside of a social bond, our physiology is reacting strongly to those changes.

Depression at its worst becomes despair. Despair says, "I will only be comforted by that which I have lost, and since that which I have lost will never come back, I am doomed never to be totally comforted again." So when people lose something important to them—a house, a job, a child, a pet, money—this loss can actually trigger a state of despair in which they will say, "I will never bond again, I will never be comforted again." This reaction is another example of how the mind's eye searches for the negative. Separation or disruption in the bonding cycle—past, present, and anticipated—creates a reaction in all mammals. However, treating the symptoms does not necessarily treat the cause. Antidepressants may stop people from feeling depressed, but they may still be dying of loneliness. The next step is to help them find the joy of life again. We must remember that depression can be a signal that something is not working correctly in the attachment process. Broken bonding can easily take people hostage in the form of depression.

5. *Burnout.* Next to food, oxygen, and water, bonding is our greatest source of energy. If the inability to bond persists, people can burn out. Burnout can be defined as a kind of exhaustion that leads to cynicism and emotional detachment. People who cannot recharge when they sleep remain physically and emotionally exhausted and may be suffering from burnout. They feel negative about everything around them, which in turn stops them from bonding. They stay emotionally detached and can prove to be major energy drainers. Everything they do seems pointless or useless, and they then experience all the people around them

negatively. They also feel badly about themselves, and this leads to an inability to feel positive emotion.

People who are burned out take others as hostages through their negativity. For example, a doctor or nurse who can no longer feel empathy toward a sick patient eventually starts to dislike sick patients. The same is true for a teacher who begins to believe every student is trying to take advantage of him, the police officer who believes everyone is a thief, or a childcare worker who actually becomes hostile and aggressive toward the children in her care. Anyone who is dealing with people in an environment of conflict can suffer from burnout.

6. *Stress reaction.* Four stressors are deeply connected to broken bonding. The first is *loss.* Sometimes the losses are obvious—someone dies, something precious is lost, or there is a divorce. While separation puts a physical and emotional strain on us, bonding protects and immunizes us against the negative impacts of stress. Stress has to do with demands on us from either external or internal sources. The key factor is not the "stressor" but the individual reaction to the stressor. Someone can go through a major loss and have a limited stress reaction. Another person can go through a small loss and have a major stress reaction. How the mind's eye responds to a loss determines how much stress people feel and whether or not they become hostage to it.

Second, in addition to loss, another powerful stressor has to do with *conflict and negative relationships.* If we are around people with whom we have an ongoing conflict, there will be extensive and destructive stress. This is because we are hostage to those people and stay in a negative state. Through positive bonding, our relationships can improve with those around us—partners, family members, friends, colleagues—and thereby reduce the stress we are placing on ourselves.

A third major stressor is *loss of direction and purpose in life.* If you do not have a purpose or goal in life and feel directionless, this can lead to feeling valueless and powerless, which will put you in a state of mind in which you can easily be taken hostage. The absence of direction and purpose ultimately leads to broken bonding.

The fourth major stressor is *loneliness.* According to author and psychologist James Lynch, loneliness is now one of the major predictors of who will suffer from major stress-related diseases.[12] We can get tremendous power over our stress reactions by understanding where we are suffering from broken bonding and are failing to maintain or renew bonds. When we go through change, even a positive change, it can put great demands on the system and bring about a need for rebonding that activates the grief process.

7. *Organizational conflict.* The difference between low and high rates of organizational conflict can be attributed to the level of bonding that exists—with managers, team members, or the organization as a whole. A healthy measure of conflict is conducive to enhanced creativity as long as the bonds remain strong or easily renewed. Can you think of a time when you were on a high-performing team or worked with a high-performing leader? Did you feel high levels of bonding? High-performing organizations and teams have high-performing leaders who create strong emotional bonds. When organizations have strong bonding, as outlined in the following list, there is the possibility of achieving exceptional results.

Ingredients for Effective Organizational Bonding

- Members who want to belong
- Emotional commitment to goals
- Dialogue with mutual respect
- Creative leadership
- Maximum self-regulation

Broken bonding disrupts organizational effectiveness in five ways:

1. A high-performing team has *members who want to belong* and are strongly bonded together. If there is fear, threat, or negativity in the team, members will struggle to feel bonded, thus generating conflict or causing avoidance of conflict.
2. A high-performing team has *emotional commitment to goals* as well as commitment to each other. If each team member is not fully bonded to the goal, the team will not achieve a high result. Failure to commit to goals can occur when goals are not clear or the person is not engaged with the goals.
3. High-performing team members use *dialogue driven by mutual respect*. This is the ability to have difficult conversations with thoughtfulness and consideration. When people can speak the

truth and keep the bond, then team members can handle the "pain" of hearing an unwelcome message because of the respect. The bonding remains intact or is quickly renewed if broken.

4. High-performing teams have *creative leadership*. When leaders only micromanage or control processes, then the workforce will not be inspired and the team will not perform at its best. Creative leadership is all about how people are brought together to create the synergy, the desire to bring out their best and achieve the goals of the team.

5. High-performing team members are given opportunities for *maximum self-regulation*. People need to and want to feel their own personal power and feel that what they are doing is worthwhile. They need to have choice in what they are doing and feel that what they are doing is making a significant contribution. When choice is taken away, that automatically brings the possibility of people feeling like hostages.

Bonding that is broken will produce organizational conflicts and ineffectiveness. Why does this have such an impact? Because, ultimately, bonding is the best vehicle leading to customer loyalty and success.

Rushing up to the airport counter, a woman anxiously tells the check-in clerk that she has to get on the next plane home because her son has been hospitalized and may be dying. The clerk looks at her ticket and says it is impossible to change, as she had purchased a prepaid apex ticket that is not exchangeable. She repeats her demand to be let on the plane, and the clerk repeats his refusal and rudely asks her to step out of the way so he can serve other passengers. She then promptly grabs an umbrella and strikes the clerk on the side of the head.

How could this situation have been avoided? If the detached check-in clerk had felt part of a team whose mission was to serve its customers as best it could, he would have responded to the woman with bonding. First, he could have made the simple step of empathizing with her problem. "Madame, I am really sorry to hear your son is in the hospital and I hope he'll be okay. You have a prepaid ticket that I am not authorized to change, but let me get you to a supervisor who can help you while I get other passengers on board. I know we can solve this problem." The woman would then hug him and forever be loyal to the airline.

Those people who have a good balance between attachment to people (ability to bond) and attachment to goals (drive to succeed) will have higher self-esteem and therefore be greater contributors to the success of a team, group, family, or organization. It is a combination of the attachment to both people (relationship-driven) and goals (task- and result-driven) that makes a well-balanced manager. Many business leaders have high attachment to goals but low and weak attachments to people. Those people with high bonding and higher self-esteem are also better equipped to manage and cope with change. Andreas's story, earlier in the chapter, demonstrates this.

BONDING AND CHANGE

With the amount of change taking place in the world today, it is hardly surprising that people are increasingly stressed and finding themselves in conflict. The initial reaction to change by the vast majority of the population is fear. Change brings with it uncertainty and doubt, leading to many questions—What will happen to me? What will happen to my friends or colleagues? When will I know the effects of the change for sure?

William Bridges created a model of personal transition that has three stages during a change: there is an ending that will involve a sense of loss and grieving, a goodbye; then there is a period when people feel they are in a neutral zone or wilderness; and finally, they look toward reaching the new beginning or new possibility.[13]

This change model reinforces the power of the bonding cycle—people have to learn to cope with separation and grieving before they can move to a new attachment and bond. One thing is clear: just as change is constant, so we are spiraling through different phases of the cycle on different levels and with different relationships.

I work with many organizations undergoing change, and the managers driving the change process share a common characteristic; they generally feel guilt and stress about what is happening and how it will affect their colleagues. These feelings lead to "the ostrich effect," when the change is announced and then management "puts their heads in the sand" hoping that everything will be fine. They hardly communicate with staff and expect everyone to "get on with it." Taking this approach creates bitterness and negativity among the staff, who feel that management "does not care" about their people.

Once managers understand the change process and take time to reflect on its impact, they are in a better position to empathize with the employees in relation to how the impact will affect them. Helping themselves and their employees to understand the bonding cycle assists both those people leaving the organization and those who remain with the organization. During mergers and acquisitions, I often hear employees complain that they have not been told what is happening. People can usually deal with negative news; what they cannot deal with is an extended period of "not knowing." It is the uncertainty that creates such stress within people. If they do not know what the change means to them personally, they are unable to progress through the stages of the bonding cycle, find resolution, and seek new attachments.

Summary

The bonding cycle is a powerful tool to help us understand motivation in ourselves and others. It helps explain why we do what we do when we are in the different stages of the cycle. When we become stuck in any stage we can easily be taken hostage, and this can lead to destructive behavior. By being aware of the bonding cycle, and the effects on individuals when they are stuck in one of the various stages, we can avoid being taken hostage. Awareness of the cycle can help team members move on and lead healthier, happier, and more productive lives.

Attachment and bonding are essential emotional components of a happy and productive personal and professional life. Creating emotional bonds with people is essential to physical and psychological well-being. Furthermore, successful leadership is based on the ability of the leader to create bonds throughout the organization. We also have to accept that all bonds come to an end and that taking into account the ensuing grief reactions in ourselves or others is essential. Working through the pain of loss contributes to building our identity and fosters the possibility of further development. Failure to grieve effectively can lead to detachment, the consequences of which we can observe in psychosomatic symptoms, violence, and burnout, and the absence of emotional engagement. For leaders to reach levels of individual, team, and organizational excellence, it is necessary to use the emotional skills in the bonding cycle. Organizations can use the bonding cycle to successfully navigate through change initiatives, whether they involve small or large transitions.

Bonding enables us to engage with the people and the world around us. Bonding is also a powerful process that lays the foundation for a successful outcome to any dispute or confrontation.

Ask yourself the following questions:

- How easily do I create bonds appropriate to the person and situation?
- How do I handle separation, disappointment, rejection, and failure?
- Am I aware of grief? Can I express it? Do I make an appropriate recovery from loss depending on the type of loss?
- How easily do I rebond after a loss?

Key Points to Remember

1. Bonding is a primary need just like air, food, and water. It is the foundation of enduring success for people and organizations. The cycle of bonding (attachment, bonding, separation, grieving) is a natural part of life that we all repeatedly go through.
2. When people become stuck in separation and grief, they can become hostages to themselves and to others. Saying goodbye is a necessary path to making new bonds and finding the joy of life again.
3. It is crucial that we learn to form, maintain, and renew bonds even in the face of profound differences or serious conflict. When appropriate, we must be capable of breaking an existing bond and finding a new one.
4. Successful leaders must help themselves as well as others go through the bonding cycle to inspire and motivate.

CHAPTER FOUR

THE STRENGTH OF A SECURE BASE

In January 1999 a ferocious storm trapped mountaineers Jamie Andrew and Jamie Fisher on a small ledge at the top of Les Droites, a ten-thousand-foot mountain range in the French Alps near Chamonix. Only after five nights was it possible to rescue the pair. During that time, Jamie Fisher perished on the mountain. Jamie Andrew was taken to a hospital with hypothermia and severe frostbite. In the week that followed his rescue, Jamie had to have both feet and both hands amputated. He lost not only his best friend but also significant parts of his body.

After the despair of the early days, when he was overcome with grief and guilt about the death of Jamie Fisher and with a certain amount of self-pity, Jamie managed to refocus his mind's eye and start the process of recovery. He was able to leave the hospital after "relearning" how to do everyday activities such as wash, dress, and feed himself.

He talks about how he focused on small steps to master simple tasks. An important person for Jamie during his recovery was Helen Scott, a physical therapist, who asked him what he wanted to do for himself the most. He replied, "Feed myself." Her response was, "Let's do it," and she devised a unique method for Jamie to hold silverware using a small nylon strap fastened with Velcro. Jamie still uses the same system.

After three and a half months, the time it took Jamie to learn to walk on his prosthetic legs, he returned to work. In June 2000, he married his fiancée, Anna. In the same month, Jamie climbed Ben Nevis, Britain's highest mountain, raising over £15,000 for charity. He returned to Chamonix in 2001 and climbed the Cosmiques Arete on L'Aiguille du Midi with one of his doctors and one of his rescuers, both of whom had also been secure bases.

In April 2002, Jamie ran the London marathon and raised £22,000 for charity. He returned to the Alps a number of times that year, climbing several mountains. In January 2004, he scaled Mount Kilimanjaro, the highest mountain in Africa, with three other disabled mountaineers and raised over £5,000 for a Tanzanian leprosy center.

"If there's one thing I have learned over the last few years," says Jamie, "it's not to dwell on what might have been. I rejoice in my good luck and in all the good things that happen in my life. Most of all I am grateful that my second chance has given me the opportunity to be with, and to marry, the one person in this world who means the most to me."

When I met Jamie in 2005, he was a proud father of a baby daughter. Anna was and continues to be a very important support for him. The other person who played a pivotal support role in his life was his mother, who had guided and encouraged him when he had expressed his desire to follow his climbing dreams.[1]

How many of us could remain as positive as Jamie has about life in the same circumstances? Did Jamie have sufficient reasons to feel like a hostage?

What can we learn from Jamie's story to help us face the difficulties in our own lives? Who are the people who have been supportive in our lives, and how have they had an impact on us?

Secure bases are those people, goals, or things to which we bond in a special way. While we create many bonds, secure bases are special in that they give protection, comfort, and energy. They serve as anchors in our lives—like the earth around the roots of a tree that provides the foundation and strength to protect it during turbulence. The stronger our secure bases, the greater our resilience in dealing with adverse circumstances. In addition, secure bases provide guidance on how to direct the mind's eye to give meaning to events. They bestow confidence and are role models in dealing with adversity. In this way, secure bases are essential in transforming negative experiences into positive ones and thus are an antidote to being taken hostage by the painful side of life. In Jamie's case, his secure bases included his fiancée (later his wife), doctors, physical therapist, mother, and even Jamie Fisher who died in the accident.

Secure bases come in many forms. They are primarily people: parents, grandparents, teachers, coaches, bosses, friends, colleagues, and so on. They can also be countries, pets, goals, beliefs, or religion. While people can have many secure bases, each person selects and finds personally significant ones. A person who has secure bases finds a sense of security. The failure to grieve the loss of a bond with a secure base or the lack of secure bases altogether can cause insecurity, anxiety, or even aggression and violence. As noted in the previous chapter, the cycle of bonding is particularly relevant to secure bases.

Bob was a fifty-year-old man who lived in isolation with his dog Buster—his only attachment and his secure base. One day, the dog ran into the street and a car hit and killed it. Watching the accident, Bob was devastated. On the one hand, he blamed himself for his failure to control the dog; on the other hand, he felt angry at the driver who had not stopped.

As he approached Buster's body, three teenagers surrounded him and laughed at his emotional distress. Contemptuously, the three boys tried to grab the body of the dog. In a deep rage, Bob pulled a gun from under his coat and took the three of them hostage in his house, locking the doors and pulling the blinds.

After the police and hostage negotiation team were called to the scene, we realized this was an unusually serious hostage crisis because Bob had nothing more to lose than his own life. This makes for the most dangerous and difficult of situations for hostage negotiators to deal with. During the eighteen-hour siege, Bob continually threatened to kill the boys.

With security around the house assured, what was the first thing the hostage negotiators had to do? We had to establish a bond with Bob even though he refused to talk. In fact, he destroyed five phones the SWAT team placed at his door by quickly opening the door and throwing them into the street. Knowing Bob was grieving over Buster, his only secure base, and believing he didn't want to kill the boys, we tirelessly attempted to speak with him.

Through his partially open window we eventually threw a stone with a note attached: "Please, let's talk." The stone accidentally broke the win-

dow. Enraged, Bob started to scream at the negotiator, who quickly realized that this response was a bonding opportunity as the focus of discussion became the window and gave an opening to create a bond and dialogue. The negotiator explained that breaking the window had been accidental. Bob demanded payment for the damage. The discussion centered on the repairs for the window and led to the knowledge that Bob's main concern was paying for the burial of his dog. The negotiator promised to find the money to bury Buster. Within two hours Bob surrendered his guns and walked out of the house on his own. The three boys were released unharmed.

Did Buster get a proper burial, and who paid for it? The hostage negotiation team raised enough money to provide a proper burial, endearing the police to Bob for the rest of his life. From this story, we can learn that loss and grief can be a source of violence and despair. What can we learn from this story about hostage negotiation that can apply in our own lives?

A secure base gives protection or comfort and is a source of energy. If there is danger, we turn to our secure bases. As adults, different from children, we can hold memories (internalize) from secure bases in our past. The bonding with secure bases, in the present or from the past, becomes a source of security. The term *secure base*, taken from military language, was introduced by John Bowlby, founder of modern attachment theory. The secure base is a cornerstone of his attachment theory. A secure base plays a unique role from which a person "can make sorties into the outside world and to which he can return" knowing for sure that he will be welcomed and safe when he gets there, nourished physically and emotionally, comforted if distressed, and reassured if frightened. In essence, this role is one of being available, ready to respond when called upon to encourage and perhaps assist, and to intervene actively only when clearly necessary.[2]

The most obvious form of a secure base is a person, either from our personal world of parents, grandparents, siblings, relatives, partners, and friends or from the professional realm, such as a coach, mentor, leader, supervisor, boss, community leader, doctor, minister, therapist, and so on. Secure bases can even involve a fantasy bond with famous people we have never met personally, such as film stars. To be a secure base for someone does not necessarily require action. It is more about being a source of comfort, and a way to organize and give meaning to our thoughts, feelings, and experiences.

It is "a role similar to that of the officer commanding a military base from which an expeditionary force sets out and to which it can retreat, should it meet with a setback. . . . it is only when the officer commanding the expeditionary force is confident his base is secure that he dare press forward and take risks."[3]

The fact is that when we are filled with anxiety and fear, this affects both mental and physical functioning and reduces our capacity to reach our highest level of performance. The purpose of a secure base is to create a sense of security and protection so that the mind's eye can be focused on possibility, exploration, creativity, and doing the things that give pleasure or satisfaction. Without secure bases, we become prone to anxiety or fear, thus limiting our potential, hindering success, and making us liable to become a hostage (or to get entrapped in a hostage state). Our brain is wired to look for danger. The secure bases in our lives enable us to switch off that radar and instead seek out opportunity rather than focus on what could be dangerous. If there is a real danger, the "internalized knowing" from experiences with secure bases helps us to know how to appropriately and effectively respond. Without good secure bases, the individual is left to the primal flight-fight reflexes. Secure bases have the power to influence whether or not we become hostages to ourselves or to events in our lives.

As we grow into adulthood, secure bases can easily be taken for granted as we venture farther and farther away from them over time. We become confident that our secure bases are reliable and may underestimate their significance in our lives.

Yet, if we lose a secure base, our emotional balance can dramatically change, and in the turmoil, the immense significance of the secure base becomes apparent.

Alexandra, as a senior leader in a global technology company, participated in my high-performance leadership program at IMD, a leading business school in Switzerland. For some twenty years, Ben had been a secure base for her. An older man, he had been a mentor who had helped her throughout her career. He was like the father she never had. The relationship was positive and constructive.

When Ben died suddenly and unexpectedly, Alexandra's motivation, enthusiasm, and willingness to take a risk diminished slowly over time, significantly affecting her leadership and performance at work. During the following four years, her effectiveness continued to deteriorate, to the point at which she was in jeopardy of losing her job.

Alexandra was oblivious to the profound impact the loss of her mentor had on her. She was unaware of her grief, even of the longing for Ben to come back. Alexandra simply said, "Life goes on and I just have to continue on my own."

She needed a positive authority figure like Ben to help her reach her highest levels of performance. However, until she could grieve and say goodbye to Ben, she was not likely to find one. She decided to do the grieving of Ben and to find a new mentor after understanding the importance of having a secure base for her to be successful. She said, "I went to Ben's grave to say goodbye and then and there, I decided to find a woman mentor."

Within six months, she did exactly what she had decided: she found Margaret, a new mentor, and began performing at levels even higher than those before Ben's death. In fact, rather than miss Ben and feel a loss in her life, she focused her mind's eye on honoring Ben with new levels of success. This is exactly what Ben would have wanted as well. The point is Alexandra could not move on without going through the stages of grief in her own way. Sometimes grief is easily and quickly resolved. However, as described in Chapter Three, not grieving can stop the entire bonding cycle.

Secure bases are vitally important throughout life, not just during our early life. Bowlby wrote regarding the need for secure bases throughout life, "Healthy personality functioning at every age reflects, first, an individual's ability to recognize suitable figures willing and able to provide him with a secure base and, second, his ability to collaborate with such figures in mutually rewarding relationships. By contrast, many forms of disturbed personality functioning reflect an individual's impaired ability to recognize suitable and willing figures and/or an impaired ability to collaborate in rewarding relationships with any such figure when found."[4]

Adults also need a network of secure bases, which are primarily composed of partners, friends, peers, colleagues, and other equals, as well as coaches, mentors, and bosses. Studies have repeatedly shown that successful people have someone they can turn to as anchors in life. Self-reliant loners, who think they can do everything on their own, often make fatal mistakes and decisions. In their book *Why Smart People Do Dumb Things*, authors Feinberg and Tarrant describe the greatest business blunders, how they happened, and how they could have been prevented. The core message is that the leaders making the mistakes either had no close support relationships, chose not to listen to those people who were their support, or had the wrong "anchors" that diverted them toward the destructive behaviors.[5]

How could the destiny of recent failed organizations such as Enron and Tyco in the United States, Ahold in The Netherlands, and Parmalat in Italy have been different had their leaders used positive secure bases to help keep them on track? While secure bases come in many forms, the two most essential for building high self-esteem are attachments to people and attachments to goals. This combination provides the foundation for a balanced approach to life. If people are only attached to other people, they may feel secure and yet feel they are not really successful. If they are only attached to goals, they may appear to be successful and yet be dying of loneliness, as often happens with workaholics. It is a tragic story to see senior leaders who are not bonded to people, having spent a lifetime striving for success only to discover that they have never really learned the richness and beauty of bonding to people. However, it is never too late to learn to rewire the brain and learn the bonding process.

On a cold and sunny March day, Derek Smith, a fifty-six-year-old successful business executive, was racing his seventeen-year-old son down an advanced-level ski slope. The day was special because Derek was "married to his work," as his friends would say, and did not often spend time away from the office with his family. His son, eager to demonstrate his skills, wanted to be the victor, and so did his highly goal-directed and competitive father.

Refusing to let his son win, Derek raced too quickly down the slope, lost control, and hit a tree. When he regained consciousness, he found himself in the hospital with a broken back. After the doctors told him he would recover but would never be able to ski again, Derek sank into a deep depression. He insisted, "If I can't ski, then life isn't worth living." He became full of despair.

His son was devastated and blamed himself. He said he had known since he was a child that his father always had to win. Feeling guilt and regret, the son believed if he had just let his father go ahead of him, then the accident would never have happened.

In my discussions with Derek, at one point I asked him a question: Did he want to be a hostage to the belief that life was not worth living if he could not ski, or did he want to recover and find joy in life? Given that direct choice, Derek suddenly realized that, of course, he wanted to live. In a flash, he shifted the focus of his mind's eye.

Derek needed to grieve the passing of his adolescence and accept his identity as a middle-aged father, husband, and businessperson. When Derek was seven, his father had died, and he had grown up without a father figure to teach him about emotions and about life. He was a typical overly independent loner who had spent his life focusing on being the best and attaching only to goals. He had stopped bonding to people after his father's death. Therefore, although he had material wealth, his relationships with people had suffered greatly.

With this realization, Derek apologized to his son and asked for his forgiveness. Then he went to his daughter and apologized for not being there for her and never telling her he loved her. She angrily slapped him and exclaimed, "How dare you, after all these years!" It took some two months for them to create a bond and for the daughter to eventually forgive him.

In looking back on his life, Derek said he wished he had known how much the death of his father had had an impact on his destiny. He was in fact living what Eric Berne called a "script," a life plan based on a decision to never risk being close to anyone because they might leave just like his father did. He now realized he could have chosen another life plan that would have meant less pain for his children, his spouse, his employees, and himself. To do this, he would have needed an attachment to a secure base.

When he returned to work, he had changed as a man and as a leader. His employees were pleasantly surprised to see how his leadership style had altered: "I lived most of my life as a hostage to success and my desire to achieve goals at the expense of my relationships. Now I see choices and face them." He managed to rewire his brain, showing that it is never too late to change behavior and choose another way of living. It is unlikely that Derek could have made this change by himself, as he needed a crisis and a secure base, like me, to help him learn a new way of behaving.

This story demonstrates the importance of balancing attachments to persons and goals. People who have secure bases are able to explore and exhibit a playful attitude toward life. This is the foundation for building self-esteem and thereby becoming truly successful (Figure 4.1).

When we have people as a secure base, we learn to love and be loved, and this leads to a sense of belonging that makes a person feel worthwhile and valuable. When we have goals as a secure base, we learn to be competent at something, which in turn leads to success that reinforces our capability to act. It is the combination of people and goals as secure bases and the experience of belonging and success that builds self-esteem in an individual.

Secure bases create success by

- Teaching us that we can trust bonding to other people
- Giving us the feeling of safety and freedom to explore the world
- Providing encouragement and protection to continually create goals to expand our levels of competence

FIGURE 4.1. SECURE BASE AND SELF-ESTEEM

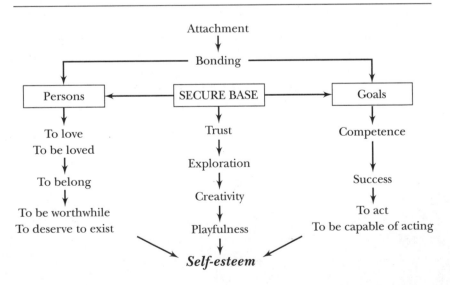

- Building our self-esteem and our positive regard for others
- Helping us to understand the roots of our identity
- Enabling us to be positive, optimistic, and constructive in interacting with others
- Modeling how not to be a hostage to ourselves, others, or life itself

As noted earlier, for adults, most secure bases are peer-related. However, there is a special group of secure bases such as mentors, coaches, and bosses—authority figures who play a critical role in our success. The foundation of success is strongly connected to the ability to build positive bonds with authority figures. Positive authority figures to whom we listen, that we follow, and that we look to as models help establish confidence in ourselves.

Over time, external secure bases enable us to become our own secure base by what we have internalized from them. We all have "mind maps" of how the world works, our views of how we are in the world, and how our relationships can best work. In *Attachment and Loss,* Bowlby used the term *internal representation systems.*[6] When attachment and bonding behavior is deactivated, for many different reasons, exploratory behavior is shut down. When attachment and bonding behaviors are active, exploration behavior begins again. This important concept has been repeatedly observed by Ainsworth (with infants), Harlow (with monkeys), and psychoanalyst Margaret Mahler (who saw children early in the second year constantly returning to mom or dad to seek comfort and energy after explorations).[7]

Exploratory behavior leads a person away from his or her secure base. However, effective exploratory behavior means that it is based on security and a feeling that the secure base will be available if needed. One cannot truly explore the world if one does not move from a base of safety. Robert Weiss elaborates on three criteria for defining attachment behavior in childhood:[8]

1. *Proximity seeking.* The infant will attempt to remain within the protected range of the attachment figure.
2. *Secure base.* In the presence of an attachment figure, as long as there is no threat, an infant will give an indication of comfort and security.

3. *Separation protest.* The threat to continued accessibility to the attachment figure or actual separation will give rise to protest and an attempt to prevent the loss of the attachment figure's presence.

These three criteria for attachment are also found regularly in adults.[9] In adults, attachment relationships involve more peers, with the vast majority of attachments being with equals or partners, and fewer with caregivers. This has profound implications for leaders in organizations who face a continuous change in attachments and separations. Leaders must be a secure base and must create a culture and social system of secure bases to create a climate of trust and ensure high performance.

Bowlby saw secure bases as "encouraging, supportive and cooperative," which enabled a child to feel securely attached and confident to explore his or her environment and develop a sense of competence.[10] Most important is the person's model of how relationships can work cooperatively. When the child becomes old enough to understand her parents' feelings or motives, she forms a much more complicated relationship with them—what Bowlby calls a "goal-corrected partnership."[11] Essentially, this means that they cooperate in helping each other reach goals. The child and parents can negotiate and cooperate in making plans together based on their respective needs. Those people who are easily taken hostage have an immature mental model of how complex relationships work. The best model for relationships is one that includes the complexity of give and take, compromise, and the subtle nature of mutuality.

There can be negative secure bases that misdirect another person's mind. Parents, teachers, or bosses can poison another person's mind. Films, TV programs, or computer games can also have a poisonous influence if positive secure bases are not available to help give and find appropriate meaning, interpretation, and boundaries.

The July 2005 bombings in London were undertaken by homegrown British suicide bombers who were "taught" and believed that it is a mystical experience and a direct path to paradise to sacrifice one's life by killing innocent civilians. Whose mind was behind their minds? An interesting aspect is that three of the suicide bombers were second-generation immigrants, who missed the values of their ancestors from their motherland. How vulnerable are second- and third-generation youths who do not feel attached and bonded to society and never establish their new country as a positive secure base? The protests and car burnings that occurred in France during 2005 are another example of disaffected youths feeling alienated from society.

How Secure Bases Influence the Mind's Eye

During a hostage negotiation, the negotiator becomes a secure base for the hostage taker by establishing trust through a bond. Secure bases are so important because we need them to shut down the radar in the mind's eye that is geared for survival and naturally searches for possible danger, pain, and negatives. The mind's eye stays fully activated, looking for danger or pain except when a secure base, either an external one or an internalized one, gives a sense of security or a useful interpretation of reality. Then we relax, feel trust, and focus on opportunity and exploration. The same process happens in an effective hostage negotiation. The hostage negotiator establishes himself as a secure base, building bonding and trust. He uses dialogue as a path toward negotiating the release of the hostages by finding common goals and interests. Thus fear, cynicism, negativity, and despair are refocused in the mind's eye of the hostage taker and replaced by trust, optimism, and hope. While the hostage negotiator must do risk assessment throughout the negotiation, fear and danger cannot take the negotiator as a metaphorical "hostage." Being a hostage negotiator means becoming a secure base. It is about having multiple mind maps and mental models that hold the hostage negotiator in the correct mental state to be effective.

How is the mind's eye shaped by secure bases? In some ways, past experiences have been locked into our brain, and these memories influence how we choose to focus. The most powerful experiences that shape our mind's eye are from our secure bases, whether related to positive or negative experiences. A person going through a traumatic event can have his or her life dramatically altered by the rewiring that takes place in the brain. However, the same event interpreted through the mind's eye of the secure base can dramatically change how the event is remembered in implicit or explicit memory, conscious or unconscious mind.

Pamela had grown up with a mother who was terrified of a storm's thunder and lightning. At the first indication of bad weather, her mother would close the curtains and unplug all electrical cords. As a result, Pamela herself grew up afraid of storms. When she had her own children, however, she was determined they would not feel the way she did about violent weather. Whenever there was a storm, she would open the curtains and "show" the children the storm, pointing out lightning and the shapes it makes, having them guess where the next lightning would strike in the sky and when the next thunder would come. To this day, Pamela is uneasy around storms, but her children, now grown, have a positive association with storms. They eagerly seek the experience of seeing a storm and encourage Pamela's grandchildren to enjoy the experience of nature at full force.

The point of the story is that Pamela could have transferred her fear of storms from her mind to her children's mind's eye. However, by not being a hostage to her fear in her mind's eye, she was able to teach her children and her grandchildren to have a different view of storms in their mind's eye. Pamela refused to become a hostage to the fear her mother had unwittingly taught her. What Pamela did, everyone can learn to do.

In his book *Magical Child,* Joseph Chilton Pearce describes an eight-year-old boy who is bleeding heavily from a cut.[12] The father simply states, "We must get this bleeding to stop," meaning in his mind that, "We must go to the hospital." However, in the child's mind, based on the deep bonding and the secure base with his father, he took this as a literal request and stopped bleeding. Many everyday stories clearly demonstrate the power of a secure base to shield another person from the negative impact of trauma.

When I work with young leaders in business, the vast majority are trained to be dubious about the power of the mind over the body. It is a challenge to offer professional training and executive education to help participants learn a robust balance between healthy skepticism and true possibility. Many people think that if something does not fit into our conception of what is possible, then it is impossible. This is a tragedy, because stepping out of the boundaries in our mind is the only real way to learn. As Einstein said, "The significant problems we have cannot be solved at the same level of thinking with which we created them."[13]

PEOPLE AS SECURE BASES

Most people are at their happiest when they are bonded to a person whom they can turn to at any time. People who are not bonded, who have never had that experience, or who no longer create bonds are generally hostages to themselves.

Secure bases give us the strength to master our mind's eye and to pursue the goals that we really want to achieve in life. From cradle to grave, as Bowlby so well described, we have a changing script of secure bases, which produces in us feelings of love, being loved, belonging, competence, and success. Without secure bases, we end up marked, wounded, or scarred. In other words, we become hostages.

Relationships and self-esteem skills develop from the secure bases that are formed initially with our primary caregivers. These early successes or lack of successes provide the foundation for the basic nature of our personalities. Our pattern of attachment is based on the early secure-base relationships (with mother, father, grandparents, siblings, relatives, and so on). After a certain period, these patterns become locked-in (hardwired in the brain) and become the basis of our attachment style. Bowlby writes, "The kinds of experience a person has, especially during childhood, greatly affect both whether he expects later to find a secure personal base, or not, and also the degree of competence he has to initiate and maintain a mutually rewarding relationship when opportunity offers. . . . Because of these interactions, whatever pattern is first established tends to persist. This is a main reason why the pattern of family relationships a person experiences during childhood is of such crucial importance for the development of his personality."[14]

Bowlby's premise was that the relationship between the child and the primary caretaker is responsible for

- Shaping future relationships
- The intrapersonal characteristics of the ability to focus, to be aware of our feelings, and to calm ourselves
- The ability to recover from misfortune[15]

THE MOTHER FIGURE AS SECURE BASE

In his autobiography, *From the Gut,* former CEO Jack Welch dedicated a chapter to his childhood. He wrote fondly of his mother as "the most influential person in my life." His mother pushed him to excel and fostered self-confidence. She famously explained Welch's serious stutter as the simple inability of her son's tongue to keep up with his quick mind.[16] At forty-five, a long-shot candidate to become the youngest chief executive in General Electric's history, Jack Welch left the podium after his first shareholders' meeting and said to a friend, "I wish my mother had been here." His mother had died many years earlier.

Welch credits his mother, Grace, with giving him the confidence to refuse to conform. He attributes much of his learning to her, including persistence. "I had a pal in my mom, you know," he says. "We had a great relationship. It was a powerful, unique, wonderful, reinforcing experience."

Did you have a mother, a grandmother, a stepmother, adopted mother, or any female mother figure who was there as a secure base for you? Could you run into her arms and be welcomed? If so, she helped to positively establish your primary mental representation, your "mental model," of women and female authority. This is how learning to give and take affectionate bonding with women is created. The mother is generally the first and most fundamental of secure bases. She is usually the first caregiver to nurture the child and, therefore, often she is the primary anchor. If a mother is not present, then it could be a stepmother, an adoptive mother, a nanny, an aunt, or another feminine figure. At this point, you may be asking, What relevance does this have for me in my life, at work, as a leader, or as a teacher? Whether you had positive or negative secure bases, in the end, it is important to understand that whatever connection you may or may not have had with female authority figures from your childhood is somehow linked to how you relate to women today, irrespective of whether you are male or female. Understanding your roots gives you powerful tools to ensure that you do not become a hostage in the present based on past experiences.

Mother-son relationship. Research has demonstrated the distinctive bond between mother and son. According to Kets De

Vries, there are many instances of successful male leaders having strong, supportive mothers and rather absent fathers. As mentioned, Jack Welch was deeply affected and motivated by his relationship with his mother.[17] Nelson Mandela had a mother who influenced him profoundly. Richard Branson's mother told everyone that Richard would become prime minister of Great Britain one day, and she convinced Branson that he could achieve whatever he wanted in life.[18]

The son knows about himself as a masculine figure through the eyes of the mother, not the eyes of the father. If the son does not have a bond with a mother figure, the most common outcome is difficulty in bonding with both men and women. A significant number of unbonded males have failed to bond to a mother or female authority figure throughout their lives. However, healing a wound with the mother is possible through a nonsexual relationship with a female authority figure at any stage of life. Male leaders must be able to deal effectively with women as examples, colleagues, or bosses. If a male leader has incorporated the wrong mind-set about women, it will negatively influence relations with females. Love by a father or father figure will never fully substitute or compensate for the bonding with a mother or female authority figure.

Mother-daughter relationship. The mother figure becomes the potential role model for every young girl—the person she looks up to and says about, "I want to be like her when I grow up." Unfortunately, this does not always happen in relationships between mother and daughter. There are many reasons for this failure linked to things such as jealousy, competitiveness, or failure to encourage emancipation, to name a few. However, it is important for the daughter to understand how the mother views femininity or womanhood. Rejection or failure to bond with the mother can lead to an alienation of the self or even dislike of the self. Making peace with the mother, having a secure base with a feminine figure, is a significant part of the path to full self-acceptance. Love by a father or male figure will never fully substitute or compensate for the bonding with a mother or a mother figure.

The daughter must learn to have a positive mental representation of femininity. No matter what happened in the past, it is possible to create this in the future by finding an authoritative woman as a secure base or as a mentor.

The Father Figure as Secure Base

After the mother, the father is generally the next secure base in the child's life. Did you have a father, grandfather, stepfather, or other father figure who was there as a secure base for you? Could you run into his arms and be welcomed? This is how learning to give and take affectionate bonding with men is first learned.

Father-son relationship. Fathers must teach sons as children and adolescents how to deal with emotions, especially the emotions of anger and grief. The socialization of males must be done by other males. The mother is limited in her ability to do this because of the son's need for gender identification with the father. Research consistently shows that young boys at risk of criminality and violence who have a secure male father figure—a loving father or loving big brother attachment that stays with a child through adolescence and young adulthood—become strongly inoculated against criminal behavior and violence.[19] Preventing violence means giving every son a healthy father figure as a secure base and a model of empathetic emotional bonding. The father becomes a role model of how men behave and handle emotions with women, with other men, with work, and across all the ranges of life. While the mother-son bond is ever so powerful, it will never be the same as the love of a father or father figure.

The father-daughter relationship. This relationship is vital for helping girls to grow up with a healthy sense of men, masculinity, and male relationships. The moment a father holds his infant daughter for the first time, a special bond is developed that will shape and mold them both. As the first significant man in his daughter's life, the father plays a unique and potent role in forming her self-image. In later years, how she sees herself as a woman, friend, lover, wife, and colleague is strongly connected to her father. What she saw in herself when she looked into her father's eyes becomes hardwired into her brain. If the father is a secure base and makes the daughter feel loved, intelligent, and attractive, then she will grow up with greater confidence. If the father was cold, distant, or critical, then the daughter may have difficulty learning to bond well with men. Research has shown that the special bond between father and daughter is significant in teaching daughters how to handle emotions.

These relationships with authority figures in childhood have been shown to play a significant role in how we choose partners and other peer-based relationships. Our relationships throughout our lives can be "held hostage" to the mental image we have in the mind's eye of what makes a mother or what makes a father. However, be clear that we do not ever have to be hostages to whatever did or did not happen with our parents. Some of the greatest stories in life are about how people overcame the most adverse experiences with parents.

Regardless of past or current circumstances (such as single parents), we can find secure bases anywhere in our developmental cycles from birth to death. Usually adults turn to peers and equals as secure bases. The good news is that the brain can rewire to correct failed bonding experiences at any point in life.

The longest attachments in life are often to our siblings, spouses and partners, and childhood friends. When I ask leaders on executive education courses who their main secure base is, the vast majority respond that it is their spouse. The most common attachments are to spouses, friends, and colleagues and bosses at work. It is also true that when leaders describe failure, they focus on broken bonds with secure bases, for example, divorce, estrangement from parents, or conflict with friends.

Often, people cite children as a secure base. However, it is vitally important that parents *not* use children as secure bases because it interrupts the child's developmental cycle toward emancipation and freedom. Parents who use a child as a secure base can place an unnecessarily heavy burden of responsibility on the child. The exception to this is the adult child who may become a secure base for an elderly parent later in life. Bill George, former CEO of Medtronic and author, gives the following example of becoming a secure base for his father after his mother died: "When I arrived home late that afternoon, my father met me at the door. I will never forget our interaction. Looking into his eyes, I knew instantly that I had to become the father of my father. This role reversal continued for the last twenty-five years of his life. In a very real sense I lost two parents in one day.

At age twenty-four I became the elder. As it is said, 'The son becomes the father of the man.'"[20]

GOALS AS SECURE BASES

One of the fundamental ways to create a secure base, and to achieve success, is to commit oneself wholeheartedly and passionately to a goal. The goal can be in sports, work, school, or learning, and can be personal or professional. What is essential is that the goal has purpose and meaning to the individual. When we have a goal, we have to develop the competence to achieve the required level of excellence. In developing the competence, we will generally experience failure and frustration on the way. Success is actually built on the ability to overcome failures. Learning to overcome barriers creates the hardwiring in the brain to act, so that we are always capable of acting and do not become hostages to failure or fear of failure. Challenging goals always carry some risk of failure. However, secure bases provide protection, comfort, and energy to make pursuing the goal a continuous learning experience. Staying focused on the goal gives positive meaning to disappointing outcomes and, in the end, teaches resilience.

Mary, a five-year-old girl, wants to learn to ride her bicycle. Her father agrees to help her and commands, "Mary, get on the bike, pedal, and don't fall." Mary gets on, and sure enough she falls. The father, who is not acting like a secure base, declares, "I cannot teach you anything," and turns away. Mary feels devastated. She is filled with shame and her self-esteem is shattered.

How would a father behave as a secure base to help his daughter learn to have goals? ? He would give protection, energy, comfort, and support by saying when Mary falls, "Hey, you're off to a great start." He would suggest, "Here, put your foot on the pedal. I will hold the bike while you cycle. I will tell you when I let go of the bike." If Mary were to fall again, he would assure her, "That's OK. I fell many times when I was learning. I'm sure you can do it."

If Mary falls five times, ten times, the father still encourages her: "You're almost there Mary! I know you can do it!" After fifteen times, she may still be falling but she doesn't give up because her father is telling her, "That is all right. I know you can do it."

He stays with her in a very positive way. Finally, Mary manages to ride the bike, and the father stands back, applauds, and exclaims with a big smile, "Mary, what a great job! I knew you could do it."

How does Mary feel? Fantastic! "Bring on the racer! I'm ready to go to the next level," she thinks. She learns that with the help of a secure base, failure is part of the path that takes her to the ultimate goal. With enough of these types of experiences in her life, Mary will learn never to be a hostage to fear of failure, and she will actually seek high enough goals that failure on the path will be likely. Failure is for learning, and if used in this way, it paves the way for greater success. And success gives confidence that we can act or be capable of acting in any situation, and never become a metaphorical hostage.

FEAR OF FAILURE AND FEAR OF SUCCESS

People who are afraid to fail are often unable to explore and take risks that may lead to success, because they are insecure. Successful people often fail many times before achieving success. However, many people have a fear of failure and may be taken hostage by it.

Other people are taken hostage by their fear of success. How does this work? Fear of success takes place when the individual is so attached to the goal or the people that he or she avoids further success, to avoid some goodbye or loss with the success. Whenever one succeeds or reaches a goal, there is always a goodbye and corresponding loss or grief. Reaching a goal means that a grief reaction follows. This may include saying goodbye to an organization, to friends when we graduate from school, to coworkers if we are promoted to another job, to the motherland if we move to another country, or to family if we leave home. It may be to all the things and people that gave us security in a time of our life. Some people do not leave home, seek a promotion, or move to another city or country because they are afraid of the grief connected to the change.

John was promoted, but instead of being delighted, he was worried. He liked his old role and the colleagues he had. Now he would be their boss and be more senior than them. He didn't want them to treat him differently.

Unfortunately, John did not say goodbye to his old role. Instead, he started failing in his new role, blaming everyone and everything around him. He became a hostage to his grief. What was the problem? Deep inside, he wanted to go back to his old role with his old identity.

As soon as he came to terms with the transition, let go of the old role, and said goodbye to it, everything changed for him in his new job. Those who had supported him encouraged him in his new role as boss. Those who hadn't supported him—well, he just had to accept that. The result was that he was no longer a hostage. He became a high performer in his new role, and he managed to let go of his old role. Most of the people around him were also able to let go of their old perception of him and view him as the boss.

If we cannot deal with the loss of a goal and then find a new goal, we can easily be taken hostage and stop ourselves from achieving our full potential. Achieving a goal, then, means having to let go of the "dream" and move on to the next one.

At the age of sixty, Henry discovered that he had prostate cancer—a great shock for him and his wife. When I spoke to him, he was in a deep grief reaction. At one point I asked him, "What is your dream? What do you want to do with the rest of your life?" His spontaneous response was, "I would love to sail the Atlantic Ocean." Well, this was not an easy task considering he was undergoing chemotherapy. However, I suggested he check with his doctor and see if it was possible. Interestingly enough, the doctor gave the OK, and Henry decided to live his dream. He got a small team together and moved to the Azores. He became greatly enthused as he worked on the details of his adventure.

When I saw Henry sometime later, after he had sailed across the Atlantic, he looked completely energized and vibrant. He said to me, "You'll never believe what has happened. I now have a PSA level that has dropped so dramatically, it is nearly like an adolescent's, and the doctors can't explain it." I asked him why he thought he had such a significant drop and that the cancer was now in remission. He responded, "It is because I lived my dream. I did what I always wanted to do."

For the next four years, Henry thrived, traveling between The Nether-lands and the United States. He then decided to sell his boat, which meant bringing it back to The Netherlands. He told me that the return trip to Europe, unlike the initial voyage, had been depressing. He advertised the boat thinking it would take a year or two to sell and was shocked when he sold it after only two weeks. Within two months of selling the boat, he had a major flare-up of the prostate cancer. At that point, he told me, "I know why this has happened. I am grieving. I have lost my dream. The boat was my secure base. Sailing, as a Dutchman, is a secure base for me, and now I know I will never do that again. I have no new dream. I have no new goal to keep myself going."

Henry had many secure bases around him: his wife, his friends, and others. However, work was more of a duty. Furthermore, he had many negative memories from World War II that had plagued him for many years and which had contributed to his finding little joy in life. The Atlantic sailing trip clearly had been one of the highlights of his life.

This story reveals the power of having a dream, the danger of losing a dream, and the ongoing life challenge to always find a new dream. Henry is now at the point of trying to find a new dream.

HIGH SELF-ESTEEM AND SECURE BASES

The foundation of self-esteem is based on a fundamental feeling of being loved and feeling worthwhile. Our primary experiences with secure bases give us that feeling of, "I am worthwhile, I belong, I am lovable, unconditionally." Attachment to goals works in parallel, when the person, acting with motivation and purposeful behavior, creates a positive emotional response to the goal.

An underlying dynamic of joy in life is to be aware of one's desires and wants, to act toward those wants, to get a response from the environment, and to find satisfaction and gratification in the result. Whether you want to be an excellent soccer player or an excellent manager, you must practice and face the challenge of continuous improvement. You must perform and receive feedback in order to reach your maximum competence. This leads to success, based on attachment to goals and the ability to create an emotional bond to those goals.

That process is what we do whenever we have emotional engagement and deep commitment to a goal. Our self-esteem enables us to act, knowing that we are competent to act, even in the face of frustration and failure, to experience a successful outcome. Secure bases with people and with goals help build high self-esteem.[21]

Manifestations of High Self-Esteem

- Displaying a joyful attitude and happiness to be alive
- Having a balance between giving and receiving energy
- Seeking new opportunities and challenges
- The ability to give and receive positive compliments
- Displaying spontaneity and flexibility
- Exhibiting a sense of playfulness
- Demonstrating creative reactions to problems
- Having satisfaction from experiences
- The ability to be intimate and close to others
- Demonstrating that others are important
- Having an openness toward life and others

Of course, even people who have high self-esteem have setbacks and disappointments, but they tend to "bounce back" quickly and display a remarkable resilience in dealing with life's challenges, struggles, and dilemmas. It is almost as though self-esteem gives a "Teflon coating" to the soul.

SECURE BASES AND RESILIENCE

Secure bases and resilience are deeply interdependent. Gilligan defines resilience as "a set of qualities that helps a person to withstand the negative effects of adversity."[22] Resilience is the process of adapting well in the face of adversity and learning from difficult experiences. As a species, humans show remarkable resilience. The day after terrorist attacks or natural disasters, people go back to their lives and carry on. When we are resilient, we go through difficulties and overcome stress. Resilience involves an ability to override the focus on pain and loss in the mind's eye in order to continue toward a purposeful goal.[23]

The son of a Kentucky sharecropper, Carl Brashear let nothing stand in the way of his dreams. When he left home, his father told him, "Never quit—be the best." Carl took those words to heart. He joined the U.S. Navy and became its first black master diver. Brashear succeeded despite racial prejudice and severe barriers to stop him.

Later, following a work-related accident, he became the U.S. Navy's only amputee master diver. Carl is one of seven enlisted men whose oral histories are profiled by the U.S. Naval Institute. His story was also made into a hit Hollywood movie, Men of Honor.

The following is an excerpt from his story: "Sometimes I would come back from a run, and my artificial leg would have a puddle of blood from my stump. I would not go to sick bay. In that year, if I had gone to sick bay, they would have written me up. I did not go to sick bay. I'd go somewhere and hide and soak my leg in a bucket of hot water with salt in it—an old remedy. Then I'd get up the next morning and run."[24]

Resilience can be learned and developed by anyone. The American Psychological Association (APA) suggests the following ten ways to build resilience:[25]

1. *Make connections.* Good relationships are important.
2. *Avoid seeing crises as insurmountable problems.* You cannot change the fact that stressful events happen but you can change how you interpret and respond to the events.
3. *Accept that change is part of living.* Accepting what cannot be changed helps you focus on what you can influence.
4. *Move toward your goals.* Develop some realistic goals and tell yourself, "What's the one thing I know I can accomplish today that helps me move in the direction I want to go?"
5. *Take decisive actions.* Act on adverse situations as much as you can as fast as you can.
6. *Look for opportunities for self-discovery.* People learn something about themselves and find that they have grown in some respect because of their struggle with losses.
7. *Nurture a positive view of yourself.* Developing confidence in your ability to solve problems and trusting your instincts helps build resilience.
8. *Keep things in perspective.* Think about the broader context and keep a long-term perspective.

9. *Maintain a hopeful outlook.* Focus on what you want rather than what you do not want, and do not let your mind worry about your fear.
10. *Take care of yourself.* Pay attention to your own needs and feelings. Engage in activities that you enjoy and find relaxing.

These attributes are most easily learned if we have secure bases from the past that give us the mental models and mind map to be resilient. Feeling like a hostage is the opposite of being resilient. Feeling like a hostage will always lower our self-esteem.

When a Secure Base Is Missing

Many people did not have secure bonding early in life. Some of them are able to solve this problem when they become adults and can go on to form happy, productive relationships in their personal and professional lives. However, many others are not able to solve the problem of failed bonding and, for most of them, they only know how to make negative bonds, or they just remain unbonded. They may be attached but not bonded. For example, insecure bonding or anxious attachment is reflected when people are unable to handle conflict, frustration, jealousy, or disappointment, or they are constantly dependent or clinging. People in constant conflict tend to have low self-esteem.

When people's secure bases have not been good enough, there are several possible outcomes. They might be afraid of attachment and avoid bonding with others in any form. They could become afraid of separation so they cling too much. They could become imitators of their fathers or haters of their fathers, so they run from their masculinity, or they could do the same based on their experiences with their mothers and run from their femininity.

They may avoid exploring or reaching out to do things because they are afraid and because they do not really feel secure in themselves. Such people can be difficult because they tend not to stand on their own two feet; they are constantly anticipating a loss and, as a result, they may worry too much. They may have feelings of panic and be unable to form secure bonds as a result.

Supervisors and managers who are not secure bases to their groups or team members will likely generate conflict, as will supervisors and managers who only attach to goals. Many people are unable to be successful because they have a fear of failure or they have a fear of success, and that comes from a failure to learn affectionate bonding from secure bases.

Symptoms of people who lack secure bases can include

- Low self-esteem
- Inability to deal with stress and adversity
- Inability to develop and maintain emotional bonds with people
- Antisocial attitudes and behaviors
- Difficulty with trust
- A negative and cynical attitude
- Lack of empathy
- Incessant chatter
- Behavioral and academic problems
- Unstable self-esteem combined with self-doubt
- Often feeling underappreciated by others at work
- Daydreams about success but often unable to sustain efforts
- Easily distracted by mood swings (even when positive)
- Can be emotional under stress
- Worry about rejection in daily matters
- A tendency to self-disclose to everyone
- Obsessions with food

STYLES OF ATTACHMENT AND BONDING

The study of attachment behavior evolved from animals to infants and later to adults. Throughout our lives, there is an ever-changing story of secure bases. Our style of attachment and bonding relates to how we select, let go of, and reselect our secure bases. Every individual has a unique style in how he or she creates, maintains, breaks, and renews attachments. These styles are based on the mental models that have endured from the past to the present and come from adaptations to various life experiences with events and people. Styles develop from the way secure bases have responded or not responded, and can be changed based on experiences with new secure bases. There are many names given to these styles, however, I find the following ones the most helpful for leaders.

1. *Secure style.* This is the ideal, and applies to adults who find it relatively easy to get close to others and are comfortable depending on them and also letting others depend on them. These people have the inner confidence to handle people and situations with appropriate degrees of trust and emotional self-regulation. People with secure styles are aware of themselves, how others respond, and the mutual impact. They tend to focus on the here and now and do not often worry about being rejected, disliked, or left. They comfortably allow closeness, not worrying about what will happen. An anxiety-free state is the fundamental sign of this style. When there is anxiety or fear, people with this style self-regulate, making it easy for others to approach them and enjoy the relationship. Leaders who have this style are far more effective because they create a sense of trust and security by being a secure base.

2. *Insecure or anxious style.* People using this style are worriers filled with doubt and distrust who will focus too much on seeking and needing approval or being liked. Their insecurity creates the feeling that others are reluctant to get as close as they would like. Getting close to people with this style can be difficult because the cloud of worry and even negativity surrounds them and makes a meaningful dialogue difficult. The paradox is that the more this person clings, the more others try to avoid the person, creating a vicious circle. Managers who use this style will pass on their fear and anxiety and will have trouble being a secure base or even a positive team member. When dealing with people using this style, it is important to be clear in what you say and make sure you do not encourage fear. The best solution is to ask questions to guide the mind's eye to a different focus rather than try to tell them not to worry. Another approach is to ask them if they are interested in another point of view and, if they answer yes, then state your view. Ultimately, insecure and anxious people have to rewire their brain to focus on benefits and positives and to learn to trust others. This will only happen when they allow a strong, positive secure base to be incorporated into their mental models. However, we should not allow anyone who uses this

style to take us hostage through their worries and insecurities. Great leaders know how to draw a boundary between healthy dependency and overdependency.

3. *Independent loner style.* Independent loners avoid emotional bonding and anything that smells of dependence or surrender. Therefore, they do not bond with others because they have never learned how to form bonds or they are afraid to bond because of anticipatory pain or loss. Adults using this style are uncomfortable being close to others and find it difficult to trust people. There is often a basic loneliness in their lives masked by activities that avoid deeper human bonding. Rather than ask for help, they prefer to do things alone to avoid any dependence or surrender of control. When managers overfocus on goals, facts, or things, they block the necessary bonding to be an effective leader or to be effective in building a high-performance team. When dealing with people using this style, it is important to avoid behaviors associated with rejection. You have to bond with respect using common goals to build the relationship. It is also good to model appropriate closeness and gently introduce emotions into the discussion. You will need to reach out to the person more than usual and understand that as a given. At some stage, you may be ready to have that heart-to-heart dialogue. This pattern is more common for men and, for them, the best antidote to being an independent loner is a deep and powerful friendship with another male as a secure base. I know of men who, after a deep struggle, have been able to let their spouses become their first secure base and teachers of bonding. In the end, the independent loner must learn that all relationships invoke pain, disappointment, and frustration, and that the benefits of a relationship far outweigh the pain. Bonding, after all, brings the greatest joy to life.

4. *Compulsive caretaker style.* Caretakers are the people who create bonds primarily through taking care of others. Their energy and focus is on helping others even to the point of self-destruction or harmfulness to others. This style goes beyond healthy helping to the compulsive need to rescue someone who can and should be responsible for themselves. The identity of the caretakers rests in helping, and, as a result, they often do not take care of their own needs. Therefore, they tend to burn out because of the imbalance

in giving and taking. Compulsive caretakers can also become bitter and resentful when they feel they are not "appreciated" enough by the people they have looked after. They can easily feel like a hostage. They can also manipulate others into too much dependency and as such take others as a hostage by using words like "After all I have done for you." In organizations, the compulsive caregivers can impede the flow of movement of ideas and the development of people. In dealing with this style, directness with boundaries will be the most effective, along with the use of consequences for helping too much.

5. *Hostile dependent style.* The hostile dependent style shows itself in the person who, as soon as he or she creates a bond, wants to push the other person away, usually by creating a conflict. Such people do not know how to maintain close positive bonding, so they protect themselves by using hostility to drive themselves or the other person away. These individuals tend to create cyclical fights and may even enjoy being in a state of conflict. As soon as they are in a bond, they want to break it or to fight. However, when the other person steps back, they then reach out and make an effort to renew the bond. They have a fear of being both close and separate. They become hostages to their own anger and fear from being close. These individuals can always find a reason to be angry and to break a bond.

In organizations, managers using this style create confusion and may show opposite and even extreme sides of their personalities, making employees feel positive and close on some occasions and then the opposite on others. One minute the person is friendly, the next he or she can be coercive and difficult. Rejection and threats are tools used to manipulate others. Ideally with this style, we must know our own boundaries and have clear goals. Defining limits in a positive way is important. Do not be a hostage to their behavior. Instead, be steady and clear, and let the consequences reward or punish. Make sure not to fall into the strategy of this style and be drawn into the "great attachment dance," that is, going back and forth, leaving and returning in a cycle of intense emotion.

As well as the styles of attachment just discussed, there are four other types of people who can be found in business that are important to understand, along with some advice on how to deal with them.

1. *The overcompliant person.* It is difficult to discover where the super-agreeable person stands on any issue. Such people tend to be overadapted, and they say yes to everything. Part of the problem is that, for them, "no" means abandonment and rejection. So they avoid disagreement. In fact, they often overcommit themselves because they are afraid to say no.

In dealing with these individuals, it is important to make honesty nonthreatening. In transactions, emphasize that you want the truth, because you would like to know how they feel or what they want even if it upsets you. These individuals do not bond deeply because over-compliance is a kind of detached dishonesty. To encourage them to be honest, you need to be direct and warm. Do not accept unreasonable commitments from this type of person. You also have to be involved in saying no, because they will not.

The problem on teams with such individuals is that they do not express differences of opinion. They have to learn that differences of opinion lead the way to better solutions. If everybody just agrees, you do not find the best solutions.

2. *The complainer.* This type of person feels persecuted and victimized. They tend to be cynical, judgmental, and critical, focusing only on what is wrong. They create negative energy. Complainers believe that if they do not do it, it is not good enough. Only they can do things right, and they also often believe that others in authority do not care.

In dealing with this type, rule number one is not to be drawn into the negativism. Remain optimistic. It is also important not to propose solutions too early. Their game is to get you to make proposals so that they can shoot them down. So instead get them to make a proposal by asking what they would do. A good strategy is to talk about the worst-case scenario. Beat them to the draw and then present the best-case scenario. If you have a person like this on your team, be prepared to do the job alone; these people sometimes just never come around to support you, and you are probably better off doing the task without them. Sometimes, when they know that you are going to do it without them, they may change their mind and join in. Using and establishing boundaries is quite important to protect yourself and others.

3. *The arrogant person.* This type of person has all the answers. Just ask them, they know exactly the way things should be done. They often tend to be negative, and they do not bond well because they take such a superior position. They are generally stuck into attachment to power and a search for unresolved personal identity. Arrogance reflects low self-esteem rather than high self-esteem.

Therefore, you have to do your homework. When you are dealing with these individuals, make sure you know the facts, because they will play with the facts. However, if you are secure and confident in your knowledge, they may back off. In general, you cannot win by confronting them unless you are willing to risk escalation. It is better to use questions. You get further through friendliness than with hard confrontation. Avoid being a counterexpert, as you are not going to win by putting them down. In fact, you have to play a little naive.

Arrogant leaders will not be a secure base and as such will not be able to create trust.

4. *The indecisive person.* This person simply cannot make a decision. These people want to avoid conflict, postponing anything that is stressful to themselves or others. They learn that through procrastination, many things requiring a decision get solved by others. With indecisive people, do not try to find another solution for them when they should be able to find one themselves. They do not realize that they put stress on people because of their indecision, and you need to make them aware of this. It is important to encourage them to solve the problem, helping them when necessary. If they are beating around the bush, because their main strategy is to stall, you need to be direct: "What are we going to do about the fact that we have no one to answer the phone?" You should try not to overload these people. When indecisive types feel they are overloaded, it makes them procrastinate even more. So if you see them struggling, help them find a structure for problem solving. For example, you could give them alternative solutions and ask them to choose one. Keep in mind that it is important to give them a lot of encouragement and support before, during, and after the decision.

SUMMARY

Secure bases give protection, comfort, and energy. There are many forms of secure bases: people, goals, countries, pets, objects, beliefs, religion. An interdependence exists between people as secure bases and goals as secure bases that provides the foundation for establishing high self-esteem and success.

Although the mind's eye is hardwired to look for danger, secure bases enable us to shut down that radar search for danger so we can see the positive side of events. In our mind's eye, we have a "memory" of secure bases that influences how we give meaning to what we are experiencing. These memories are known as mental models or mind maps. The secure bases in our lives influence our values and help us learn to find meaning and purpose in painful experiences.

It is important to understand our secure bases from the present as well as the past. Understanding past influences gives us valuable insight into understanding our identity. It is a shortcut to understanding how we bond to people, to goals, or to a whole system around us.

As we look at the key secure bases we had in our past, we can see the patterns that have developed in our brain related to how we bond to men and women. We learn styles of attachment and bonding from and through the secure bases in our life. If you did not have secure bases in the past, the good news is that it is never too late to find one—a person, a friend, an authority figure.

Ask yourself the following questions and take time to reflect on your answers:

- Who and what have been the secure bases in my life?
- Who and what are the secure bases in my life now?
- What have been my most important learnings from my secure bases, past and present?
- Who and what have been the secure bases that I lost in my life?
- How did their loss affect me?
- Who have been the secure bases in my career?
- When have I been a secure base for someone else in either a personal or professional capacity?

Key Points to Remember

1. Know and use your secure bases to help manage your mind's eye for success. Leaders must be a secure base to build trust in a team or in the organization.

2. Understand who the secure bases were in your past and what strengths and barriers they have helped to create in you.

3. The loss of a secure base can be one of the deepest griefs we face. It is necessary to go through that grief to recover the joy of life or to find new secure bases.

4. Secure bases enable us to have a sense of security and protection so that the mind's eye can be focused on exploration, creativity, and doing those things from which we derive satisfaction or pleasure.

CHAPTER FIVE

THE ART OF CONFLICT MANAGEMENT

Hossam, a senior leader for a telecommunications company, attended a high-performance leadership program at IMD. Involved in a serious conflict with his boss, he had become frustrated with his job and was preparing to resign.

"I was on a one-way path with my manager," Hossam revealed. "Our communication was so difficult and tense that he could not understand what I meant, and I interpreted what he said or wrote in a preconceived manner. Everything he said I took personally, and I ended up building a wall to protect myself."

Due to his background and culture, Hossam strongly avoided conflict. However, after the program, he decided to raise his concerns with his boss even though he believed he had no option other than to leave the company. He also felt stressed because he had just relocated from his home country with his wife and two children. He inferred that his boss considered him unimportant, and he was rated the lowest performer on the team. He thought the manager did not like him and did not want him on the team.

He arranged a one-hour meeting with his boss to discuss his concerns. Unexpectedly, it turned into a four-hour heart-to-heart dialogue. He later told me that this had been the first time in his life he had found the courage to tell someone the truth about what he was thinking and in turn to hear the truth.

"It was painful, very painful," he admitted, "but somehow that pain triggered a dialogue between us. It was the most rewarding and radically changing event in my relationship with my manager."

He discovered that his perception of his boss had been wrong. Further, the boss also had misperceptions of him. After a long discussion they clarified their issues and renewed their bond. Over the next twelve months, Hossam's performance improved significantly. In fact, he became the highest performer in the group, and his boss became his sponsor in the company.

Hossam had always avoided conflict, but he discovered he could actually raise issues in a nonconfrontational, nonaggressive way. Direct and honest, he renewed the bond between his boss and him, and as a result, he decided to stay with the company.

He believed this experience deeply affected his own character, as he had never learned to deal with conflicts. Now in his mid-forties, he was able to rewire his brain and manage conflict in a productive way.

This ability to manage disagreement efficiently also helped his relationship with his wife and children. For many years, his wife had been frustrated because he had avoided conflicts in his personal life. Hossam revealed, "This experience has had tremendous cascading effects on my personal life, not only with my wife and children but also with my mother and brother and sisters."

Hossam now is successful in both his job and his private life through learning the positive benefits of dealing with conflict.

Avoiding conflict is one of the most common ways to become a hostage to it. Ironically, if you avoid conflict, your brain is actually working correctly. At the primitive reptilian level, our brain is hardwired to avoid conflict. The mind's eye tells us, "Conflict could be dangerous." However, it is important to rewire our brain so that we can learn to step toward conflict instead of stepping back and away from it. Conflict must be seen as a challenge, a problem to be solved, an opportunity, and, in that sense, something positive. Everyone can learn to see conflict with a positive mind-set just as Hossam did in his story, otherwise we are vulnerable to being taken hostage. How did he do it? First, he had to be shocked enough to become aware of the problem: "I avoid conflicts at work and home and it's going to cost me my job and maybe my marriage." Second, he needed a secure base, in this case his friends and me, to support the change. Third, he then had to focus on the benefit of the change: "I will get a solution and, however it goes, I will be in control of myself, I will not be a hostage." Fourth, he made a plan and then he needed to act, act, act. He had to keep the bond, be totally honest, and look for common goals. He learned to change an enemy into an ally or friend. He did this through repeated role playing with immediate feedback. Fifth, he had to understand the benefit and, finally, celebrate his success. Hossam did all of these things successfully. He took the first step in rewiring his brain with significant consequences for his boss, his work, his wife, and his children. By repeating this new behavior, he will override the conditioned pattern that kept him a hostage to his fear of conflict and, eventually, rewire his brain.

When you think of conflict, what comes to mind? Fighting? Aggression? Hatred? Fear? Struggles? Battles? Or can you think of conflict positively, as challenge, opportunity, energy, passion, creativity, engagement? Leaders, teachers, parents, coaches—everybody engaged in dealing with other people must learn to like handling conflict. For many people, it is a shock to think of the idea of learning to like dealing with conflict.

Peter Senge in *The Fifth Discipline* wrote, "Contrary to popular myth, great teams are not characterized by an absence of conflict. On the contrary, in my experience, one of the most reliable indicators of a team that is continually learning is the visible conflict of ideas. In great teams conflict becomes productive."[1]

Conflict occurs as a natural, and inevitable, part of human relationships. It can stimulate us to search for a basis of compromise and cooperation. It is possible to use conflicts to teach and develop ourselves. Conflict is also a major stimulus for curiosity and creativity. With this mind-set, conflict is positive. It is a process to be managed so that the destructive potential is converted to a positive outcome.

Conflict reflects energy and is a potential source of commitment to a team and an organization. Teams become high performing because they are able to have intense arguments or constructive fights and because they maintain the emotional bonding involving rules of respect and engagement and focus on common goals and the positive outcome. To create an environment of cooperation, a "win-win" attitude is an essential ingredient for effectively managing conflict. Respecting the dignity of the individual is also essential to resolve conflict. It involves finding the best solutions to a problem while maintaining the relationship through the emotional bonding.

Handled well, the differences that arise between people will lead to creative problem solving and successful deepening of those relationships. When we address a conflict and take action to resolve it, it has a positive effect; there is a better result and a better long-term relationship. Effective conflict management stimulates creativity and fosters personal and professional growth. Learning to speak from the heart, putting our differences on the table, and engaging in dialogue with mutual respect and dignity will lead us to conflict resolution. At the heart of conflict resolution is the ability to respectfully negotiate toward common goals and mutual benefits.

The negative effects of not confronting conflict include reluctance to exchange information, poor performance, stress, loss of self-esteem, and destructive relationships. When mismanaged, conflict can lead to serious and costly consequences in our companies, schools, and homes. Violence, illness, depression, and addiction can result, affecting the long-term health of individuals and our society as a whole.

THE NATURE AND ROOTS OF CONFLICT

Conflict can be defined as a difference between two or more persons or groups characterized by tension, emotionality, disagreement, and polarization when bonding is broken or completely lacking. At the root of all conflict is broken bonding and failure to handle loss. There are people with major differences and disagreements who are able to keep a bond and, as such, do not have a conflict. For example, there are couples with different religious, political, and cultural beliefs who remain happily married because of their strong emotional bonding.

James Carville, a staunch Democrat, and Mary Matalin, a fierce Republican, oppose each other politically. When the couple fell in love and married, people were perplexed. They still wonder how the relationship works.

Matalin insists that "the problem is people look at us as though we're opposites. We're not. We're actually very similar people. We're both advo-

cates. We're both passionate. We both like a good, fair fight. My opposite is someone who doesn't have a philosophy of life, someone who doesn't get fired up about anything."

Says Carville, "Sure, we have different ways of looking at politics. No doubt about that. But Jews and Catholics who get married probably have a different way of looking at God. It's just not a deal-breaker. If most everything else is compatible, you've got the makings of a damn good relationship."[2]

Some people turn small differences into huge conflicts and ongoing battles, sometimes even leading to violence. I once spent many long nights with the police mediating a dispute that started with a small difference that escalated and then led to violence and the need for police intervention.

The resolution of conflict comes through creating and maintaining a bond with the other person irrespective of differences and of any dislike of the person. We do not have to like someone to form a bond with him or her. We only need a common goal. Here I draw on the wisdom that, as human beings, we all have something in common that we share and that may be the starting point of creating a bond.[3] Hostage negotiators learn to override, in their mind's eye, any natural feelings of disliking someone to focus on the person as a human being in order to create a bond. They learn to suspend judgment about an individual, as their goal is to get the hostages out alive. This can be very challenging when dealing with a criminal who has engaged in the most heinous crimes. If you believe doing this is impossible, then you have not yet understood the power of your mind's eye to focus on a goal. If the goal of a hostage negotiator is to free the hostages, he will do whatever it takes to create a bond that is strong enough to build a dialogue toward a common goal as the way to get the hostages free. Remember, this works in 95 percent of hostage situations.

Ronald Reagan and Mikhail Gorbachev, once enemies, eventually became friends. Asked in an interview what had happened that they could become friends, especially after Reagan had previously described Gorbachev as "the head of an evil empire," Gorbachev said the answer was simple: "We stopped demonizing one another."

As an example, he described a tense 1985 meeting in which their talks were going nowhere. After a fiery exchange, Reagan angrily stood up to walk out of the room. As he reached the door, he stopped, turned around, and in one moment switched his focus, his mental state, his emotion from anger to engagement.

In a changed state, he then said calmly, "This isn't working. May I call you Mikhail and will you call me Ron? I would like to talk man to man, leader to leader, and see if we could really accomplish something worthwhile."

Gorbachev's response was to reach out his hand and say, "Hi, Ron."

Reagan responded, "Hi, Mikhail."

That was the beginning of a friendship that lasted until Reagan's death. Gorbachev later said, "His words were so persuasive, I could not say no."[4]

This story demonstrates the power of changing a mind-set about another person from a demonizing perspective to an ally-making focus. It also shows the power of one person's state influencing another to move toward common ground. Successful, confident people who do not become hostages achieve this by being able to switch states almost at the snap of their fingers, rather like actors getting into character. The secret is to do this with authenticity.

In addition to broken bonding, there is always a loss or an anticipated loss (meaning that the person grieves before the actual event occurs) at the root of every conflict. If you can understand how people deal with loss, you will understand the origins of how conflict escalates or is resolved.

Many conflict management interventions jump too quickly into negotiation without understanding the losses behind the conflict. In dealing with conflict, we need to understand not just the differences at the root of the conflict but also the emotions around various losses lying underneath the conflict. By understanding how losses can touch the deepest levels of a human being, we are able to appreciate better how people behave before, during, and after a conflict intervention.

Figure 5.1 shows the types of losses that can trigger a conflict and create fierce emotions. Understanding the loss and the cor-

FIGURE 5.1. TYPES OF LOSSES AND THEIR ROOTS

Loss of attachment (Who am I connected to?)	Need to feel connected, bonded, secure, or belonging
Loss of territory (Where do I belong?)	Need to feel a sense of belonging or grounding to a place, a home
Loss of structure (What is my role?)	Need to feel important, involved, and valued
Loss of identity (Who am I?)	Need to know who I am as an individual, what I stand for, my values
Loss of future (Where am I going?)	Need to know direction and have hope and a positive expectation
Loss of meaning (What is the point?)	Need to find meaning and purpose to all situations
Loss of control (I feel overwhelmed)	Need to feel in control of the situation or my destiny

responding grief emotions that you or another person feels, and where they come from, can be immensely helpful in resolving conflict. Managers frequently overlook the hard reality that grief occurs every day in organizations through things such as loss of promotion, loss of office space, loss of parking privilege, or even the ending of a successful project and the disbanding of a team.

VIOLENCE AS AN EXTREME RESPONSE TO LOSS

I have never seen a hostage situation or any act of violence that was not preceded by some loss—a person, territory, a pet, money, an object, a self-image, a goal, freedom, and so on. And I have seen countless examples of violence prevented by having a secure base—a grandparent, teacher, friend, therapist, police officer— who walked the violence-prone person through the rages about life's losses successfully. The idea of understanding loss as the entry point to bond to a person is extremely important and one all hostage negotiators have learned. If business and community leaders and parents could use the same insight in dealing with conflicts between themselves and others, how different could the foundation for resolving conflict be?

People do not kill people—they never have and they never will. People who kill perceive other people as objects; they are killing in a state of detachment or broken bonding. The killer must see the other person as nothing more than an object or enemy to be eliminated. If at any moment that object becomes a human being—a person provoking empathy in the killer—the act of violence is stopped cold. The problem arises with those individuals who are so wounded in their attachment capacity that they cannot feel empathy, form human bonds, or maintain bonding under high emotional stress.

In April 2002, Robert Steinhauser, a German student who had been expelled from his school, returned to the building in Erfurt, Germany, and killed thirteen teachers, two students, and a police officer before shooting himself. Steinhauser's murder spree ended when Rainer Heise, a sixty-year-old history and art teacher, confronted him.

When Steinhauser began walking around the school shooting teachers and students, Heise locked himself in a room. Hearing a sound in the corridor and fearing it was a student, he opened the door and came face-to-face with the masked gunman, who was pointing his weapon directly at him.

When the gunman then took off his mask, the teacher recognized his former student. "Robert, what's all this about? Was that you shooting?" asked Heise. Then he looked at the nineteen-year-old and calmly said, "If you're going to kill me, look me in the face."

Steinhauser looked at the teacher, dropped his gun, and responded politely, "No, Mr. Heise, that's enough for today."

Heise then invited the student into the classroom to talk about what he had done, but as the police moved in on the school, Steinhauser shot himself in the head.

Later, the police insisted the teacher's bravery had prevented an even higher death toll. "A courageous teacher involved the assailant in a discussion and most probably prevented a far worse massacre," declared police spokesperson Manfred Etzel.[5]

For the murderer, the sense of detachment is clear, but for the police officer or soldier it is similar. Proper law enforcement and military training demand that individuals learn how to reach a state of detachment so that they see another person as an object in order to kill in the line of duty. However, there is always a price to pay to the heart, mind, and soul of the person who kills, regardless of how well trained he or she is.

Verbal aggression or aggressive actions filled with depersonalization and detachment have the potential for escalating into violence. The violence-prone person has a history of poor attachment behavior and easily sees others as objects to manipulate. At the same time, the violence-prone person is very manipulative and yet can easily feel humiliated and rejected.[6] This framework becomes especially explosive when two such persons meet and quickly act to defend their own integrity by attacking and treating each other as an object or thing. The violence-prone incident can be deescalated by someone refusing to be depersonalized, as did Mr. Heise.

The root causes of violence are the lack of healthy social bonding and the failure to handle loss. Violence, then, is a form of grieving or, in some situations, of grief avoidance. The losses can be connected to the present or to the anticipated future, or to the past, or even to those of past generations that are carried into the present by way of resentment, hatred, feelings of injustice, prejudice, or lack of forgiveness. Violence-prone people live on the edge of chronic loneliness or masked depression, lacking the personal power to get what they want in a positive way through social bonding and interaction. They are hostage to themselves and to the events triggering the violence. In the end, violence becomes an act of power to deal with whatever emotional volcano is inside and to escape from the feeling of being a hostage inside. It gives temporary relief to the feeling of victimization and powerlessness. However, it is not a solution and actually ends up deepening the feeling of being a hostage. Healthy grieving is a social process occurring in a tribe, clan, or group in which other protecting, dependable people help the individual who suffered the loss, be it large or small, to fully rebond to life.

When people feel that conflict is imminent, they may continue to find reasons to avoid bringing it into the open. For example, there may be a fear that confronting a boss, colleague, husband, wife, or sibling will lead to increased tensions. In the mind of the individual, open discussion of the conflict may cause irreversible damage to the relationship. Fear of rejection, retaliation, embarrassment, or humiliation or a sense of isolation may lead such people to avoid conflict. Other possible fears include being labeled as a troublemaker, as disloyal, or as selfish. Fear of being personally attacked may lead some people to avoid any risk of provoking this possibility.

People can be taken hostage by the desire to overprotect harmony as a reason to avoid conflict. When feelings of entrapment, powerlessness, or ongoing resentment continue and nothing is done to solve the problem, people may begin to act like hostages. Repeated attempts to solve a conflict without success can result in increased frustration and resentment, which reinforces the feeling of being a hostage. Here is where conflict management techniques used by hostage negotiators in dealing with real-life hostage situations can provide powerful understanding, insight, and tools to break a deadlock. However, this will require tackling the real problem and confronting the people involved.

"Put the Fish on the Table"

While working in Sicily teaching conflict management, I enjoyed visiting the fish markets on the Mediterranean coast. The fishermen have a strong bond with each other, their work, and the sea. As the men brought the catch in, they would clean some of it for market. They would put the fish on the table, which soon was a gory bloody mess.

Early one morning in Catania as I stood watching, they invited me to join them, and I found myself with an apron and a knife helping to clean those fish. Suddenly I realized this was what good conflict management is all about: "putting the fish on the table" and going through the bloody mess of cleaning the fish to prepare for the great fish dinner at the end of the day.

Each time we eat a fish dinner, someone has had to clean and prepare that fish. If you leave a fish under the table, it starts to rot and smell. Unfortunately, many people leave a lot of fish—conflicts and issues—under their table. They do not face the discord, hoping it will vanish. However, leaving the fish under the table not only does not remove the conflict but also makes the odor worse and worse.

What every person needs to do is reach under the table, grab the fish, put it on the table, and go through the mess of cleaning the fish (the conflict) to have a great fish dinner (the solution) at the end of the day. Now, it is true that sometimes we may reach under the table and find a shark or a whale, so we must be aware of the size of the conflict in order to handle it properly. Putting the fish on the table does not mean to be aggressive and hostile. Instead, it means being able to raise, openly discuss, or, as *Good to Great* author Jim Collins says, "face the brutal truth" to allow a resolution to follow.[7]

We need to approach conflict management believing that the adversarial person is willing to put a fish on the table. However, choosing the right time to bring that fish into the open is imperative! If your boss is walking out the door late for a meeting, this is not the best time to put a fish on the table. When you do it, how you do it, and where you do it—all are tactics. However, if we rewire our brain in such a way that we are willing to put the fish on the table and go through the smelly, bloody process of cleaning it, then the relationship and the environment can return to a positive base.

The "put the fish on the table" metaphor works for problems at home, in the office, or anywhere in our lives. If an issue is not raised, it will begin to fester and can lead to a much larger and more critical problem. The motivation to participate in "cleaning the fish" is critical. There must be a true benefit and reward for enduring the process and getting the "great dinner-solution" that reunites the involved parties. This metaphor that I coined is now adopted by many organizations and many people in helping them to understand the process of conflict management. They use "put the fish on the table" as a prelude to raising concerns to prevent either party being on the defensive.

Jane was concerned that Martin, her direct report, was "not pulling his weight" in the organization. He was hard to reach, slow to answer e-mails, and unresponsive to customers. Other people commented on his "absences," and Jane felt she had no choice but to raise these concerns with Martin. She feared the conversation, for it might become very unpleasant.

Time passed, and then the organization introduced the concept of "putting the fish on the table." Jane now felt she had the route to open a productive dialogue with Martin. She approached him by saying, "Martin, I have a fish that I need to put on the table."

Martin was immediately tuned into the fact that a sensitive issue was going to be raised; therefore, he was able to handle the conversation rationally rather than defensively or aggressively. Jane was able to communicate her concerns and those expressed by others and asked Martin how he felt about these comments.

By asking a simple question, Jane was inviting a dialogue and treating Martin with respect rather than putting him into a child mode. In the end, Martin put his own fish on the table and disclosed that he was very unhappy in his job due to personal circumstances. After a deep dialogue, Jane and Martin were able to find options that allowed Martin to become reengaged with the team.

The truth was that Martin was not a bad employee, but he had become a hostage to his personal situation involving child custody issues and had allowed this problem to affect his work performance.

Make it a rule to learn to put the fish on the table. You may choose to not do it each and every time, but you should be willing to do it. Choosing not to put the fish on the table is a matter of tactics and would not represent conflict-avoidant behavior because you would have thought about it and made a conscious choice. A word of caution to those people who tend to be adversarial: "put the fish on the table" is not permission to slap the person in the face with the fish! Rather, it is permission to be direct, engaging, and respectful in working toward a resolution. Treat conflict as a joint problem and work together to find solutions, rather than being a hostage to the issue at hand. You will be amazed at how often this method actually works, as seen in the examples of Hossam, Jane, and countless others.

Sources of Conflict

What are the differences that provoke conflict, keeping in mind that the root of all conflict is broken bonding and failure to handle loss, be it actual or anticipated? There are people with great differences who are not in conflict because their desire to maintain a relationship is greater than any personal goal, and there are people with minor differences who end up violent with each other because they put a personal goal ahead of maintaining the relationship. For most people, conflict does not lead to violence. However, unresolved differences and barriers can prove to be major forces of disruption and negativity in our lives. Bonding can be broken for a number of reasons, thereby creating conflict, as outlined in the following list:

- Differences in goals
  Example: Wanting to take a promotion working in another country versus spouse wanting to continue in his or her job
- Differences in interests
  Example: Interest in family time versus interest in overtime
- Differences in values
  Example: Distorted reporting versus accurate reporting of economic figures
- Differences in perception of the problem
  Example: "It's a quality control problem" versus "It's a production problem"
- Differences in communication styles
  Example: Someone who is analytical and rational versus someone who is highly intuitive and creative
- Differences in power or status, or a rivalry
  Example: A colleague who is jealous, interfering or blocking the success of another colleague
- Insecurity
  Example: Someone who feels incompetent; an indecisive leader unwilling to make a decision, negatively affecting a team
- Resistance to change
  Example: People who want change versus people who want the status quo
- Role confusion
  Example: Discrepancy between what you and I think we should do: "That's your job" versus "That's my job"
- Search for ego identity
  Example: Leaders who manipulate others to build their own identities and self-importance

- Personal needs
  Example: A sick child taking time and energy away from work
    performance
- Poor communication (or lack of communication)
  Example: Failure to inform others of necessary information,
    excluding them through the withholding of data or
    information

Historically, when resolving conflicts, the two disagreeing parties simply had a fistfight, a duel, or an all-out war, and the winner was "right." Although there are many new ways to handle differences, "might makes right" or the use of force or coercion is still used by too many managers in the world today. Fortunately, due to globalization and interdependence, the concept of win-win and cooperation and collaboration as opposed to win-lose is certainly more prevalent today in the general mind-set of leaders than ever before. However, the truth remains that many people still feel like hostages to conflict and fail to resolve differences in an effective way.

The content of the conflict is generally not the problem. The real problem has to do with the difference, the underlying broken bonding or lack of bonding and loss that drive the emotions to escalate the conflict or to block the resolution. In the end, all conflicts can be solved. However, many people are simply not willing to pay the price involved in solving the conflict. In most cases, the reason has to do with a failure to see the benefit of maintaining a good working relationship, or even of ending in a positive manner.

THE DYNAMICS OF A HEALTHY RELATIONSHIP

Dealing with conflict means attention must be paid to the relationship as well as to the goals. Hostage negotiators learn to do this and so can others. There are a number of actions we can take to keep the relationship intact.

Balance reason and emotion. Many aspects of a relationship are not rational. We often act emotionally, not logically, in pursuit of a purpose. Emotions such as fear, anger, frustration, or even love may disrupt otherwise thoughtful actions. Emotions are normal, necessary, and often essential to problem solving. They can convey important information, help us marshal our resources, and inspire us to action. Wisdom is never found without positive emotions of the heart being involved. Two people will deal well with their differences if reason and emotions are in some kind of balance, managed and used as a constructive force.

When emotions overwhelm reason, we cannot work well with other people. We cannot make wise decisions in the middle of a temper tantrum. However, logic alone is not sufficient for solving conflict and building a relationship. Rather, we need reason informed by emotion and emotion guided and tempered by reason. This balance between reason and emotion is a practical path to not being held hostage. I believe this balance can be best learned from the secure bases in our lives who help us develop the internal models we can borrow and use to balance reason and emotion.

Understand each other. If we are going to achieve an outcome that leaves both parties feeling fairly treated, we need to understand each other's interests, perceptions, and notions of fairness. Unless I have a good idea of what you think the problem is, what you want, why you want it, and what you think might be fair, I will be groping in the dark for an outcome that will meet your interests as well as mine. You will be seriously handicapped unless you understand me and what I think. Whether we agree or not, the more we understand each other, the more likely it is that a solution to a conflict can be found.

Communicate well. Conflict resolution requires effective communication to understand how to create, maintain, and renew the bonding during the process. Although we may understand each other in general, the quality of an outcome and the way it can be reached depend on effective communication about the "fish" under or on the table. The more effectively we communicate our differences, and our areas of agreement, the better we will understand each other's concerns and the better our chances for reaching a mutually acceptable agreement. The manner and extent of our language build trust and reduce the basis for suspicion in the mind's eye. We have the power to change the state of another person through our transactions with each other. There are many examples in which the entire destiny of a conflict has rested on one word or one sentence. Hostage negotiators are trained to understand and to use transactions with great respect. Typically, the greater our communication, the better the working relationships we have. The best communication is that which becomes a heart-to-heart dialogue.

Be reliable and honest. Our communications are worth little if we do not believe each other. Commitments entered into lightly or disregarded easily are worse than no commitments at all. Blind trust will not help us work with others; instead, it can damage a relationship more than can healthy skepticism. Well-founded trust, based on honest and reliable conduct over time, can greatly enhance our ability to cope with conflict. The more honest and reliable we are with each other, the better our chance of producing good outcomes. We must be reliable and honest in order to be a secure base.

Persuade rather than coerce. In a particular transaction, we may be more interested in the immediate outcome rather than in the long-term relationship. Each of us will try to affect the other's decisions; the way we do it will have a profound effect on the quality of our relationship. For example, one person might try to inspire voluntary cooperation by information, logical argument, or moral persuasion. Another person might try coercion through worsened alternatives, warnings, threats, extortion, and physical force. The more coercive the influence, the less likely the outcome will reflect both our concerns, and the less legitimate it will be for at least one of the parties. The less coercive and the more cooperative the influence is, the better our ability to work with each other. The shortcut of coercion leads to disrupted bonding. Taking the time to engage in a persuasive process reaps mutual benefit and goodwill. Historically, this was the foundation of hostage negotiation. When force was used, people were killed. The introduction of the skills of persuasion and negotiation saved lives and works in 95 percent of cases.

Feel mutual acceptance. If we deal well with our differences, we accept that dealing with the other person is worthwhile. Feeling accepted, worthy, and valued is a basic psychological need. The foundation of the deepest bonds has what eminent psychologist

Carl Rogers called "unconditioned positive regard."[8] For example, unless I listen to your views, accept your right to have views different from mine, and consider your interests, you probably will not want to deal with me. And if we do not deal with each other, we will not even begin to resolve our differences. Understanding how to communicate acceptance of the other person while saying no or disagreeing with a specific point is a skill that can be learned. Being able to say "no" while keeping the bond by communicating acceptance of the person is a secret to never being taken hostage.

Acceptance is not an either-or phenomenon but a matter of degree; the higher the degree of acceptance, the more chance there is of working out differences and producing positive outcomes.[9]

CONFLICT OF INTERESTS VERSUS CONFLICT OF NEEDS

Donohue and Kolt view conflict as "a situation in which interdependent people express (manifest or latent) differences in satisfying their individual needs and interests and experience interference from each other in accomplishing their goals."[10] This idea frames several key thoughts regarding conflict.

While most conflict-management writers blend the concepts of interests and needs, psychologists, from Freud to Maslow, point out an important distinction. Interests are viewed as more transitory and superficial, while needs are seen as more basic and enduring. Interests are tangible things that can be traded and compromised, such as land, money, or jobs, while needs are intangible things that are not for trading, such as identity, security, respect, or recognition. The most conflict-provoking losses have to do with needs, and these needs may connect to the deeper wounds someone carries in their mind and heart.

Since needs are more intangible, they are often hidden underneath more visible conflicts over interests. But when human needs are also in conflict, resolving a conflict about interests will not make the conflict go away. Sometimes attempts to deal with a conflict about interests will actually make the situation worse, when, for example, people get angry at the thought of having to compromise, as is sometimes the case with interest-based conflicts. Conflict about interests can often become emotional. It is not surprising that real or perceived conflicts about interests can lead to painful and emotional battles. The issue of trust lies below the surface. Preexisting anger, resentment, perceived unfairness, and communication breakdowns can be aggravated by a lack of trust or bonding.

The underlying problem is the assumption that many conflicts are perceived as conflicts about interests, when in reality they are conflicts about fundamental needs. Usually conflicts cannot be adequately managed if needs remain latent because they are repressed by the individual. Often, ways can be found to meet these needs, without having to compromise.

RESOLVING CONFLICT

Another secret of successful conflict resolution is the ability to continually maintain the bond and to rebond when a bond is broken too quickly for whatever reason. Taking a positive approach to conflict involves understanding that bonding is fundamental to any resolution. Being curious and creative, and searching for compromise and cooperation, have their own rewards. Tackling conflicts head-on is basic to avoid being taken hostage. When we do not address a problem and take action to solve it due to passivity or the inability to make a clear choice, we are acting like a hostage. When we have a hostage mind-set, we come to believe in the mind's eye that a problem cannot be solved and so, interestingly enough, find ways not to solve it. In fact, the opposite is possible—learning to enjoy solving conflicts is a possibility for everyone.

The manifestations of conflict are many, yet the principles for resolving conflict are simple. Understanding and knowing the complexity of conflict and, at the same time, understanding its simplicity is an essential mind-set that I have observed in the great peacemakers, mediators, and hostage negotiators. It can be dangerous to see only the complexity or see only the simplicity. Managing this paradox is the dilemma in every conflict situation. As used by hostage negotiators, there are four fundamental principles to resolve conflict successfully:

1. *Never create an enemy.* Where there is an enemy, transform that person into an ally and partner. This is a fundamental principle of transactional analysis, as expressed by Eric Berne's phrase "I'm OK, You're OK."[11] This idea is both a central truth and a fundamental tool in communicating mutual respect, positive regard, and cooperation. Every transaction must carry the power of this message even when using strong, limit-setting boundaries referred to as "tough love."

2. *The person is never the problem.* Separate the person from the problem and focus on the issues to be resolved, not the individual. This is a basic principle to avoid escalations in the conflict resolution process. It can be counterintuitive because our culture drives the "demonizing" of individuals in the political and religious arena, in children's literature, and in Hollywood films. It is hardly surprising then that we tend to personalize a conflict at work or at home unless we have learned another model from strong secure bases. Often, the thinking is that if only we can get rid of the person, then everything will be okay. This is a mind-set challenge and, once mastered, will prevent us from being taken hostage in the emotions of a conflict.

It is all too easy to view someone who is different from us in any way—be it appearance, language, culture, attitude, or approach—as a potential threat or enemy. This is a poor base for dialogue and is likely to lead to an emotional standoff. As our businesses are increasingly global and our workplaces and cities become more and more diverse, the possibilities for misunderstanding are immense. It is easy for a person to feel attacked or threatened, and therefore every effort must be made to separate the person from the problem.

3. *Maintain a sincere desire to help the other person get what he or she wants or needs.* It is all too easy to become hostages to ourselves by overemphasizing what we want without first communicating a sincere and authentic desire to help the other. We must maintain the bond with the other person in every transaction, verbal and nonverbal, by showing interest in what they want as well as what we want. Saying no or putting the fish on the table can be done as part of showing interest in the other person's wants or needs. Sometimes the underlying battle in the conflict is to get the detached manager to show appropriate and authentic interest in

the well-being of team members. The independent loners must learn to bond and show interest in people if they want to become effective leaders.

4. *Never be hijacked by attacks and intense emotions.* Never take aggressive words or actions personally. Keep your thoughts clear and never lose sight of the goal. When you feel like withdrawing or attacking someone, quickly cancel that thought in your mind's eye and replace it with a desire to help or a desire to carry on in your personal or professional role. Have you ever done or said something that you regretted later? You were quite simply taken hostage.

Thirty years of hostage negotiating and managing violence has made me a believer in conflict management, even to deescalate the most violence-prone people through dialogue. The secret is the ability to continually bond and rebond and to work authentically within the process, even if it takes hours or days, patiently, intensely, and with full knowledge of the power of each sentence, each word, each pause, and each transaction. The following international examples demonstrate these principles of conflict resolution very well.

In 1993, Yitzhak Rabin and Yasser Arafat signed the Oslo peace accord with a handshake that "shook the world." Those who know the inside story say that this was without a doubt one of the most difficult moments in Yitzhak Rabin's life. Here was the prime minister of Israel, the former chief Israeli warrior, making peace with the enemy. Before his assassination, Rabin repeatedly said Arafat was Israel's ally in peace and they had a common goal: to exchange land for peace.

Over time, Rabin and Arafat developed a bond with one another as reflected by their behavior and language. This bond was further reinforced by Mrs. Rabin's warm welcome of Arafat into her home after her husband's murder by one of his own countrymen because of his belief in exchanging land for peace.

Yitzhak Rabin is a model of a warrior becoming a peacemaker by using his mind's eye to look into the future, knowing the past, and seeing another possibility. Many in Israel, Palestine, and around the world wonder what would have happened in the Middle East had he not been killed.

Broken bonding and the lack of bonding have been at the heart of the Middle East conflict, combined with the powerful grief over loss of territory, loss of people, loss of security, and loss of identity across many generations. Another example of political leadership working to repair a broken bond comes from Great Britain.

In Northern Ireland in 1997, when British prime minister Tony Blair merely shook the hand of Gerry Adams of Sinn Fein, some Protestant loyalists became enraged, called Blair a traitor, and asked how he could shake hands with a terrorist. Blair stated, "I treated Gerry Adams in the same way I treat any human being. Before talking, I shook hands. What is important about the situation here in Northern Ireland is that we do actually treat each other as human beings."

Blair understood the necessity of entering into a dialogue. Further, he recognized that every good dialogue starts with a handshake to establish respect and goodwill.[12]

Tony Blair was able to separate the person from the problem and focus on the end goal, peace. He also recognized that dehumanizing any individual is not the way to resolve conflict.

Applying Conflict Resolution Techniques in Business

By understanding the roots and nature of conflict and creating a climate in which people feel secure in raising personal concerns and fears, anyone can successfully apply conflict resolution techniques. This will ensure that the harmony and long-term viability of any relationship, be it a personal one or a business one, will be preserved.

In business terms, management must encourage a climate of trust and openness in which people feel it is safe to raise questions and concerns without fearing the consequences. If this climate does not exist, the concerns will become fish *under* the table and result in tension and other disruptive behaviors.

*Appointed CEO of a large multinational company, James was eager
to take the helm and launch the company on a new, strategic direction.
After he and his immediate senior management team had worked out a
new strategy, he called together fifty global senior managers to reveal the
plan and discuss the challenges they would face in implementation. He
sent out an e-mail with a clear message: "We're coming together to discuss
the strategy, not to change it; to clarify the approach and not criticize it."*

*The meeting began positively and energetically. Then Dorene, a young
high-potential manager with great enthusiasm for her job, expressed concern that part of the strategy was confusing, for it seemed to be pulling
the company in opposite directions. Feeling personally attacked, James
immediately responded by stopping the meeting and chiding Dorene for
not listening to him, not following his directions, and not supporting
the company's goals.*

*Shocked, the group became passive and never recovered from this harangue.
In fact, James stopped the meeting a day and a half into a three-day session because of the negative ambiance.*

*After seeking external coaching, James understood what had gone wrong:
by his breaking the bond and losing sight of a common goal, he allowed
himself to be taken hostage. Six months later, he called the same group
back and handled the session in a very different way.*

*James was a quick learner. He understood to do what every good hostage
negotiator does: keep the bond, ask a question when attacked, and stay
focused on a common goal. He apologized in advance to Dorene, and,
in front of the group, he apologized to her again and to the group, saying
he had made a mistake and wanted an open and honest dialogue about
the challenges the company faced. The result was a three-day meeting
with a deeply engaging dialogue about the company's direction.*

*James was so happy with the outcome that he continues to bring senior
leaders together for open discussions about leadership decisions related
to strategy. Yes, he did rewire his brain to never be taken hostage again,
regardless of what was said to him, and to understand that one transaction can change the destiny of a whole process, for better or for worse.*

James's style of leadership has changed dramatically from a
coercive approach to an inspiring one because of how he learned

to create bonds and manage conflict. He now knows how to deal with conflict in a constructive way, and that by nurturing and cultivating bonds through an apology, a word of praise, or a moment of recognition, there is no destructive conflict.

SUMMARY

Conflict is everywhere around us—in our personal lives, in our professional lives, and in the world at large. This is a reality. The good news is that we can learn to manage it so that the idea of conflict has a positive rather than negative connotation. All conflicts are solvable with the right degree of bonding, cooperation, engagement, and willingness to "pay the price" of letting go of something for a greater benefit. The brain is hardwired to avoid conflict because it can be dangerous. However, we can rewire our brain to learn to enjoy dealing with conflict. Some people have a natural ability to handle conflict based on the secure bases they have had in their lives. Others find themselves knee-deep in conflict because of avoidance or because they are repeatedly "contaminated" and held hostage by negative feelings and unable to turn disagreement into agreement, making the same mistakes over and over again.

The skill of handling conflict begins with bonding and bridge building, acting from one's own authentic state. During a conflict, we must stay engaged; understand the other's interests, wants, and needs; and listen to the pain. Learning to manage conflict will make our own lives richer—we can live hostage-free, without fearing disagreements and by turning energy-draining arguments with family members, friends, and colleagues into relationship-enhancing experiences.

When we understand and appreciate the constructive side of conflict, we are empowered to identify problems, engage in a dialogue, and seek ways to resolve differences, quickly and clearly. We look for and find friends and allies instead of enemies and rivals. We look for common and shared goals and objectives. We are hostages to no one, least of all ourselves, and we welcome conflict, because we know how to manage and deal with differences. We do not allow conflict or fear of conflict to ever take us hostage.

Key Points to Remember

1. Make it a rule to "put the fish on the table" to bring out tensions, conflicts, and problems, to resolve differences and harness the positive energy of conflict.

2. Learn to get along with everybody by looking for a friend rather than an enemy. Of course, it is true that we might not get along with everybody. However, if we start with the thought in mind that we will not get along with somebody, it is too easy to put that person into the category of dislike.

3. The root causes of conflict and violence are broken bonding and failure to deal with loss. When dealing with conflicts, attention must be paid to losses and the price to pay, as well as to the benefits, both individual and shared.

4. Leaders must understand that conflict can be a major source of creativity and a potential for innovation. Teams can reach a high-performance level because they are able to have constructive "fights" in an environment of cooperation and trust in which a win-win attitude becomes the goal of conflict management.

CHAPTER SIX

EFFECTIVE DIALOGUE

At a Swiss hospital, I held a training session on crisis intervention and violence management. Monica, one of the nurses who attended the training, later told me how she had applied the techniques in a real situation.

The Swiss police had stopped a man driving a motorcycle. A homeless member of the European Hell's Angels, Jacques was traveling alone. When he refused to show his papers, the police attempted to arrest him, and in the process of restraining him, they broke his arm. In addition, they confiscated his motorcycle.

The police took him to the hospital emergency room. As Monica tended Jacques's arm, suddenly he pulled a knife and shouted, "I'm getting out of here. If you try to stop me, I'll kill you!"

Monica told me she remembered about "bonding" and immediately put her hands up, saying, "Jacques, I don't think that's a good idea. The police are out there, and they're going to stop you again. I know you're upset about your motorcycle."

She recalled what she had learned about loss and realized the bike's symbolic significance: his secure base. So she said, "Look, I'm here to help fix your arm. If you cooperate with me and let me do my job, I'll try to help you get your motorcycle back."

"No, you are lying!" he responded.

Remembering that his words were a small concession to a positive event even though they sounded negative, Monica continued, as any good hostage negotiator would, by repeating her desire to help him. Within ten minutes, she had engaged him in a dialogue, and he started to cooperate. Finally, he agreed to put down the knife.

Through her bonding approach, she was able to create what she called a "profound dialogue" that prevented an escalation into further violence. In the end, she helped him sort out the problem with the police and get his motorcycle back.

Six months later, when he was driving through the city, Jacques stopped at the hospital to say hello to the nurses and the emergency room team. Through Monica's attitude and approach, a potentially dangerous situation had turned into a positive one in which Jacques could actually create in his mind a positive association to hospitals, doctors, and nurses.

Fortunately, few of us will find ourselves in this type of situation. However, the power and effectiveness of dialogue as illustrated in the preceding story is something everyone can learn and use in daily life. There is no greater tool than the skills of dialogue to help keep someone from becoming a hostage. What is the difference between a dialogue and a conversation, you may ask? Why put so much emphasis on dialogue? Is it not just about talking to each other? Actually, it is so much more and involves all aspects of our mind and body.

The root of the word *dialogue* is from the Greek words *Dia,* meaning "through," and *Logos,* meaning "word" or "form." Logos for the Greeks was an attribute of the human soul that "gave form to what would otherwise be without form," to make definite that which was previously undefined. Words are "formulas," containers, packages for carrying and conveying the meaning inside the human being. Dialogue is then two people sharing words, formulas, or containers for meaning and the energy inside them. Dialogue is about shared inquiry, a way of thinking and reflecting. It is not something you do *to* another person, it is something you do *with* another person. It requires a shift in mind-set about what the relationship with others means. The focus is on understanding the other person and not only on their understanding us. Dialogue is an exchange in which people think together and discover something new. It is the seeking of a greater truth. The depth of dialogue brings the participants to a different level, through which they come to a deeper understanding of each other.

According to author and lecturer William Isaacs, "Dialogue is a living experience of inquiry within and between people." He continues, "People come to dialogue for many reasons. Some want to resolve conflicts. Others wish to get along better with a particular person, a business partner, a boss, a parent, or a child. Still others want to solve problems more effectively. Dialogue can enable people to bring out differences and begin to make sense of them."[1]

In March 2003, John Mackey, CEO of Whole Foods Market, tried several times to cut off the animal rights activist who was disrupting his shareholder meeting. Lauren Ornelas, director of Viva! USA, a group dedicated to improving the living conditions of farm animals, was making a speech about the lives of the ducks that ended up in the display cabinets of Mackey's stores. Ornelas was lecturing a man who had already done a substantial amount to improve the quality, sustainability, and purity of farm food. Mackey cofounded and heads Whole Foods, the largest organic and natural foods grocer in the United States. His initial response to Ornelas was dismissive. "I said to her, 'We have the best animal standards in the country—go bother somebody else'," he recalled. After the meeting, he found Ornelas in the crowd and they had a polite chat. The CEO gave the animal rights activist his e-mail address. For the next few weeks, they traded arguments through e-mails about the way animals were treated. Finally, Mackey got fed up and wrote to Ornelas that they would never agree and they should end the correspondence. However, Mackey then did something unusual. Instead of dismissing Ornelas completely, he tried to understand her beliefs and why she thought the way she did. Over a period of months, he read a dozen books about the way animals were raised. Said Mackey, "The more I read, the more I was interested in it. I said, 'Damn, these people are right. This is terrible.'"

The CEO then did two things. First, he changed his diet from vegetarian to vegan, and second, he sent Ornelas an e-mail telling her she was right—not just about the ducks, but also about chickens, pigs, and cows. He said that Whole Foods would immediately begin to use its influence and buying power to demand that the meat it sells comes from animals that have been treated with a measure of dignity before being slaughtered. He invited Ornelas to help his company in this task.[2]

SEEKING A GREATER TRUTH THROUGH DIALOGUE

Having an authentic dialogue with someone requires a mind-set of discovery. For some people, especially in a business environment, it is easier to get into a debate or an argument. In both situations, people are looking either for the right answer or to prove a point. In a dialogue, we want to keep a connection with the person to whom we are talking. True dialogue also involves questioning and sharing doubt. In debating, we keep looking at the issue that is most important to us, which easily leads to disagreement. In times of constant change and increasing complexity, where we cannot act as self-sufficient individuals anymore, we need to take into account our growing interdependence, and dialogue takes us there. Dialogue is an important means to develop a culture of collaboration. Creative dialogue can also be used as a means to search for new ideas, ultimately leading to innovations in any field. Another purpose of dialogue is to resolve differences. Through dialogue, two or more people can reach agreement by communicating with one another to reach a shared understanding about a problem.

Dialogue is a powerful combination of listening and talking. In many cultures, dialogue is the principal means for coming together to resolve conflicts that are bound to arise between human beings. This process of dialogue starts with an attachment and a bond between two or more people, to listen and respond. The most important sign of dialogue is how mutual influence occurs in the process. If I do not let you touch me, influence me, change me, then I am not in a dialogue. The same can be said of the other person. If you do not let me touch you, influence you, change you, then you are not in a dialogue.

As depicted in Figure 6.1, the energy from the body, the emotions, the intellect, and the spirit is given form through words. Words carry energy and make an impact. How do we communicate, put into words, what is inside us so that someone else can easily understand what meaning those words carry? For some people, it is more difficult to put into words what is inside, because they do not know what they are feeling or they block the truth of what is inside. People who cannot put words to the pain and sadness inside of them are more likely than others to get sick, be aggressive, have addictions, become depressed, burn out, have stress reactions, or create organizational conflict. If we communicate only with our intellect, we will be too rational and lack empathy. If we communicate only with our emotions, we will be too irrational. It is when we communicate with our whole being that we can really enter into

FIGURE 6.1. AUTHENTICALLY ENGAGED TRANSACTIONS

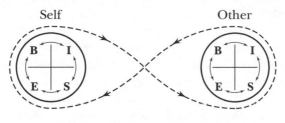

Talking—Dialogue—Negotiation

B   Body

E   Emotions

I   Intellect

S   Spirit

a fully engaged dialogue with another person for shared learning through shared meaning.

According to psychologist James Lynch, "dialogue consists of reciprocal communication between two or more living creatures. It involves the sharing of thoughts, physical sensations, ideas, ideals, hopes and feelings. In sum, dialogue involves the reciprocal sharing of any and all life experiences."[3]

If an individual believes he or she knows everything, then there is no benefit to dialogue. In reality, no one person has "the truth." There is a perception, an interpretation, a subjective part. There should always be room for dialogue. There is a time to engage in dialogue, to decide, and to act. Leaders must be able to do all three. It is also correct to say that there are times to limit dialogue. Leaders must make a decision. The question to consider is, Have all viewpoints been heard, especially the opposing or minority opinions?

The power of dialogue is to enter a deeper exchange even when the parties are in major disagreement. Dialogue resolves many disputes and conflicts simply through this process of listening and talking to each other. There are many examples of people sitting and talking and finding that the differences or conflicts between them are dissolved through understanding each other and having a "heart-to-heart" exchange.

A large multinational introduced a diversity initiative. At first, many in the white male majority were extremely dismissive and skeptical, making comments such as, "So now I have to have a sex change to get promoted." However, when the company ran diversity awareness sessions and explained that the goal of the program was to create an environment in which all employees felt included and in which people were appointed to roles based on their competence rather than their contacts, many of the skeptical employees became less defensive and even supportive of the activity. Through a dialogue on a potentially explosive and divisive topic, employees came to understand the motivations of the company behind the initiative. "Oh, I didn't realize that was what you meant by diversity. What I'm hearing is fine," was a common response heard after the dialogue-based meetings.

Negotiation is an extension of dialogue in which a process of bargaining is added to help further resolve differences. Hostage negotiators do not immediately begin with negotiating. They start by asking questions, listening to the other person. They invite the hostage taker to engage in a dialogue by this offer of questions. The hostage taker is seeking a way to create a positive association that will form the basis of trust and establish the negotiator as a secure base. At this point, the hostage negotiator is working at two levels: the content level, discussing what the hostage taker wants, and the nonverbal process level of building the relationship bond. One problem for many people is that they do not know how to express themselves in a dialogue. A person unable to build a positive bond may speak with words that carry fear, anger, or sadness. How can you tell when someone is doing this? It shows up in the behavior and words. Such people speak with coercion, aggression, anxiety, low energy, and detachment. They are argumentative, they interrupt without listening, they defend, and they think ahead, and the result is that dialogue is blocked. The words people use sometimes do not match their actions. Negotiators are experts in the use of words, transactions, and dialogue to help people get past their natural defenses and into a genuine bond.

For many people, talking becomes a habit, a ritual rather than a personal exchange. It is like driving a car. They get into the car and just drive. They meet someone, open their mouth, and they just talk, not thinking about the impact or the effect their words are having on themselves or other persons.

When we are actually aware and thinking while talking, something different happens beyond just reporting a memory or repeating memories to fill in silence. Thinking is about seeing something new, seeing the potential, the possibilities, or something different. Thinking also requires a kind of self-awareness. What is the emotional state that I feel when I am thinking? When people stop thinking, they are likely to be taken hostage because they are operating out of memory and not personal engagement to the other person. In fact, if someone is operating only out of memory, the exchange is likely to drift to the negative. Gossip serves this kind of purpose. It is rare to hear gossip about positive aspects of other people. People many times just talk through playback—the mind is unaware, nonthinking. Genuine thinking is less automatic and moves more slowly—it has "freshness," and it flows like a river of soft water through the mind. Body, emotions, intellect, and spirit combine into a stream of consciousness that flows out from the self to the other and then is absorbed and returned as an extension of the stream. We can choose to block the flow of the current going out or coming in, and the other person can do the same.

INTERNAL AND EXTERNAL DIALOGUE

Looking at Figure 6.1, we must remember that there is an internal dialogue that occurs within ourselves—within the body, the emotions, the intellect, and the spirit. If we are disconnected or detached from a part of ourselves or, as psychologists say, we "disassociate" from part of ourselves, we will have difficulty in creating genuine dialogue.

The internal and external dialogue come together when we accurately and authentically put words to what is inside us. The first step in creating a bond is managing ourselves even if there is a strong anger or fear reaction. When a hostage negotiator feels fear at a sudden unexpected reaction or event, it is natural to have that feeling and yet not to be taken hostage by it. As part of my work as a police psychologist, I was involved in over three hundred fitness-for-duty evaluations. Any time a police officer participated in a shooting or life-threatening situation, I was part of the process of determining whether he or she was allowed to continue carrying a gun and return to the street for active duty. The most troubling of all to evaluate were those police officers who described feeling no fear at all. This was not because of a state of peak performance, which can happen in high-focus situations, but because of alienation to the part of themselves that intuitively screens the world for danger. In fact, those officers who were not allowed to return to duty were those completely out of touch with their own fear and often presenting themselves as overly aggressive. The learning here is that it is necessary to be in touch with fear and to use fear as a part of dialogue with self and others. In fact, fear was the most difficult emotion for police officers to be aware of and to talk about.

If you can articulate your feelings and thoughts with another person, you are able to have a dialogue, meaning that you can put words to what you have inside and listen to the words that come from someone else. A true dialogue is a feeling of togetherness, a unity because you speak and you are understood, and you listen and you understand. With each transaction, there is a mutual influence.

In 1984, a Kuwaiti airliner was hijacked. From the hostage takers' point of view, to be a good hostage you have to believe you are going to die. You do not make a good hostage if you are not afraid. This is why terrorists intimidate and torture hostages and often kill one as an example.

In this case, the terrorists chose twelve men and, with great ceremony, took them to the front of the plane to be seated and wait to be killed. One of the twelve selected was a Kuwaiti man. In his deep grief, he sat quietly with tears streaming down his face. One of the terrorists, who was wearing a mask—not just to protect his identity but also to block bonding—walked up to the man, pointed his gun at his head, and commanded, "You are an Arab. Die like a man. Die with dignity. Don't die like a coward."

Accepting his imminent death, the Kuwaiti looked into the eyes of the terrorist and said, "Sir, if you had as many people waiting for you back home as I do, you would cry too."

The terrorist immediately pushed the gun to the man's head and started to engage the trigger. Then he hesitated. After a short period of silence during which eye contact was maintained, the terrorist put down the gun and walked to the back of the plane. After some two hours, this Kuwaiti man was freed.

Later, when investigators asked the hostage why he had been released, he explained, "I think the terrorist felt sorry for me. I could see it in his eyes."

The point of this story is that, though he faced death, the hostage was able to remain calm enough to look at the terrorist with the grief and sadness for the people waiting for him, and that look along with the words somehow connected, influencing the hostage taker to let him go. Indeed, the power of his words and the bonding he created through this short dialogue had saved him. I think you would agree that this is dialogue at its greatest impact.[4]

Effective dialogue cannot be measured by the length of time spent talking together. The quality and authenticity of the exchange determines whether a bond is established and mutual influence occurs. Sometimes that can happen quickly, as in the previous story. People who have trouble bonding often cannot speak effectively or cannot listen attentively. This becomes a primary barrier to resolving conflicts and differences. Anyone who cannot talk effectively or listen intently will not be good at negotiating.

What do we mean by *negotiation* in the context of dialogue? Negotiation means I continue to assert myself, even in the face of being told "no," while maintaining and deepening the bond. This process continues until we find an agreement. People who have difficulty bonding often overemphasize their own wants or they give in too easily out of fear. Persons who cannot assert themselves will not negotiate effectively and are likely to become hostages. Human conflict develops because people are unable to talk, engage in dialogue, and negotiate effectively. Negotiation is essential to deal with the people around us, whether it is at home, with friends, or at work. Parents should teach children how to speak, to put words to what is inside, to use dialogue, and to negotiate. Ideally, these skills are first learned in the family environment. It is wonderful for children to see parents and the family as a secure base for the mind's eye to capture the picture of effective conflict resolution—talking, making dialogue, and negotiating. Negotiation is covered in detail in Chapter Seven.

Authenticity is the art of speaking the truth in a dialogue. It is finding what is deep within us and giving voice to it. In this way, we are all unique—we have our own experiences and senses, and this is why dialogue can be so rich. Authenticity means that we are true to our inner natures. According to the work of James Lynch, human beings can tell the difference between people who are true to their inner nature and people who are not. In states of authenticity, people are comfortable in their own skin. They interact with "truthfulness," and they are able to let the energy of life flow through themselves, into their words and then their dialogue. Authentic dialogue, when people are speaking from their hearts, requires good self-esteem and enables powerful bonding to take place. Good dialogue feels good! And great dialogue feels even greater!

BLOCKS TO DIALOGUE

Often, we are not aware of blocks that can interfere with dialogue. These blocks are ways to stop the dialogue and thereby rupture the bonding process. We have all met those people who, when we ask them for the time, tell us how to make a watch. Or when we ask for direct feedback, they give us generalized platitudes. Or we talk about a problem, and they dismiss it as not important. These are all blocks to dialogue. Whether with a statement or a question, the responder needs to link directly to what preceded. That way it is possible to follow (or trace back) sentence by sentence to the point at which any block intrudes. One of my favorite expressions when people do not answer a question directly is to say gently, "That's a great answer, but to a different question." Most times, the other person does not even remember the question. My research shows that in organizations about 70 percent of communication is filled with blocks to dialogue. This reflects a major problem in communication and indicates why so many meetings take too long without adding any value. When in dialogue, the bonding is strong. When dialogue is blocked, the bonding is limited or broken.

Hostage negotiators must excel in dialogue by avoiding all blocks or using a block only with full awareness and a clear goal. The most powerful model and tool I know related to understanding transactions in a dialogue comes from transactional analysis, developed by Eric Berne and refined by others.[5] This system involves looking at each sentence and each response to determine the level of dialogue or lack of dialogue. By understanding the states behind the content of the words, it is possible to see where one is going and even to predict what outcome there may be in the future. The valuable part of analyzing transactions is the opportunity to interrupt and change the process and thus the outcome. Each transaction offers an understanding of where we are going and an opportunity to interrupt and change the direction. For example, if the hostage taker demands a car "right now," the negotiator usually would not say no but would ask a question about who the hostage taker would allow in the car and who would be the driver. The negotiator must also be aware of the blocks from the other person and respectfully deal with them in an effective way. All trainings I undertake for hostage negotiators and most trainings for leaders in organizations include this powerful approach, that with practice, anyone can learn. Have you ever been "stuck" in a conversation, going around in circles, or just plain bored? Then you were a hostage to the other person and maybe to yourself as well. You can learn to never be a hostage in any conversation.

There are four primary blocks to dialogue:

1. *Passivity.* This is when a person displays and uses language of withdrawal or nonresponsive behavior. The focus of the person is on inhibiting himself or herself rather than engaging in problem-solving behavior. For example, Mary says to Tom, "I am angry that you are late for our meeting." Tom, looking scared and detached, does not respond. So Mary gets increasingly uncomfortable and continues by saying, "What were you doing?" and Tom keeps his passivity and says, "Not much." Silence itself is not necessarily passivity when used constructively for reflection or adding impact. The nonreactiveness of Tom to Mary is the passivity.

2. *Discounting.* When people say something to minimize, maximize, disrespect, or put down another person or themselves in some way, they are discounting. For example, the husband offers to take the children to school, and the wife says, "You can't. You don't know where your head is much less where the school is." Or a six-year-old wants to take care of the plants in the house, and the parent replies, "You can't water them because you are too young." It can also include attacks such as, "You are really stupid. Don't you have a brain?" The words, "Yes, but . . ." are usually a discount of whatever was said before. In organizations, managers and team

members alike may fill conversations with discounts, thus blocking any chance of a good dialogue.

3. *Redefining.* This involves changing the focus of the transaction by manipulation to avoid something that may be uncomfortable or emotional. It can be a form of defensiveness to maintain an established mind-set about one's self, other people, or the world. Jacqui Schiff, Ken Mellor, and others called this "forcing your frame of reference on someone else."[6] The stimulus and the response refer to different issues. If this is allowed to run full course, the dialogue shifts focus away from the point being discussed. Participants appear to "talk past" each other and not "with" each other, or they simply just go in circles. The original point may even be forgotten. For example, Mike says to a colleague "Did you leave the confidential report at the photocopier?" Paul responds, "What time was it left there?" Or Mary asks, "Are you upset with me?" Geraldine says, "What do you mean by upset?" What is missing in these exchanges is the linking of thoughts. This shows up regularly in hostage negotiation. Asked if he is hungry and would he like some food, the hostage taker says that he will not eat "poisoned food." He inserts his frame of reference on being poisoned without a link. The direct answer would be, "Yes, I am hungry and no, I don't want any food because you may poison it." English psychiatrist R. D. Laing said that these kind of transactions can drive people "crazy" because there is no common ground on which to move forward.[7]

4. *Over-detailing.* Simply put, the speaker gives too many details. The problem here is that the dialogue does not proceed because the person gives excessive detail, overwhelming others with too much information, and the important point is lost or hidden. It can also be recognized by exhaustion in listening to the speaker going on too long. For example, when asking where the hospital is, the answer is a detailed explanation of the history of the city. Over-detailing is common in businesses, in which many leaders give presentations that have far too many slides and far too much detail for any one person to reasonably assimilate. When asked why they make things so complicated, they respond that that is just the way things are. The speaker and the listener both have a responsibility for helping each other know the important points in the transaction.

There are six secondary blocks to dialogue; these may or may not occur in conjunction with one of the primary blocks.

1. *Being too rational.* Conversation is conducted too analytically, without any personal warmth, emotion, or bonding. It discounts the feelings connected to the topic. For example, in facing a closure of an office, the leader cannot understand the pain and simply says to an employee, "You know, you can always find another job. You can't expect to be employed here forever." By not seeing both sides of the issue, the leader has failed to understand the emotions and the need to offer support at a difficult time. This type of block includes being overly simplistic in responding to complex emotional dilemmas people in organizations often face.

2. *Being too emotional.* This is when an emotion such as anger, sadness, or fear takes over in the dialogue and the person stops thinking clearly about the subject. Emotions drive the person to say and do things he or she later regrets. An example would be when a manager recommends changes to a report and the colleague stands up, rips up the whole report, and throws it in the trash, screaming, "I can't ever please you." Over-emotional blocks should not be confused with passion or the appropriate expression of emotion someone has when caring about a subject.

3. *Over-generalizing.* If someone takes a small piece of truth and exaggerates it to an extreme or absurdity, they are overgeneralizing. This involves avoiding a topic by using "general" statements rather than being specific about an issue. It is making statements that are meaningless, overwhelming in their massiveness, and lacking in relevance. Statements that over-generalize often involve the words *always* or *never*. "You are always late for meetings," "You are always interrupting me when I speak," "Nobody ever does what I want around here"—all these are over-generalizations.

4. *Abstraction.* This occurs when the conversation moves too far off subject and the focus and train of thought are lost, or ideas and concepts are not connected to a specific incident, are disconnected from reality, or are too philosophical in nature. There is an aloofness or detachment in thought and thinking so that there is no connection. For example, a person asks the time and gets the response, "Within our universe, time is a vague and abstract concept formulated by humans to provide structure and meaning."

Some professions are prone to teaching its members an abstract jargon that may work well within the profession but not outside of it, for example, lawyers, economists, and engineers.

5. *Lack of directness.* Avoiding an issue or problem, or talking around the subject, is a lack of directness. It differs from over-detailing in that the sentences are clear but avoid the subject. Instead of saying, "Will you give me a ride to the train station?" you ask how the other person got to work, what time they are leaving, how they would travel home—anything on the related subject but without asking the specific question, "Will you give me a ride to the train station?" The person wants something specific but is afraid of asking for it in case the answer is "no," or fears that the person being asked may get upset.

6. *Lack of honesty.* When one or both persons are unwilling to be honest with the other, then an open dialogue becomes impossible. This may involve a lack of self-disclosure, distortion of true feelings, or lack of authenticity that can be reflected in a simple or a serious lie. An example is when someone asks, "What is your reaction to my presentation?" and you say, "It seems okay" (when in fact, you did not like it or you like it very much).

Blocks to dialogue are significant at two levels. First, they break the flow in content or subject matter. Second, they rupture the fundamental emotional bonding needed in dialogue. The basic reason people block dialogue is to keep themselves or others at a distance through a disrupted or limited bond. People who block dialogue often have trouble in making attachments, staying engaged, and maintaining bonding in the relationship. Blocking dialogue is usually a habit, sometimes learned in the family. However, it is still possible to rewire the brain and learn to speak effectively, directly and without any blocks.

When analyzing blocks to dialogue, you may find that more than one block exists at the same time. The important thing is to be aware when you or others are blocking dialogue. Hostage negotiators are trained to be near perfect in the effectiveness of dialogue. Most organizations, however, engage in mutual monologues and other forms of ineffective communication as reflected in meetings that are too long and boring, adding little value and making participants exhausted and frustrated.

By recognizing when people are using blocks to dialogue, leaders can reduce meeting times dramatically and, even more important, bring enjoyment back to meetings. How many meetings do you attend that are filled with blocks to dialogue? How would these meetings look if effective dialogue replaced all the blocks?

When people tolerate blocks to dialogue, they can easily be taken hostage. However, the choice to interrupt and put the "fish on the table" and take the dialogue deeper can stop the hostage-taking process. Find time to practice. I like to do this at cocktail parties or dinners, at which the challenge is to move into a deep and more meaningful dialogue with someone. I have also used this exercise when training hostage negotiators.

TOOLS TO REMOVE BLOCKS TO DIALOGUE

To help remove blocks to dialogue, there are four tools you can use:

1. *The red card game.* I often recommend that organizations or families introduce "block to dialogue" red cards, an idea borrowed from the referees in soccer matches. During a meeting or discussion, if someone uses a block to dialogue, he or she gets a red card from others. This technique helps people to learn to be conscious of language and to engage fully in dialogue, assuming, of course, that people want to make it easier for others to listen to them.

2. *Banning the "Yes, but . . ."* One of the most common phrases heard in business conversation is "Yes, but . . ." A colleague has spoken his or her opinion on a topic and another colleague interjects with the opening words, "Yes, but . . ." Next time you are at work, count how many times you hear "Yes, but . . ." in any given day. This is actually a classic case of discounting—one of the four primary blocks to dialogue. It does not mean yes at all. Instead, it is a way to disagree and move away from the previous comment and state a different personal view. It is, in fact, a nice way to say "No." It is the classic means of ensuring that people talk in monologues and not in dialogue. Far more effective is to say "Yes, and . . ." or just "And." This response requires the person to *build* on the previous point rather than *destroy* it. It is a simple, yet powerful, tool to ban the use of "Yes, but . . ." in your organization or your family. Sometimes it

is helpful to be quite explicit: "Here is what I agree with and what I disagree with."

"Yes, but . . ." is reflective of a person using the mind's eye for a negative focus and acting as a "destroyer." The opposite, "Yes, and . . ." is to use the mind's eye for a positive focus and be a "builder."

3. *The "Yes, but . . ." game.* In many of my courses, we show people how to play the "Yes, but . . ." game to demonstrate the blocking effect of these words. You can play this game at home or at work. There are two parts to the game. First, invite three people to the front of the room and tell them that they have been given $1 million to throw a party. Their task is to decide how to spend that money, and they have ninety seconds to do it and agree on the approach. The only rule of the game is that each person must start the sentence with the words "Yes, but . . ." What happens is that each person has lots of ideas. However, they do not reach any sense of agreement because they are constantly disagreeing with each other and offering a different approach to the solution.

Second, then ask the same people to repeat the task, only this time they must start each sentence with the words "Yes, and . . ." The outcome of this discussion is not only that the participants come up with a result and a solution, the energy and bonding between the people is greatly enhanced. This simple game is a powerful demonstration of how our language can either block our creativity and bonding or enhance them.

4. *The four-sentence rule.* The truth is that less is more when it comes to dialogue. Making it easy for people to listen to and understand what you are saying is vital. Therefore, introduce the four-sentence rule into your discussions, team meetings, or large group meetings. Each person speaks in four sentences or less (except, of course, when someone is making a presentation). Keeping to four sentences encourages people to think clearly about what they want to say before they speak, thereby enhancing understanding and dialogue. This rule does not mean that you only speak in four sentences on all occasions but rather that you have the ability to engage in clear and focused interpersonal exchanges. I have seen extraordinary results with this rule—teams reducing meeting time by as much as 70 percent.

PRINCIPLES OF DIALOGUE

Paul Grice, a philosopher on dialogue theory, introduced some helpful principles for conducting a dialogue. From his point of view, every move or act of speech in a dialogue should be evaluated in terms of its contribution, at the stage of the dialogue when it was expressed. Drawing on the work of Grice, Lynch, and Isaacs, I emphasize five principles of dialogue.[8]

1. *The principle of quantity.* Make your contribution as informative as the people, context, and situation demand. You have probably met people who just plain speak too much. Leave a little space for others to speak and to ask questions. Watch for the reactions in others. It is a delicate process to know how to give the right amount of information and when to stop.

2. *The principle of quality.* Make sure what you contribute is clear, interesting, easy to listen to, concrete, informative, and truthful. Do not exaggerate or divert.

3. *The principle of relevance.* Make your contributions add value; make sure they are fitting, pertinent, proper, related, relevant, and significant to the situation.

4. *The principle of personal presence.* Avoid obscurity of expression; avoid ambiguity; be brief and orderly; use your eyes; smile; use your body, your personality, your manner, and your attitude. In other words, use your body, emotions, intellect, and spirit to communicate. Be authentic, spontaneous, and natural. The more at ease you are, the more presence enters the dialogue. While some people are known for their positive "presence," others unfortunately are known for the negative impact of their presence.

5. *The principle of brevity.* This refers to the structure of your responses and questions. Dialogue involves full attention. When entering a dialogue, most people find that they do more listening than talking. When you do speak, be clear and concise. Remember the four-sentence rule. If you can get your message in three sentences, that is good. Two is even better. One is great!

Historically, people would engage in dialogue, debate, and converse as forms of entertainment. The Native Americans would regularly hold "pow-wows" at which they would sit in a circle and talk with each other. In Victorian times, after dinner, people would converse, and, up until recent times, families would have dialogues with each other at the dinner table.

The hectic pace of our lives today, combined with the proliferation of television, computers, and videogames, means that many people are no longer taking time to "really talk," much less have a dialogue. Unfortunately, talk between family members is all too often merely for relating information or asking questions on mundane matters: "Your shoes are in the cupboard." "I'll be home at seven o'clock." "Do you have your schoolbooks?" I encourage everyone to put time aside to rediscover the joy of true dialogue and the strengthening of bonds that arise as a result.

As Anne Mulcahy, president and CEO of Xerox once said, "I learned some of my most valuable lessons in leadership at the family dinner table, where my father presided over nightly debates with me, my mother, and my four brothers. The topics would vary—politics, business, literature, current events, civic issues—but everyone was expected to articulate a position and defend it."[9]

THE ART OF LISTENING

Listening is becoming a lost art in today's hectic world. However, we all can improve the quality of our lives by improving the quality of our listening. By watching and listening, we can learn more than by talking. The Chinese character for listen contains the sub characters for heart, eye, and ear—all of which we must use to truly listen. Listening is the first step in making dialogue fully effective.

Hostage negotiators ask many, many questions for this reason. They know that the power of questions will get them far more influence with someone than "talking to" that person. Hostage negotiators monitor carefully how they themselves listen and present themselves. Listening and responding are the important foundations for an effective dialogue. Asking questions is also the quickest way to get into the mind's eye of the hostage taker, understand motivation, and evaluate danger and risk to the hostages. If you can find out what is at stake, what is motivating the other person, you are well on your way to using dialogue for many purposes, including resolving conflicts.

To be able to engage in an authentic dialogue, it is necessary to have four basic listening skills.

1. *Sensing.* This is listening at its most basic level. The ears perceive the speaker's voice and take in the message. The person is listening with his or her entire body and listening to the other's body language as well as words.

2. *Interpreting.* The message is decoded into ideas, and a meaning is assigned to the words and phrases received, again using the body, emotions, intellect, and spirit.

3. *Evaluating.* Once the message is understood, it is evaluated based on the evidence and facts decoded. This results in either agreement or disagreement with the speaker in the mind of the receiver.

4. *Responding.* The listener's verbal and nonverbal behaviors signal to the speaker that the message has been absorbed and that, after reflection and thought, the listener is ready to respond.

Good talkers do not always make good listeners, and good listeners do not always make good talkers. Active listening requires that we go beyond hearing just words. It means rather that we aim to understand also the meaning and energy the words carry and not think about what we are going to say next. Listen carefully, instead of thinking about what you are going to say next. Active listening requires concentration and body language that says you are paying attention.

There is a difference between passive listening and active listening. Listening passively means letting your mind wander and becoming distracted, letting your emotions lead you to boredom. In how many meetings do you participate in which you are a passive listener, thinking of something else, and being emotionally disengaged? Active listening, conversely, seeks engagement, focus, and concentration with our whole selves. Do you believe that you can listen with your whole being? Every hostage negotiator believes so.

Being a good listener also involves listening for the right reason. Even if you think that someone is completely off the mark, you can find value in the question, "Why do you think that?" Remember that the goal at this point is to continue to create a bond and to understand what is in their mind. This will allow you to build on what the other person has said rather than to block it or destroy it.

The best cure for leaders who, after so many courses on active listening, still do not exhibit good listening skills is to get an agreement with them that they will ask a clarifying question before speaking. For example, they could paraphrase what was just said, asking, "Can I just check that you are saying x, y, or z?"

Good listeners repeat the message in their own words to ensure that the message has been accurately received. By giving feedback, and understanding through listening, we can reflect, understand, and respond in a truly authentic way and demonstrate our engagement in the process. People recognize that their listening skills are essential to affecting and maintaining the bonding necessary to both prevent and resolve conflicts.

THE IMPACT OF DIALOGUE ON HEALTH

In 1785, Dr. John Hunter, at age sixty-five, began to suffer chest pains. An astute observer of his own medical condition and of the factors contributing to his angina attacks, he stated publicly, "My life is in the hands of any rascal who chooses to annoy or tease me."

On October 16, 1793, after a colleague teased him at a medical staff meeting, Hunter got into an argument with the board of governors at St. George's Hospital. He angrily left the room and immediately fell dead.[10]

This story demonstrates the impact words can have on our health. It also shows that allowing others to take us hostage can sometimes have fatal consequences.

It is worth exploring how talking and listening both have a far deeper connection to our physiology and biology than most people realize. Research shows that when we speak, our heart rate and blood pressure go up. When we listen, however, our heart rate and blood pressure go down. Listening is relaxing and lowers the level of arousal in the body. The response of our heart, blood vessels, and muscles when we communicate with our spouse, children, friends, colleagues, and the larger community has as much to do with our cardiovascular health as do factors such as exercise or diet. Human interaction, especially emotionally upsetting conversation, can undermine cardiovascular health or lead to premature death.[11]

Effective listening skills activate the cardiac-orienting reflex that allows a person (speaker) to lower his or her physiological state of arousal. The cardiac-orienting reflex was named by the Russian physiologist Y. E. Sokolov.[12] Studies he conducted, confirmed by subsequent researchers, showed that focusing one's attention on the external world in a nondefensive way caused heart rate to slow down and moved blood circulation in a positive way. This signals the importance of being outwardly focused, to "look up, look out," and to listen to others.[13] To listen is good for our health. In his groundbreaking research, James Lynch describes the effects of listening in detail in his book *The Language of the Heart: The Impact of Human Dialogue.*

This line of research, starting with Pavlov, has highlighted the relationship between social interaction and human physiology. Pavlov is famous for his work with dogs and the "conditioned response," as discussed in Chapter One.[14] During these experiments, Pavlov noticed that when people entered or left the room, there was a change in the physiology of the dogs. This interfered with his goal of measuring the physiological parameters of the dogs. His solution was to remove all contact with people or other dogs, studying the animals only in isolation to ensure the validity of his measurements. He observed and understood what later came to be called the "person effect" perfectly well but chose to ignore it and, as such, missed a powerful aspect of understanding the social nature of physiology.

After nine years of dedicated study in Russia, Pavlov's student James Gantt returned to the United States. He believed it was critical to study this "person effect" more deeply to understand truly the physiology of dogs. For Gantt, our biology and physiology had a strong social component. Under Gantt's supervision, people would enter the room under many conditions, and Gantt would study the physiological reactions of the dogs before, during, and after— especially the barking. What he observed was that when the dogs barked their heart rate and blood pressure would go into a state of arousal, which he labeled "state of reactivity." This makes sense. However, what he discovered next was one of the most important biological discoveries ever made. When the dogs stopped barking and took a listening stance, their heart rate and blood pressure would go back to their base levels and sometimes even lower. To listen is to relax. After reactivity and arousal, listening and lowering of arousal is known as the cardiac-orienting reflex.

James Lynch, a student of Dr. Gantt, asked the question, "Is barking like talking?"—an extraordinary question that led to another profound understanding of the social nature of cardiovascular reactivity in humans. In a series of studies, Lynch made the aforementioned discovery that blood pressure and heart rate go up when we speak and go down when we listen. In fact, this happens in the most ordinary of conversations far more than it does during intense physical exercises. He demonstrated how, during the "vascular see-saw of all human dialogue," blood pressure is raised when we talk to others, and falls whenever we listen to others. However, many people are not able to listen. Lynch developed a highly effective program to treat hypertension by helping the affected person change how he or she spoke and listened.[15]

The way we talk also has a direct impact on blood pressure. When we speak too quickly, blood pressure increases more than when we speak slowly. Lynch discovered that type A personalities are more vulnerable to heart diseases because of how they speak.[16] A type A person is one who has a tendency to be highly competitive, an overachiever, always under time pressure, and unable to relax. As a result, such people tend not to be able to listen and, therefore, cannot reduce cardiovascular arousal with the cardiac-orienting reflex activated by the listening in dialogue.

Speaking without taking a breath generally leads to higher levels of blood pressure than speaking with an even-balanced rhythm. Lynch introduced "talk-quiet-talk" training for patients with hypertension and had dramatic success in lowering blood pressure by teaching hypertensive people to speak differently.[17] All this comes down to the importance of making a dialogue "heartfelt"; in other words, to talk "with" a person, instead of talking "at" a person.

As further evidence of the "person effect," studies show that when a doctor takes a patient's blood pressure, the measurement is 20 percent higher than when the person self-measures at home. This is termed the "white coat" phenomenon.[18] When a nurse takes the blood pressure, the reading increases by 10 percent over what it would be if taken at home by the patient.

This state of arousal includes narrowing of vision, hearing, and other senses. So when a hostage negotiator asks a question requiring the hostage taker to listen, if the hostage taker does listen, he begins to lower his blood pressure and heart rate. If the hostage taker blocks the dialogue, that either raises the blood pressure or maintains extreme levels of heart rate and blood pressure. This is important because, as the hostage negotiator knows, violence occurs when the person is in a hypertensive state. The hostage negotiator uses questions to focus the mind's eye and to lower states of arousal, blood pressure, and heart rate by helping to regulate listening. Listening is an excellent diagnostic tool to predict violence; when someone is listening, it has a positive effect of lowering heart rate and blood pressure, whereas when someone does not listen, it can raise heart rate and blood pressure. Answering a question is a form of listening. Refusing to answer a question is usually a form of nonlistening.

The person effect means that when we talk to someone our blood pressure is automatically going to rise. When we listen, it automatically falls. It is important that we regulate our levels of listening because if we become hostages, our heart rate and blood pressure are likely to rise. In healthy dialogue, with bonding, there are tremendous benefits for our well-being (see Figure 6.2).

Furthermore, in line with Lynch's research, J. Pennebaker has conducted research on the health benefits of confession and confiding in others. By asking people to talk about traumatizing events in their lives, he has shown that people who are high "disclosers" show a pattern in which many stress hormones are lowered after the person has disclosed a painful event. However, it should be

FIGURE 6.2. THE PSYCHOPHYSIOLOGY OF TALKING

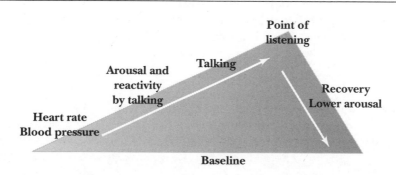

noted that the person effect demands that the person being confided in be a positive secure base. Lynch found that hypertensive people find it a threat to talk about emotion to just about everyone, thereby making self-disclosure potentially dangerous.

"Overall, when (and if) people really let go and disclose their deeper thoughts and feelings, a number of immediate and long-term bodily changes occur. Skin conductance, which is an indicator of inhibition, drops during the confession. Blood pressure, heart rate, and other cardiovascular changes increase during the confession. After high disclosers confided, however, their blood pressure dropped to levels below what they had been before they entered the study."[19]

Lynch explores the links between loneliness and premature death, and describes the biological power of human dialogue—which, he says, can be more intimate than sexual intercourse, because dialogue involves the heart, not just the body. Lynch postulates that the prohibition of emotional self-expression, based on lack of self-awareness, leads to emotional detachment in childhood and adolescence.[20] Denial is a form of self-concealment and leads to emotional detachment from others that blocks a person from bonding to another person. The result is a feeling of isolation and abandonment, "a seemingly numbing loneliness," according to Bowlby.[21]

The extreme of this state is alexithymia, found mostly in males, whereby the individual is not aware of feelings or sensations in the body and remains detached in dialogue, unable to create bonds.[22] This condition shows up primarily in independent loners who have difficulty knowing and expressing what they feel.

Due to the work of Gantt, Lynch, and others, many hospitals and retirement homes today have Pet-a-Pet programs in place to combat loneliness. Patients and residents receive "visits" from dogs or cats, as well as people who stop by to talk and listen to them.[23] After the September 11 terrorist attacks, dogs were used to comfort and calm survivors and relatives.

SUMMARY

Have you ever noticed how friendly words, said with authenticity, can lift your spirits, even when they are from people you do not know well? It can be from the neighbor who smiles warmly and greets you as you leave the house, or the waiter in the coffee shop who says how well you are looking, or the receptionist at your office who seems genuinely pleased to see you. It is so simple for us to lift each other's spirits and bond through words.

I always begin my lectures and seminars with a cheery "Good morning!" as I want my participants to feel welcome and appreciated. I am careful to call students by name, to look at them directly when they are speaking. When we disagree, I often reach out and shake their hand to model that the disagreement is positive, and that we still have a strong, viable bond to each other.

Many of my students are leaders in high-stress jobs, not the people you would think need to be encouraged. But they do. That is why it is important to remember that posture and bearing are a powerful language to inspire or discourage. We are in control of our speaking and listening behaviors, and we are responsible for inviting others into a dialogue by how we speak and listen. Leaders may block the dialogue without realizing it, thereby blocking the emotional bonding that is required in effective bonding. By learning to recognize and change blocks to dialogue, we can move our conversations into productive, efficient, and respectful dialogues. When avoiding the pitfalls of dialogue blockers, leaders can engage in a true dialogue for mutual benefit and effective problem solving.

Dialogue is one of the most challenging and rewarding exchanges between people. It is much more than plain conversation. Dialogue is the seeking of a greater truth. In dialogue, we experience ourselves as bonded to the person with whom we are speaking, making understanding and meaning flow beyond words. Shared meaning is the glue that holds people and organizations together. Good dialogue is not just about the words we use, it also involves talking with our body, emotions, intellect, and spirits. Body language can reveal more about what we are thinking and feeling than does our actual vocabulary.

Listening is a crucial element of effective dialogue. There is a profound difference between active and passive listening based on how much we are searching to understand the other person. It is important to demonstrate what you have heard from the other person by repeating back his or her message in your own words or through the use of clarifying questions. The cardiac-orienting reflex is a physical test of whether we are truly listening or not.

Key Points to Remember

1. Whenever we speak, our heart rate and blood pressure rise and our body moves into a state of arousal. Whenever we listen, our heart rate and blood pressure go down and we relax. To listen is good for our health.

2. Dialogue is a way to find meaning conveyed through words. Words are containers for carrying energy, ideas, and emotions from within the person. Each person has his or her own unique set of experiences and perceptions that when captured can make dialogue rich and rewarding.

3. Take the time to have true dialogue with those around you. Set aside time when you can fully engage with someone else to reach a deeper understanding and learn something new.

4. Dialogue is an important part of successful negotiating. Dialogue allows us to know exactly what are the needs and interests of our negotiating partners.

CHAPTER SEVEN

THE POWER OF
NEGOTIATION

On June 14, 1985, shortly after the take-off of TWA flight 847 from Athens, two Lebanese men who had smuggled guns and grenades aboard hijacked and diverted the plane to Beirut. One of the hijackers kicked cabin attendant Uli Derickson, first in the chest and again as she lay on the floor. After the other hijacker had kicked down the cockpit door, the first forced her to watch as he pistol-whipped the pilot and the flight engineer.

Although the Lebanese men spoke no English, Uli was able to communicate with one of them in German. She tried to calm him, and at one stage, she sang him a German ballad he had requested. For the next fifty-five hours, Uli found herself at the center of the drama as she translated the tense communication between the plane's crew and the hijackers.

According to individuals later interviewed by the New York Times, *when the hijackers started beating passengers, Uli intervened with commands such as, "Don't hit that person," and questions such as, "Why do you have to hit those people?"*

During the plane's refuel stop in Beirut before leaving to fly to Algiers, Uli pleaded with the hostage takers to release the passengers. They eventually freed seventeen elderly women and two children. When the ground crew refused to refuel the plane unless they were paid, the hijackers threatened to kill a passenger. Uli intervened once more, handing over her Shell credit card to charge approximately $5,500 for six thousand gallons of jet fuel.

The hostage takers asked Uli to look through the passports of the passengers and single out those with Jewish-sounding names. Although initial reports claimed she had followed orders, she had in fact hidden the passports of those people. After reaching Algiers, the hijackers released another twenty passengers and then directed the plane back to Beirut.

On the flight, the hijackers identified three U.S. military personnel: two navy divers and an army officer. The three men were bound and beaten. Upon landing in Beirut, the hijackers shot navy diver Dean Stetham in the head and dumped his body on the tarmac. Next, they turned to Clinton Suggs, the other navy diver, and began beating him. According to Suggs, Uli put herself between the hijackers and him and screamed, "Enough! Enough!" After that, they left him alone. Last, a dozen Islamic militiamen boarded the plane, which then flew back to Algiers.

After thirty-six hours, the terrorists released another sixty-five hostages, including Derickson, and headed back to Beirut with the remaining thirty-nine hostages. Eventually, the hostages were handed over to a moderate Shiite leader who freed them on June 30, 1985, following the release of thirty-one Lebanese prisoners held by Israel.

Widely credited with saving many lives, Uli Derickson received the Silver Cross for Valor from The Legion of Valor, a veteran's organization.[1]

Whether by instinct or training, Uli knew one of the golden rules to follow when one finds oneself in a hostage situation. Hostages owe their lives in part to their capacity to create a bond to the hostage taker, maintaining personal power to influence, persuade, and negotiate. Hostages must not let their minds and emotions put them into the situation of feeling helpless. Following her double kicking at the outset of the drama, Uli could have withdrawn because of fear and become passive or submissive, or she could have acted out of aggression and violence herself. Instead, she kept her personal power and used it to influence, persuade, and negotiate a change in mind-set in the hijackers.

Negotiation is the process whereby interested parties resolve disputes, agree on courses of action, bargain for individual or collective advantage, and attempt to craft outcomes that serve their mutual interests.

Negotiation is the ability to engage in a dialogue that can lead to resolving the real issue in conflict. In other words, negotiation is the art of saying "no" while maintaining bonding until an agreement is reached. A good negotiator is able to say, "No, and let's keep talking." During negotiation, dialogue creates an atmosphere in which mutual needs are recognized, common interests are understood, and solutions to conflicts are discovered. Both parties work together to get what they need. To resolve or settle a conflict through negotiation, the parties involved must express what they need, want, feel, and think, and listen to what the others need, want, feel, and think. Negotiation does not mean we surrender our personal power. We can negotiate and still maintain our power.

The hostage taker held a knife to the woman's throat and screamed, "I'm going to kill her for what she did to me. She destroyed my whole life." The hostage negotiator dealing with the conflict asked Peter, a former employee whom the woman had fired, to put down the knife.

"No, I'm going to kill her now!"

The hostage negotiator calmly responded, "Peter, can you speak to me for a few minutes so I can help you?"

"You can't help me! I have no life left. I'm going to cut her throat. She deserves to die for what she did to me."

"Can you speak with me for just one minute? I'm sure I can help you."

"Nobody can help me now."

"Peter, I know you have a family. How do you want them to remember you?"

Breaking down and sobbing as the police entered the room, Peter asserted, "I love my children. I cannot do this to them."

Was this fast-paced exchange of transactions a good negotiation with a good outcome? The answer is yes. Why? The woman is still alive. And she owes her life to the capacity of the hostage negotiator and his personal power to negotiate. What did the negotiator do? He asked questions, changing his goal repeatedly from the knife to time to Peter's children. With each concession that Peter makes, the likelihood of success increases. And, as we learned in the last chapter, Peter's blood pressure was lowered each time he listened and responded to a question. These are all things that hostage negotiators do every day and that you can learn to do as well.

TEN STEPS IN THE NEGOTIATION PROCESS

On the one hand, negotiation is a simple process and, on the other hand, it is a complex process. Negotiators need to be able to keep both in mind—to see both the trees and the forest—so they are not overwhelmed by the complexities, emotions, or dilemmas presented in the negotiation process.

Talking and dialogue can solve many issues in conflicts. However, when the situation has moved beyond talking and dialogue, then the negotiation process becomes the focus. There is a growing body of knowledge based on the invaluable work of Fisher, Ury, and the Harvard Negotiation Project.[2] Using this knowledge, I describe the negotiation process as ten clear steps.

1. Forming a bond
2. Separating the person from the problem
3. Identifying needs, wants, and interests of self
4. Identifying needs, wants, and interests of other person(s)
5. Using focused dialogue
6. Creating a goal and finding common goals
7. Finding options, generating proposals, and making concessions
8. Bargaining for a mutual benefit
9. Coming to an agreement
10. Ending or continuing the relationship on a positive note

The first basic step is to *form a bond* with the other person or persons. These bonds go beyond just talking. Bonding is that underlying emotional synergy that creates the process for mutual influence. Remember, as we saw earlier, you do not have to like someone to bond with them. Bonding is about an exchange of energy that keeps people engaged in a way that holds the relationship together during difficult moments. The inability to bond is often the root cause of failures in many negotiations. A bond goes beyond verbal communication; it can be measured by the degree of engagement.

Second, you must *separate the person from the problem or the demands*. Remember, the persons in and of themselves are never the problem. It is the challenges presented to you that must be resolved. For example, in a hostage situation the problems presented may be the need for food, the demand for a car, an aggressive attitude, or threats to the hostages. The best approach is not to focus on the person as the problem but rather on the hierarchy of the problems to be dealt with. Normally you start with the easiest to resolve in order to build a bond. So, for example, you might start with the request for food. What would they like to eat? The point is that as soon as you say that the person is "crazy" or "stupid," you have depersonalized them in your mind's eye. The challenge is how to keep a bond to the person, maintain a positive focus on the person while solving the problems. It is important to communicate that you are focusing on the problems and not on judging the person. Leaders who learn to do this can become really effective negotiators.

Third, you must *identify the needs, wants, and interests of self.* Think carefully about what you want from a negotiation. Self-awareness, clarity of mind, and managing emotions are all important to maintaining focus. This might also include knowing your limits and knowing what you do not want. Only after you know what you want, what your interests are, are you then ready to move on. Negotiation is the means of attaining what you believe is an important purpose, aim, mission, or objective that you have as well as the other person. An example of this is reflected in a passage from *Alice in Wonderland* by Lewis Carroll in which, when Alice comes to a fork in a road, she sees the Cheshire cat up in a tree. "Which road do I take?" she asked. "Where do you want to go?" was his response. "I don't know," Alice answered. "Then," said the cat, "it doesn't matter."

If you do not know where you want to go, you may well get lost. Your expectations, defined in advance, will be your guide for action in negotiation.

I am asked sometimes why we think about our own interests before the other person's, and the reason for this is that it is important that the hostage negotiator can act as a secure base. To be a secure base requires having a clarity of mind and purpose that ensures that we are not thrown off by other things that happen. If we are confused in our mind's eye, it will confuse the other person. The clarity of our mind will also help clarify the other person's mind.

Fourth, by listening to the other person and understanding, you *identify the needs, wants, and interests of the other person.* By using empathy, you reinforce the bond you are building. You must show a sincere and authentic interest in what the other person wants. If you do not know or have clarity about what the other person wants, what his or her interests are, you are also not ready to negotiate. When you exhibit empathy, you continually reinforce the bond you are building. You demonstrate that you are focusing on the problem rather than judging people when you actively want to understand their needs. Doing this also demonstrates your interest in helping them get what they want.

The fifth step is when you enter into a *focused dialogue;* the clarification of the first four steps is done through continuous dialogue. As discussed in Chapter Six, dialogue helps clarify your own needs, wants, and interests as well as helping the other person understand his or her interests, needs, and wants. The other person may want things that are opposite to what you want, or you may both be confused about what you want. Dialogue helps create a shared knowledge of each other so that you can move from a foundation of understanding to the bargaining toward mutual benefit. The next five steps depend on the value of the dialogue between the two parties up to this point.

Sixth, you use all of the preceding steps in *creating a goal* and understanding common goals. This goal becomes the focus of the process. In the earlier story about Peter holding the knife to the throat of his former boss, the first goal of the hostage negotiator was to get Peter to put the knife down. Then the goal was changed to time and amounts of time to talk. Finally, the focus shifted to understanding the impact on Peter's family.

It is important to differentiate between a position and a goal.[3] A position is when one digs in and fights for territory, symbolic or real, as opposed to fighting for goals based on common interests. As the needs, wants, and interests become clear, with all their complexities from all sides, the common goal becomes the focal point.

The seventh step is to *find options, generate proposals, and make concessions.* What are all the alternative ways that you can find to resolve the differences and bring the common interests together? These options can and should change during your conversation as you go back and forth discussing what to do to reach resolution, and this automatically leads into the next stage.

In the eighth stage, you *bargain for a mutual benefit*. In a successful negotiation both parties win something and both parties give up something. This is a challenge because it means you must have a cooperative mind-set and be thinking about how both sides can gain. This is sometimes referred to as a win-win solution as opposed to a win-lose solution. Being able to say to someone with whom you are negotiating, "I want to help you get what you want," is a powerful way to win them over.

The ninth step is when you *come to an agreement,* a contract or an understanding of what has been negotiated. The agreement can be informal and verbal or formal and written. Regardless, a handshake and your word are the deepest bonds any human being can make and the foundation for the best agreements.

Finally, the negotiation process is one that allows the two parties to *end on a positive note*. It allows two people who have never met before to negotiate and end the relationship positively. If, however, you work or live with someone, once you have negotiated successfully together it is usually easy to continue negotiating on future occasions. With a successful negotiation, the relationship can continue on the amicable terms that were present at the beginning of your negotiation or grow even stronger.

Negotiating does not have to take a lot of time. Negotiation can be clear and quick. When you have a good bond with the other person involved, know what you want, and are clear about it, you can express your goal succinctly. If they also know what they want and can express it succinctly, you will get a great deal accomplished in a short amount of time.

Jean Baptiste Lamarck, an early pioneer in biology, suggested that evolution and progress follow four elements: being goal-centered, being adaptive, making major changes when needed, and having memories of the past.[4] Effective negotiation involves the same principles.

TAKING A POSITIVE APPROACH TO NEGOTIATION

Successful negotiation requires a goal-oriented strategy. To build your negotiation strategy, you must have the proper foundation—and the proper positive attitude. That includes the following:

- Show respect for the other party
- Have a win-win mentality
- Develop patience and timing
- Avoid "fighting" with your opponent

Show Respect for the Other Party

Respect comes from the Latin *re* (back) and *specere* (to look). Perception is everything. The way one sees, looks, and perceives gives life to all that follows. In fact, one gets exactly what one looks for. If you are looking for an enemy, you will surely find one; if you are looking for an ally, one will appear. Wars first start in the mind. I interpret "back" to mean with foundation and esteem based on a solid grounding and integrity.

An attitude of respect involves seeing and accepting another as a separate and unique human being, with a right to thoughts and feelings independent of our own. This does not mean agreeing with or liking everything the other person offers. However, it demands that one be secure enough to respect the other person's version of reality and to separate behavior from the person so that differences can be handled without attacking or belittling.

Treating someone without respect leads to all kinds of potential damage, including resentment, hostility, and retaliation. The focus on the topic, issue, or problem to be solved is lost in the defense of self or in the attack of the other. This is the basis of destructive conflict.

Many years ago, while I was training police officers, the team I was riding with in a patrol car had to arrest a violent assailant. During the struggle, emotions became heated. As the assailant passed me on the way to the car, he shot a large wad of spit in my face. My gut reaction was rage and an instinctive desire to retaliate. Whether as a result of my own integrity or a desire to model appropriate behavior, I managed not to do so, instead maintaining a state of respect through self-discipline. This was what I was trying to teach police officers everyday. The assailant continued this behavior even in the police car, until finally the officers tied a cloth around his mouth. Through this experience, I learned personally what it demands emotionally to maintain the demeanor of a law enforcement professional. My respect for police officers who do so was greatly enhanced that day, as was my own self-respect.

Disrespect comes in the form of prejudice, personal attacks, emotional outbursts, humiliation, depersonalization, and resentment. More subtle forms of disrespect are when roles, territory, boundaries, and rules are not respected. Using language meant to hurt, attack, or belittle is also a way of being disrespectful.

Respect is a fundamental value and attitude in dealing with people and should be at the heart of every transaction to ensure a hostage-free outcome.

HAVE A WIN-WIN MENTALITY

The key to a win-win attitude is deciding on how to meet each party's needs instead of focusing on the problem or forcing a solution on someone. For example, consider the couple who are planning a trip. The husband wants to get away from the telephone and rough it in the wilderness by backpacking in Alaska for two weeks. The wife enjoys swimming, relaxing, and reading, and she does not want to eat freeze-dried food or carry a heavy backpack around. She wants to be comfortable and relax, possibly at a resort.

The couple could fight about this indefinitely. One of three things might happen: one might give in to the other, and two very unhappy people would either go backpacking in Alaska or sit by the pool at a resort. Both would be unhappy because one would resent giving in and would probably sulk and make life miserable for the other.

Alternatively, the couple might get tired of arguing and either forgo a vacation altogether or choose a place neither really wants to visit. While the location would not meet either of their needs, both would save face by not giving in. The result of this "negotiation" would be the loss of a perfectly good vacation, time, and money. Or the couple may decide to go on separate vacations, with the loss of potential bonding opportunities between them.

How can a win-win strategy change this? First, both need to focus on what they really want out of the vacation—isolation, relaxation, swimming, good food, and so on—and not limit their discussion to a specific location. Once they identify what they want from the vacation, they can start evaluating locations together to find one that meets their collective needs.

This approach works because the couple must first agree on the objectives for the vacation; then they can move forward in the same direction. The result is a win-win solution: a destination that offers the kind of vacation each wants.

A relevant story concerns a group of Japanese and Americans who were working for the same company and were going on vacation together. Their first important decision was where to go.

The Japanese, who outnumbered the Americans, were eager for fresh air and hikes; they proposed a trip to the mountains. For the sake of avoiding conflict and maintaining their friendship with the Japanese, the Americans, who wanted to go to the seaside, suggested voting on the issue. As the Americans were in the minority, they accepted defeat as inevitable.

The Japanese kindly but firmly refused to vote, however, and began a discussion that delayed the group's departure by a day. In the end, the Japanese found a lake in the mountains and the Americans were happy because this lake provided opportunities for swimming, canoeing, and water skiing.

When asked why they refused to vote, given they had a winning majority, the Japanese explained that voting would have taken them to the mountains sooner, but also would have threatened their vacation with their American friends. The Japanese believed the Americans would have become dissatisfied, thus lowering the morale of the whole group. They further felt that if the two groups were to go on vacation together again the next year, their American friends would have more power over the decision about their destination because they had lost this year.

Voting can create winners and losers. Unsatisfied losers may find they are no longer interested in the task for which the decision was made; they may slow down the implementation with their poor participation or, in worst-case scenarios, active sabotage. Moreover, the split that inevitably results becomes a "fish under the table" and shows its consequences in future group decisions. Although decisions reached by consensus require more time and a willingness to relinquish individual positions, ultimately they belong to every member of the group. This allows everyone to feel "on board" and responsible, which motivates group members to stick to the decision. When time does not allow for consensus, then hearing out the minority opinions and asking for concessions is an alternative. When high engagement exists, one rule of working together is that the persons with the minority opinion can agree to join in with the majority opinion because of the trust that exists.

In a negotiation, many options may not give you exactly what you wanted but will satisfy your needs and the other's quite nicely.

Two children were arguing at school over who was going to have an orange. The teacher came into the room and cut the orange in half, giving each child half. However, it turns out that one child wanted the segments to make juice, while the other child wanted the peel to make marmalade. If both children had been able to discuss what they wanted with the orange, they could have fulfilled their needs and met each other's needs as well.[5]

It is important to think of negotiating in terms of what you have to gain, not what you stand to lose.

DEVELOP PATIENCE AND TIMING

Patience and a good sense of timing go hand-in-hand. To exercise good timing, you need to be sensitive to the nuances of negotiating and thoroughly understand the people you are dealing with. Timing is being able to identify the optimum moment to make a key point, suggest a solution, or present an issue that moves the negotiation process forward. The optimum moment is when the other party is most receptive to what you are saying and most likely to respond favorably.

If you have not developed the patience necessary to wait for the optimum moment, it is difficult to use timing to your best advantage (in other words, haste makes waste).

Developing good timing will help you be a successful negotiator because

- You will communicate more effectively and efficiently.
- You will ultimately shorten the negotiation process.
- The other party will be more likely to understand your position.
- You will reach a win-win solution more quickly.

Can you pinpoint the optimum moment to suggest a new idea or solution? While there is no surefire way, the more negotiating experience you gain, the more acute your timing will become.

Developing good timing in negotiating is like developing good timing in dancing, golf, or tennis: it takes practice. In the meantime, you can watch others for clues suggesting that they are receptive to your ideas. Clues can be verbal or nonverbal (body language such as nodding in agreement, leaning forward, and so on).

Ron was involved in sensitive customer negotiations. When entering the room, he chose to seat himself away from his colleagues on the other side of the table and closer to the customer. He turned his body toward the customer chairman and listened attentively to what was said. As the discussions progressed, the customer began to turn toward Ron and return his eye contact. When the customer had finished, Ron asked a few clarifying questions and then proposed a solution that he believed to be mutually beneficial for both parties. Ron recalled realizing there would be a positive outcome when he noticed that the chairman's body language became similar to his own.

Avoid "Fighting" with Your Opponent

During a negotiation, ignore perceived subtle attacks, and keep your comments and attention focused on the issues; otherwise it is easy to become a hostage to the other party. Your mind's eye must remain focused on the goal. This tactic unsettles opponents and erodes their credibility. If this approach fails, you can matter-of-factly deal with the behavior by confronting others about their actions. For example: "I think my focus is on (*the issue*) yet your priorities and interest seem to be elsewhere. Will you tell me what's bothering you so we can resolve it and get on with the negotiation?"

Or, if the attacks have been blatant: "I sense you are focusing on personal aspects rather than (*the issue*). I'm interested in discussing the problem and resolving it to our mutual satisfaction. If you don't want to take this approach today, perhaps we should reschedule this meeting. If you have some unrelated issues you think need to be resolved, let's clear them up now."

Remember, the key is refocusing the conversation on the fundamental issues—those that can be expressed in objective terms, not through the shortcomings or actions of the other party. By being objective, you can avoid "getting into the ring" to battle with opponents on their terms.

Besides restating the issue in objective terms and ignoring the verbal assaults of your opponent, direct the conversation to the future. The other party may focus on past injustices or problems. Keep your comments directed toward the fundamental issues and future resolution. Because you will not fight back, your opponent may become frustrated. Patience is important.

One of the most powerful experiences of my early days of working with the police occurred in 1968 before the police had hostage negotiation teams. I was accompanying a senior police officer, whom I respected, and we arrived on the scene where a paranoid man had locked himself in his house and was shooting a gun out of a window.

Neighbors had called the police, who were preparing to fire tear gas into the house. It had become a tense escalation. The senior police officer fortunately intervened and walked up, with me, to the front door. He knocked and asked the man if he could come in.

"No. There're people spying on me and my mind is being infiltrated and controlled by electrical circuits used by the city."

"Really—why would they want to do this?" asked the officer.

"They want to kill me."

The police officer gently commanded, "Listen to my voice. Do I sound like I want to kill you?"

"No, you seem concerned enough."

"Look, let me help you. Take off the locks. Let me come in with my friend to see where the electrical currents are coming into your room. We have to find a solution to this problem."

The man undid some of the locks and asked what the policeman would do when he found where the interference was coming from. The officer indicated that he just wanted to get the currents stopped so "you can live in your home peacefully. Everyone has the right to live in a quiet, peaceful home."

The man took off the rest of the locks and let us into the house. The police officer simply introduced me as a friend.

What I witnessed next contradicted everything I had learned in the class-room or thought someone did with an exceedingly paranoid person. The police office brought his finger up to his lips and whispered, "We have to be careful what we say because they can probably hear us."

Successfully entering the world of this paranoid man, he quietly asked, "Do you have aluminum foil?"

The man gave him some foil. Then the police officer crawled around on his hands and knees and put foil over the electrical sockets. Last, he turned the television around so it faced the wall. "We do not want any currents coming through the TV screen," he said.

The police officer asked, "Is there any chance we can get a cup of coffee, as we have to wait to see if we've stopped the infiltrating currents from coming in?"

After the man had brought us coffee, the three of us sat silently for a few minutes. Then the officer and he agreed the noises were no longer coming into the house. "Yes, I think you've got them stopped. I never thought to use aluminum foil."

After further conversation, what became clear was that this man lived alone, had no one to take care of him, and had lost his only friend a short time ago. He was under treatment for paranoia but had stopped taking his medicine.

We continued the dialogue, agreeing that the goal was to give the man a peaceful home. By now a primary secure base, the police officer suggested we go with the man to find a doctor who would give him medication he could trust.

An hour later, the man peacefully walked out with us. We took him to the emergency room at a hospital where I introduced him to a doctor who knew me very well, and I built a bridge between them to deescalate this patient.

What so impressed me about this experienced police officer was the way he established himself as a secure base and then persuaded the man to agree to a solution. The officer did not focus on talking away the currents. Instead, he entered this man's world of paranoia to form a bond and to walk him out of the house to the hospital.

How do you build bonds in a negotiating situation? First, avoid a common mistake: do not wait until you begin negotiating to start building a bond. The relationship-building process must begin before you start hashing out the problem at hand. The more time you spend building relationships before negotiation, the more effective your negotiation will be. Moreover, you will reduce the tension and hostility that might otherwise be present.

As you become more skilled in negotiation, you can begin to better understand the motivation behind what somebody is seeking. Dialogue becomes the process of listening and then speaking, creating a specific goal—knowing what you want.

The following story shows how quickly someone can learn to negotiate even with violent criminals.

Eric Singer, a former radio show newscaster, found himself in the shoes of a hostage negotiator when escaped convicts demanded time on his talk show to air their grievances. Seven convicts had escaped from a Texas prison. Four were recaptured after being recognized on an episode of Fox's America's Most Wanted. *A fifth committed suicide. Murphy and Newbury, the two remaining escapees, were tracked to a hotel room in Colorado after killing an Irving police officer. They demanded to be allowed to talk on the radio show before surrendering. Singer was chosen to interview them.*

He spent two hours being coached by police negotiators, who told him to avoid certain hot-button words such as "surrender." They also instructed Singer to use words like "honor" and "commitment," to ask the two prisoners certain questions in a certain way, and to give the convicts a few minutes to speak their minds in exchange for no more bloodshed.

"There was no room for error," said Singer. "I look back and I think, 'Wow, what if I had put one wrong word in? Or one wrong inflection? What would have happened?'"

In the end, Singer told the men they had to turn themselves in "to honor their agreement." Murphy and Newbury surrendered.

Ury suggests five clear steps of breakthrough negotiation that will help to ensure that the outcome of any dialogue is satisfactory.[6]

1. *Do not react to provocations.* Step away from the scene, calm down, and carefully plan your response. Do not respond automatically, because most automatic responses are negative and may escalate the situation further.

2. *Step around obstacles, do not walk right into them.* Use active listening to defuse negative feelings, and use "I messages" to express your feelings. Agree whenever you can, but stand up for your principles as well.
3. *Ask people "Why?" "Why not?" or "How is that fair?"* Try to move people involved in a conflict away from positional bargaining toward principled negotiation.
4. *Make it easy for your opponent to agree.* Make the offer as attractive as possible.
5. *"Bring them to their senses, not their knees."* Respect will work better than humiliation.

In the "heat of the moment" when you are in a negotiation, this commonsense advice may be more difficult to apply than it sounds. However, by following and practicing these steps you can take greater control of both yourself and the situation, ensuring that you are never taken hostage in a negotiation.

APPLY THE LAW OF RECIPROCITY AND CONCESSION MAKING

A friend of our family, an Italian named Alfredo, is a trainer who works with wild animals in circuses. Watching him with the lions and tigers is educational and amazing. With respect and gentleness, he watches and listens carefully, taking in every movement of each animal.

He knows the personality of each lion or tiger. He calls them by name; he jokes with them as if they could talk back. In a sense, of course, they do. Alfredo and his lions and tigers are engaged in a dialogue beyond words, the heart of which is a series of concessions in which trainer and animals move back and forth in a kind of dance of bonding, cooperation, and understanding.

Although Alfredo is clearly in charge, he is not dictatorial or authoritarian. He does not order the animals around the cage with harsh commands or emotional detachment. Instead, he recognizes the power and authority of the animals and treats them with respect.

When he steps forward and cracks that whip to get its attention, the animal steps back and stops. Then Alfredo steps back, making a concession. The animal comes forward. Then Alfredo takes a step back again. The tigers make a concession; Alfredo makes a concession. Gently, but insistently, Alfred encourages these potentially dangerous animals to move around the cage in this give and take manner. One missed concession—one time in which Alfredo does not step back to acknowledge the power and strength of these creatures and to accord them respect—and he could be attacked.

Alfredo's philosophy is simple: know each animal's personality and motivation, always show respect for and earn the respect of each animal, create cooperation through a "dance" of mutual influence, and never violate the integrity of an animal's boundaries. Alfredo always remembers to thank his wild animals.

Much of Alfredo's training is based on the law of reciprocity and concession making. He gives something; he gets something back. The law of reciprocity is the foundation of cooperation and collaboration, and it comes naturally to many species. The monkeys who groom each other, the meerkats who take turns to watch out for predators while their comrades eat—nature has many examples of the law of reciprocity in action. Humans have a deeply hardwired pattern of reciprocity. As it is so natural for humans, the law of reciprocity is also the foundation of all bonding.

Concession making is a related part of the process of creating a bond. As mentioned before, you do not have to like someone to bond with them. Some people find this hard to understand, but it is a fact. If it were not true, hostage negotiators would be unable to do their jobs. They are paid to talk to someone they have never met to stop that person from harming other, often innocent, people. The only way that they can possibly succeed in their task is to create a bond with the hostage taker to drive toward a common goal, irrespective of what the person has done or is threatening to do. One technique to smooth the way toward attaining the goal is to recognize when someone is making a concession and reward it. It does not really matter if the concession is a small one—it is still significant, as it demonstrates the desire to start a bonding process.

"Will you approve this request?" one employee asks his boss.

"No, but I will think about it."

Although not the answer the employee wants, the manager has made a concession that should be rewarded.

"Thank you for considering it," says the employee. "If I can provide you with any more information to help you in your decision, please just ask."

One powerful technique to master in any kind of dispute situation is to recognize the feelings and views of the other individual by making the first concession.

A business meeting becomes tense when one colleague bluntly disagrees with another about a proposal. A stand-off situation could quickly arise in which neither party wants to give ground to the other. As the defensiveness increases, so does the aggression.

By being the first to make a concession, you can assist in getting the conversation back onto a business-like footing. "I can see that you feel strongly about this. Can you help me understand why you have concerns?" You are not endorsing the other's opinions but recognizing that they have a different view. Immediately, the other party feels they have been heard and treated with respect and, therefore, they are likely to take a less hostile stance. You have made a concession and it is likely that the other party will make one, too. Now you have entered into a dialogue rather than two monologues.

Remember to make concessions and thank people for taking a step, no matter how small, toward seeing your point of view. Use respect and courtesy at all times; treat others as you yourself would wish to be treated. People are able to see things more clearly and act more rationally when they feel they are respected. Conversely, it is often perceived disrespect that causes people to react irrationally. At the heart of all conflict resolution is the art of concession making.

Unfortunately, many people often view making concessions as a sign of weakness. However, applying the law of reciprocity actually allows a greater control over the conversation and enables anyone to exhibit greater leadership.

Sean had recently taken over as the vice president of marketing. He called together his team for a kick-off meeting and planned a workshop to get buy-in to his approach. He felt he was exhibiting leadership.

However, one of the workshop team members criticized some of Sean's suggestions about the role of marketing in the organization. Rather than thanking the people for their contribution and discussing the implications of their ideas, Sean felt attacked and responded aggressively by telling the team to change its attitude, work with the rest of the group, or leave.

Sean was so angry at having his judgment questioned, so outraged at having an error in his thinking pointed out before the group, he allowed himself to become hostage to his own emotions. Somewhat insecure about his new role and worried his people would see him as a weak leader, he decided to deploy an approach of eliminating any questions—even the most harmless.

This style immediately led to tension and the uncomfortable feeling that something was amiss or had been left unsaid. Sean's emotions kept him from thinking clearly about his real goal and caused concern and resentment among the team, which in turn produced more disagreement. As others became afraid they, too, would find themselves the victim of Sean's anger, the climate of trust vanished. The team became polarized, and the original purpose of the meeting—to get everyone engaged with the task— was lost. A simple concession to his colleagues would have precluded this situation and helped him get into a dialogue to find "a greater truth."

As mentioned earlier, in hostage negotiation, food and basic requests are given as a way of establishing a bond and an act of stimulating the law of reciprocity. However, at the right moment, a hostage negotiator asks for something back. If someone wants something significant, then it is the hostage negotiator's opportunity to ask for something significant back.

This give and take applies in negotiations at home or at work.

A colleague asks, "Will you come to my presentation and give me feedback?" You respond, "Yes, I would be happy to. In exchange, would you be willing to attend a working dinner, in my place, so I can be with my daughter on her birthday?" "Sure, I can do that for you," is the response. This negotiation is a simple exchange in which both parties win through the process of concession making.

The law of reciprocity is a universal rule. Concession making forms the foundation of cooperation and collaboration, the kind of relationship that Alfredo masters every day when he works with wild animals.

The Impact of Influence and the Power of Persuasion

How effective are you in influencing and persuading other people? One of the most important ways to deal with someone who wants to take you hostage is through influence and persuasion. The best way to get control of our world is by learning to be effective in influencing and persuading other people. A powerful tool is to understand the dual pressures of reward and punishment and the link between pain and pleasure. For example, you may say to your child, "If you go to bed now, I'll read you a story," or "If you don't eat your vegetables, you can't watch television."

A good hostage negotiator knows how to use both the power of reward and the power of pain, at the same time. The hostage taker must realize that although the negotiator can help him, he can also hurt him. The combination of being both a source of support (a secure base) and a potential threat to the hostage taker enables the negotiator to maximize his worth in a hostage situation. With the threat of violence or force from the police, the negotiator can be seen by the hostage taker as an "ally," who will help or assist the hostage taker. The contrast effect is a powerful tool of influence.[7] Reward power is often present, but a word of caution: it can get expensive as the value of the reward diminishes and you have to increase it to get the same effect.

When you are a leader, people doing business with you get rewarded by working with you. The moment you think you are rewarding them you become arrogant and set yourself up to be a hostage: "If you don't do business with me it is your loss, not mine."

Credibility is part of effective influencing and persuasion. It is important to tell the truth, even if it hurts. However, if you tell the truth and the other person does not believe you, then it will not work.

Psychologists have studied the effectiveness of fear as a tool of persuasion. What they found was that mild threats were just as persuasive as extreme threats. Fear is a powerful persuader only up to the point that people feel genuinely threatened. When they begin to doubt that the threat is as great as it is made out to be, the power of the threat diminishes. Any parent who overuses a threat will soon find that their children do not believe it and it loses its effect.

When trying to influence others, many people use the idea of punishment or loss to bring in an element of fear. The effect of this technique is to take the other person hostage. The person's mind races ahead to the fear—perhaps the loss of an account or the threat of loss of bonus—and the person becomes more stressed at the thought of the anticipated loss. The mind's eye then puts the person into a negative state where he or she fears losing face, or rejection, or ridicule, or embarrassment, or loneliness, or abandonment.

Fear is not a good motivator for sustained high performance. Excitement is a far better motivator for maintaining a workforce of loyal, high-performing colleagues.

Honesty is a cornerstone of bonding and of influence and persuasion. When we are aware of someone's true intent, we have the power to control the situation or at least not let it take advantage of us. Hostage negotiators are trained to know how to get to the message behind the words. In influencing and persuading, we have to be able to protect our own mind's eye so that we are not unduly influenced and not taken hostage.

Influence can be understood as a power affecting a person, thing, or course of events, especially one that operates without any direct or apparent effort. Influence is the power or capacity to produce a desired result.

Exercising Informal Authority

Leading a team, a division, or a company involves thinking and interacting with others and, at times, exercising your power and influence within the group. The more self-aware a leader is, the more able he or she will be to bond with colleagues, employees, and supervisors. The leader will be able to exercise "informal authority"—leading from within rather than from above. Anyone can exhibit leadership irrespective of his or her position or seniority. Leadership is measured by the impact and contribution leaders make to those around them rather than by the experience, knowledge, or skills they exhibit.

Business managers have to be measured on performance figures, and at the same time excellent leaders understand that their job is really about managing relationships. While our qualifications are often related to our competence or skill, the secret to managing relationships is to understand the need for bonding and to be able to encourage workers to contribute to the best of their potential. A leader needs to foster an environment in which people want to belong to the organization, in which they feel they are working toward a common goal, in which dialogue is conducted with mutual respect, in which creative leadership exists, and in which team members are self-regulating.

Those people who have a balance between attachment to people (ability to bond) and attachment to goals (drive to succeed) will have a higher self-esteem. It is this combination of hard and soft skills that turns a competent manager into an effective leader. Any time we are able to influence and persuade someone without the direct "power" or official command to do so, we are using informal authority.

The power to influence and persuade is as vital in our personal lives as it is in our professional lives.

Lis Pringle, a dear friend and colleague, shared this personal story with me. "When I first came to Dayton, Ohio, from our small town of Leesburg, Florida, a man at the Dorothy Lane Market offered to fix my car, which was 'spouting fire out the tail pipes.' While he knelt on the floor of the front seat fooling with 'wires under the dashboard,' I told him how warm and wonderful I had found the people in Dayton, when I had expected cold 'city folk.' Finally he got out, said it was all fixed, and refused any money. I told him again how kind he was, how much I appreciated his help, and waved goodbye as I left.

"When I got home and told my husband what had happened, he read between the lines and completely shocked me by saying, 'There are no wires under the dashboard,' 'fire doesn't come out of tail pipes' and 'your story makes no sense.' The next morning a composite picture on the front page of the Dayton Daily *showed the same man, who had picked up a woman at the Dorothy Lane Market, taken her to the woods, and raped her. I always said, 'We must have bonded during that time, and he didn't have the heart to take me hostage.'"*

Persuasion is the ability or power to induce or get someone to undertake a course of action or embrace a point of view by means of argument, reason, or entreaty.

Being a good persuader does not mean being pushy or manipulative. People will want to do what you want them to do and feel good about it. As author Napoleon Hill said, "Persuasion is the magic ingredient that will help you to forge ahead in your profession or business and to achieve happy or lasting personal relationships."[8] The act of being persuaded is to be moved by argument and reasons offered—anything that moves minds or emotions.

Author, speaker, and expert on influence and persuasion Robert Cialdini talks about the "science of influence" and cites six principles of persuasion to enable you to negotiate more effectively:[9]

1. *Authority.* People will defer to experts. They are more easily influenced by those they perceive to be legitimate authorities with expert knowledge. How much authority do you carry in your presence? Do you speak with authority? An important distinction here is to separate authority from arrogance—to have authority also involves humility—in order to authentically create a bond using this principle.

2. *Consistency.* People generally behave in a steady, regular, reliable way. We like to be consistent and to uphold stated commitments. If you have any doubt or uncertainty, the rule of consistency drives you to decide on a course of action so as not to appear weak or indecisive. If people publicly vocalize commitment or sign a document, they are more likely to keep to what they promised. After signing a petition in support of a social cause, for instance, people are more likely to donate to that cause when asked later. Individuals feel obligated to back up a public statement of support.

3. *Liking.* "You are nice to me, so I'll be nice to you as well." People like other people who like them. People are more likely to buy products from a friend than from a stranger. Finding common interests and offering praise are two ways to foster liking. Hostage negotiators will spend time trying to find connections or parallels to enhance a positive person effect.

4. *Reciprocity.* People will repay in kind. Just like Alfredo with his lions and tigers, if you give something, others feel obligated to give something back. For instance, when the Disabled American

Veterans began sending free mailing labels with their fundraising letters, the response rate nearly doubled, from 18 to 35 percent. People feel obligated to reciprocate when they receive a gift or favor, even when it is unsolicited.

5. *Scarcity.* Items and opportunities become more desirable as they become less available. People want things that are rare or scarce. Ads that say "limited time only" or "while supplies last" capitalize on this principle. Sales representatives who claim to have exclusive information also use this technique. In negotiation, time is always on the hostage negotiator's side. However, convincing a hostage taker that "a moment in time" offers "a rare opportunity" is essential.

6. *Social proof.* People follow the lead of their peers. We often look to others to see what should be done and then copy that behavior, especially in situations of uncertainty or the unknown. It is the "safety in numbers" mentality. If others are doing it, then it must be okay. For example, a door-to-door charity campaign was found to be more successful when prospective donors were shown a list of neighbors who had already contributed.

Cialdini states that these six key principles are universally applicable.[10] By understanding them, we are better able to recognize when others are using the same techniques and better able to deploy them ourselves. Using the six key principles, we have a strong chance to persuade others effectively. However, they can only work, either individually or collectively, if they are used in an authentic manner. Authenticity is the secret weapon to successful influence, persuasion, and negotiation. By knowing these principles, you can avoid being taken hostage. Most of us can look back at examples of instances when we bought things because of a persuasive salesperson using one or all of these principles.

Sell the Benefits of Pain

In the 1990s a large, multinational firm adopted a casual dress code. However, as business became more competitive, management felt that more polished, professional-looking competitors were gaining an advantage. Therefore, a memo went out ordering the men to wear ties to work. The directive seemed simple.

This was not a law firm in which people were more comfortable in a suit and tie. And no one was told why the rule had been put into effect. People just knew that starting on a particular day they had to wear ties.

Some men on the staff had thrown their ties away; others objected to the policy because they did not meet with customers and did the majority of their business on the phone. Most just thought the whole thing was silly.

So a group showed up on the first day the memo took effect wearing Mickey Mouse ties. The lack of discussion had created polarization. Sure enough, the next day a memo appeared saying, "No more Mickey Mouse ties."

Then the men wore ties with naked women on them, upsetting the female staff members, who started wearing ties with naked men on them.

The office was in uproar—all over some neckwear!

Eventually, peace was declared when the employees learned that management was worried about their competitors' more professional appearance. The necktie directive was not a signal that other perks—the free drinks and the open coffee bar—were going to be taken away. And, no, the company had not lost any business. It was just concerned about changes in the market.

When the employees understood why they needed to improve their appearance, they accepted the new dress code. They needed to understand the benefits to them and to the organization.

When we ask friends, family members, or colleagues to go through any type of change, resistance is a typical reaction. The ability to influence and persuade can avoid unnecessary conflict. People need to be encouraged and motivated. The more we are able to explain the reasons behind why we are asking for something to be done, the more empathetic and sympathetic people will be to our needs. People are best able to follow a leader when a clear picture of an end goal is communicated; in other words, we need to "paint the picture of the uplifting future."[11] The expression "no pain, no gain" is one that is well understood in the field of sports. Individuals and teams have an end goal in mind (the trophy, gold medal, record) and they are then able to put themselves through weeks, months, or years of pain to achieve the desired result. Business leaders must also learn to think in terms of benefits to keep employees engaged and committed to a clear end goal.

SUMMARY

Negotiation is a powerful technique to resolve conflict, make deals, and conclude contracts. It can also be applied more broadly to everyday circumstances to help us achieve what we want from life. Every parent knows that one of the most effective ways of dealing with children is through negotiation—this in turn means that children learn to negotiate as well. Often, children are far more effective negotiators than their parents, as they are clear about their specific interests, needs, and wants!

Negotiators start by creating a relationship, a bond through which people can work together. A clear understanding of what both parties want must be reached before the actual bargaining can begin. We must know what we want. We must also know what the other person wants. Hostage negotiators focus their questions on finding out precisely what those wants and needs are. We must be able to put ourselves in the other person's shoes.

It is important to remember the law of reciprocity; someone gives us something, we give something back. This concession making allows the dialogue to move forward with mutual respect.

Negotiation normally involves some concession or loss. Every win-win has concessions behind it. Therefore, sell the benefits of those concessions to help people understand how a change will be better in the long term even though it may be painful initially.

Influence and persuasion are also powerful aspects of negotiation. Authenticity is essential in being able to influence and persuade effectively, giving the leader more "informal authority" to guide others.

Hostage negotiators are experts in the skills of negotiating, influencing, and persuading. These skills also have great value to leaders when applied to business processes and situations. By regularly practicing negotiation, influence, and persuasion techniques, we can increase our skills and ability to not be "taken hostage" by the stresses and conflicts omnipresent in everyday life.

Key Points to Remember

1. All effective negotiations start with the creation of a bond between people. Through a bond, it is possible to handle any conflict that interferes with the negotiation process.
2. Leaders using informal authority achieve higher levels of success through negotiating.
3. Effective negotiation is about seeking an outcome that provides mutual benefit through the understanding of our wants, needs, and interests as well as the other person's wants, needs, and interests.
4. Acknowledge the value of concession making. You give something; you get something back. The law of reciprocity is a universal rule. In general, reward all concessions one way or another.

CHAPTER EIGHT

MASTERING OUR EMOTIONS

Late one evening in New York City, Joyce, a twenty-six-year-old woman who was training to be a psychologist, was walking to her apartment. A car suddenly stopped at the curb, and two young men grabbed her, threw her into the front seat between them, and pushed a knife to her throat. The two spoke to her aggressively and excitedly, telling her they were going to take her to New Jersey to rape and kill her. They demanded that she tell them how she felt about the fact she was going to die.

Joyce recognized their extreme agitation and realized they were serious about their threat to kill her. Displaying an intense mixture of fear and anger, they shook while jabbing at her throat with the knife.

After initial panic, she inferred the futility of her position, and calmly accepted her imminent death. Answering their questions serenely and thoughtfully, she became intrigued by the men's fear and lack of physical control. An odd feeling of maternal concern began to dominate her thoughts.

Joyce started asking the men about themselves. At first, they ignored her, repeating their demand that she tell them what it felt like to be about to die. She revealed that she was sorrowful she had to die, for she was young, but she knew the severity of the rape-kidnap laws and realized they would have to kill her.

As they drove to an isolated part of the Jersey tidewater region, the men grew increasingly exasperated, confused, and belligerent, all but pleading with her to tell them what it felt like to be about to die. She continued to ask questions, however, while confirming that she knew they were going to rape and kill her. Inquiring why they were so distressed, she assured them they must not feel troubled on her account, for she had come to terms with what was going to happen to her.

When the car stopped, the men took Joyce out of the vehicle and showed her mounds of earth where they claimed they had buried previous victims.

Again demanding she tell them how it felt to be the next one to die, they stripped her and threw her to the ground. As one of them lay over her, she put her hands to his face and said, "It's all right. You don't have to be afraid."

At these words, the man collapsed, sobbing uncontrollably. The other man sat pounding the ground with his fists and shouting, "What is it? What's gone wrong?" Then he, too, began to sob.

After some time, she sat up and said, "Boys, we may as well go home."

She dressed, and the two men silently drove her back to the city. At the first subway station, she asked that they let her out.

Although she had $300 in her purse, they had not seen it, showing no interest in money. On impulse, she asked if they would lend her the fare for the subway. They did.

As she walked into the subway, she heard them drive away.[1]

With the calm acceptance in her mind's eye of the inevitability of her situation, Joyce was able to use the power of bonding and words to engage her kidnappers in a dialogue that led to survival. By talking with the men in a way that they did not expect, and by not allowing their states of mind to overpower hers, she was able to influence them and persuade them to let her go. In other words, while physically a hostage, she was in fact never a hostage psychologically. She used what can be called "paradoxical intention"— doing one thing and at the same time, doing another. By accepting the inevitability of her death, Joyce sent a nonverbal "you win" message to the men. However, her behavior, staying engaged and attached, brought her closer to what she really wanted—to do everything she could to live.

Imagine facing a situation like this and being able to apply the mind-set and skills to manage your emotions. What would you do? I realize that there is a lot involved in this story, including chemistry and synchronicity. Yet we can learn the skills Joyce used and apply them to our own situations when we are metaphorical hostages.

Understanding and managing our emotions and those of others is one of the most important things we can do to avoid being taken hostage.

How Emotions Work

Emotion can be described as a mental and physiological state that arises spontaneously rather than through conscious effort and is often accompanied by physiological changes.

Emotion is the realm where psychology and physiology are inextricably intertwined and where the "self" is inseparable from our subjective perception and evaluation of others. Emotion is the ultimate result of the mind-body connection.

Emotion is sometimes thought of as the opposite of reason—a person is either emotional or rational. Phrases such as "Don't be carried away by your emotions," imply that our emotions override our thought processes.

Emotional reactions can create internal states and cognitive streams that are out of control. It should be noted that the human psyche can express an entire spectrum of emotions, from pure logic to pure emotion. We can become hostages at either extreme or anywhere in between. Emotion is strongly rooted in conditioned behavior, associations hardwired in the brain based on our past experiences. The mind's eye is able to retain these "emotional memories" and is strongly influenced by them.

Neurologist Antonio Damasio suggested that neurological mechanisms of emotion and feeling evolved in humans because they create strong biases to situationally appropriate behaviors that do not require conscious thought.[2] He argued that the time-consuming process of rational thought often decreases one's chances of survival in situations that require instant decisions. Memory both explicit (conscious) and implicit (nonconscious) is a powerful and rapid source of automatic influence. Reasoning, after all, does have its drawbacks: it takes time, there may be insufficient information from which to draw a conclusion, and the brain may not be sufficiently developed for reasoning to take place.

Emotions, therefore, provide the person with a way of working around the limitations of reasoning. People often describe instances when, contrary to all the knowledge or observable facts, they had a "funny feeling" about something, acted on it, and saved lives.

Andy Kirk has been a firefighter in Leicester, U.K., for over twenty years. On October 5, 2001, he and his team were called to a fire at an unoccupied bingo hall. Although the fire was big, Andy decided his crew would be safe if he sent them into the building. Smoke was everywhere, but after five minutes, the team thought they were getting the fire under control.

Then, for no apparent reason, Andy had a strange feeling. "I couldn't put my finger on it, but I thought something was going to happen, and it was time to get the team out." Despite the protests of his crew, he ordered them to leave immediately. Suddenly, there was a very loud rumbling and a massive fireball began chasing them as they rushed to safety.

Without warning, a huge explosion had ripped through the building, bringing down the walls and the roof. An area the size of a football field was affected, and flames shot forty feet into the air.

"I'm sure if Andy hadn't pulled us out of that building, we would have been killed," said one of his colleagues.

When investigators examined what had happened, they realized Andy had saved his men from one of the most dangerous phenomena in firefighting—a backdraft, which occurs in enclosed fires when all the oxygen has been burned up and the fire becomes explosively unpredictable. Backdrafts are incredibly rare, so how could Andy possibly have known what was going to happen? He knew, because his mind was aware of the signs of danger even though he did not consciously read them.

A part of our brain is always scanning the environment for danger. Without his conscious knowledge, Andy's brain compared the fire to every other one he had ever seen, and it noticed three significant differences. First, the color of the smoke was very orange, unlike that of most fires. Second, air was rushing into the building through the open doors, though normally it rushes out. Third, though a fire crackles as it burns oxygen, there was no such sound.

Unconsciously, Andy's mind recognized the differences in this fire and sent him a warning signal. As he described it, "I had a feeling of uneasiness, an intuition."[3]

Just because we cannot explain a feeling does not mean we should ignore it. Our emotions can provide us with valuable information about what is happening. Listening to our intuition is a skill we can all use.

Five Stages of Emotion

Understanding the process of how emotions move through the body and mind becomes critical for both self-awareness and awareness of the states of others. The work of Wilhelm Reich, as described by David Boadella, indicates that there are five stages involved in the flow of emotion from creation to resolution.[4] The flow involves charge, tension, discharge, relaxation, and flexibility of emotion (Figure 8.1).

1. *Charge.* Emotions must go through a charging process. When the emotions are charged in the body, it involves the whole network of being, mind, body, and spirit, leading to a state of physiological arousal. The arousal process creates energy in our state of being. The question is, How do we charge our emotions? Everybody has emotions. Some people charge them quickly, and easily flood with anger, joy, or any of the emotions. Other people are slower, requiring more time to charge. Some people do not charge at all, so they do not experience emotion and are often low-energy or very

FIGURE 8.1. Five Stages of Emotion

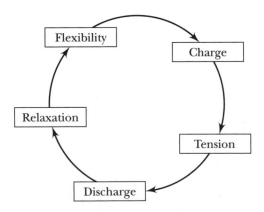

detached people. They can also present themselves as cool, aloof, and detached because their emotions lie dormant deep inside.

Other people overcharge and are easily and quickly overwhelmed with emotion. In itself, this is not a problem. The problem may come in what they do with the charge. Emotions are always present in some way in our being. It is essential to track emotional levels whenever facing a threat, for safety, self-regulation, and knowing how to respond. Thinking, by itself, is not enough once the charge takes on a "life of its own." Eva Reich, daughter of Dr. Wilhelm Reich and a renowned doctor herself, used the terms *over-charged* and *under-charged* to describe how emotions start their journey through a person.[5] Hostage negotiators must be assessing themselves as well as the hostage taker as to the level and style of charging. In fact, the quiet loner, showing only a small amount of agitation, may be more dangerous than the hysterical person.

2. *Tension.* Emotions move from the charging process to a point of tension. Any physical organ, any muscular system, any chemical system can hold the tension of an aroused emotion. For example, with anger, the person might clench his or her jaws, tighten neck muscles, create chest pains from the lungs or heart, and overactivate the adrenalin system. The holding in of the tension is not a problem in and of itself. The issue arises when the holding cannot be released and becomes chronic or habitual and thus becomes part of our character.[6]

When we are holding tension in an unhealthy way, psychosomatic problems may develop. There is a strong connection between biology, physiological chemistry, emotions, and mind. When people describe themselves as tense, agitated, uncomfortable, or nervous, these words all describe a charged emotion being held in some form of tension. Hostage negotiators must manage their levels of charged tension so that they are not overcharged or undercharged in the bonding relationship with the hostage taker. The use of words is constantly applied to help regulate the level of charge and tension. Another good example is the temper tantrum. People who quickly react because they are already holding anger or fear or sadness in their bodies find that the new stimulus merely opens the floodgates to previous emotional energy. The key thing to remember is that emotions are energy. Once energy is created, it must go somewhere. One major misunderstanding about emotions is that they will just disappear. They cannot; instead, they are transformed in one way or another, and they will stay in our bodies until we release them.

3. *Discharge.* In the emotional discharge, the person releases the emotion and the energy of the emotion. This letting go means the emotional energy comes out of the body through talking, acting, or doing something. For example, if there is pressure in the chest, this can be released in the form of shouting or crying, or it can be transferred internally from one system to another, as, for example, when fear turns into stomach cramps or back tension. Discharge is extremely important. It can be intense or minor in its expulsion. The question is whether it is a partial or complete discharge. If the discharge of emotion is inadequate, it may mean the person stays in a state of tension, thus blocking the charge of another emotion. Wilhelm Reich also had the idea of physiological expansion and contraction.[7] The body expands through the charge of emotion, and the body contracts as the emotion is released and discharged; somewhat like a balloon that is inflated and then, as the air is let out, it deflates. The breath in is expansion, and the breath out is contraction. We need to make sure that we are discharging emotion in an effective way or the entire flow of emotion can become blocked. The river is another metaphor for understanding emotional energy, the current or the wave as it contracts and expands and yet keeps on flowing. The question is, If there is a dam in the river, what is being held back? What happens if the pressure gets so strong that the dam breaks? Or what happens downstream if too much water gets blocked? Hostage negotiators are experts at managing the discharge of emotions in both themselves and the hostage taker. A hostage negotiation is one of the most charged, intense emotional dramas that can occur. And yet, as described earlier, hostage negotiators achieve a positive resolution in 95 percent of cases because they are able to manage the stages of emotion in themselves and others.

4. *Relaxation.* The best outcome to an effective discharge is relaxation. When the mind-body system can relax, it creates a calm and lower arousal level that is necessary for the health of the individual. This is what Gantt and Lynch meant by the cardiac-orienting reflex explained in Chapter Six. It is when the body

returns to a state of calmness. Relaxation benefits the mind and body. Extensive and numerous research studies have demonstrated the evidence for the benefits of relaxation. As stress hormones suppress the immune system, relaxation allows the immune system to recover and function more effectively. Relaxation lowers blood pressure and thus decreases the likelihood of strokes and heart attacks. Relaxation also gives people a break from the pace of life and lowers activity in the emotional center of the brain (the limbic system).

5. *Flexibility.* This final stage rounds out the cycle, allowing the person to act and move with ease and elasticity. It can be seen in how the person walks, talks, and stands. We cannot act if we are totally relaxed. Flexibility is a kind of regulated relaxation in which we are ready to act. What is the difference between someone who acts from a state of overcharged tension and someone who acts with a positive amount of pressure? In situations when people are under pressure to perform, they need to do so in a state of flow, which enhances the likelihood of success. Athletes and artists refer to this state as "being in the zone" or "the sweet spot." Someone who remains fully flexible under pressure will feel a vibration, a flow that is pleasant and satisfying, as discussed in Chapter Nine.

It is virtually impossible for people to completely hide how they are feeling. The emotions seep from the body, even when people try to block them. People can be taken hostage by their own emotions. It is important for people to understand that one emotion can block another emotion. If we cannot feel love, we may be blocked with anger or fear. If any emotion is blocked, it affects all the others. As mentioned, it is like a river: if there is a block in the flow of the river, then the whole flow is affected. When one of our emotions is blocked, it affects the flow of other emotions. This fact is often overlooked. We cannot ignore one aspect of our emotions and expect the others not to be affected.

To avoid being taken hostage by our own emotions, the first step is to be aware of them. Without awareness, there is little hope of regulating them effectively. Second, we need to be able to accurately perceive and respond to the emotional stages of another person. We all know what it is like to have a good cry, a good scream, or a good laugh. To express our emotions is important. It should also be noted that for some people, how they express anger or any other emotion does not bring relief. Instead, it only increases the charge of the emotion. This is why it is important to observe violence-prone behavior. No aggression or violence can occur without an emotional charge. For some people it is an internal charge, and the escalation can be observed through a twitch in the face or a rubbing of fingers and other agitated behavior. Agitation is the most important sign of emotion a hostage negotiator or anyone facing potential violence must monitor, as it indicates what is beneath the surface and what may be threatening to explode. The most dangerous persons are those hiding an internal charge showing few signs that a volcano is building for a big explosion. You may often read about stories of young men, described as quiet loners, who suddenly explode at home, at school, or at work, all too often killing someone in the process.

During a negotiation, hostage negotiators will charge, have tension, discharge, relax, and be flexible in order to be emotionally attuned to the hostage taker. It is important that the negotiator is not cold and detached, because this would make it impossible to build a bond. It is also important that negotiators manage their emotions so that they are not taken hostage by them.

FIVE PATTERNS OF EMOTIONS

Emotions are a dominant force in learning. They are powerful and meaningful. What happens inside us when we "jump for joy" or when our hearts are "broken"? While there is broad agreement among researchers that emotions are essential, it turns out that labels are somewhat arbitrary. The idea of "core" or basic emotions is still a point of discussion. What is known is that emotions operate at many different levels, both physically and psychologically. The emotions I have found most useful in dealing with conflict are fear, sadness, anger, joy (including love), and sexual feelings. Each of these manifests itself physically in our bodies.

Fear. Fear happens to us all. It is nature's way of protecting us from being hurt by others or ourselves. It is an emotion that immediately alerts us to danger, for example, if we are about to fall off a cliff or step in front of a car, or if we hear an unknown and unexpected sound in a dark room. Fear can range from a small scare to paralyzing terror. When we experience fear, our blood rushes to the large skeletal muscles, making it easier for us to run should we need to do so. The heart starts working harder, we increase our breathing rates to bring more oxygen into the body, and a large amount of adrenalin is pumped into our systems to put us in a state of increased alertness. At the same time, the body freezes, even if only for a split second, to allow the mind's eye to evaluate danger in a nonrational manner. Persons startled by a mugger will hesitate for a moment before running. Their stomachs contract, their extremities get cold, and blood rushes to the central parts of their bodies. The fight-or-flight mechanism jumps into action. Afterward, it is common to hear the person say, "I couldn't control myself." Hostage negotiators know that someone who is afraid of them is far more dangerous than someone who is angry with them. I personally saw a woman in such a high state of fear. She was only about five feet two inches tall, weighing about 120 pounds. In thinking she was going to be killed, her fight-or-flight mechanism had been activated and she had twisted a metal bed frame. It took six police officers to restrain her. She thought they had come to kill her and her baby.

In a different situation, a woman backed her car out of her driveway and hit her eighteen-month-old son. She was able to lift the rear of the vehicle to get the child out from underneath it, drive him to a hospital, and then collapse once he was safe with the medical staff. Fear activates the most powerful emotions. It can move someone to kill or to act with the greatest courage.

Sadness. We feel sadness over loss. When we lose someone or something, sadness is the part of the grief when we cry and long for the return of what has been lost. Sadness can also happen when we come to realize that we cannot have or achieve something we had hoped for, especially when we might have invested a lot of time or effort in it. Losing something of high value to us, such as a secure base, an item of jewelry, or any person or item to which we are attached, can lead us to feel sad. With sadness, there is a feeling of pressure in the stomach, an ache inside, moving up to a pressure in the chest, a lump in the throat, and then, finally, tears and sometimes sobs that flow out. According to Dr. William H. Frey, author of *Crying: The Mystery of Tears,* "Perhaps the reason people feel better after crying is that they're removing chemicals that build up during stress."[8] If people try to suppress their feelings of sadness, keeping the tension and not allowing the discharge, then they may retain the feeling of pressure in their chests or a lump in their throats. Remember the story of Hannah and her pet pig in Chapter Three. Elisabeth Kübler-Ross, the well-known author on grief, believed that crying is an important need in all humans.[9]

Anger. Anger stimulates an intense emotional reaction. It is a response to the frustration and part of the fight-or-flight reflex. Anger is a positive emotion because it stimulates the person to action. People who cannot feel their anger will have difficulty setting boundaries. However, the person with too much anger will create ongoing problems for himself or herself. When angry, we may feel a rising swell of pressure that spreads to our limbs, making us want to kick our legs, throw up our arms, shout, and scream. It is as if a fire is blazing in our eyes. People often find ways of venting it in different places, so, for example, if they are frustrated at work, they may take it out on their partner when they get home. This action is termed *displacement.* When we have anger, it is important to discharge it in a constructive way to release the muscular, biological, and chemical tension, so that we can return to a relaxed state. A Chinese proverb wisely says, "If you are patient in one moment of anger, you will escape a hundred days of sorrow." The secret to good anger management is not too much and not too little.

Joy and love. When we feel joy, there is a sense of delight, a "lightness," a "tingling" and "weightlessness" that radiates outward. The entire body is involved. We want to "sing and dance with joy." The energy lifts us up. The chest expands, the eyes glow, the head is held high, and then the tension is discharged through a smile, a laugh, a hug, or a shout. When we look at people experiencing joy, they appear to be shining and radiating from within. Joy gives us a sense of expansion and possibility. Eva Reich talked about love as an emotion directed toward a specific person, pet, or thing.[10] Joy is more general and universal. Joy and love are the most powerful of all emotions and should be the source for most of our energy.

Sexual feelings. Sexual feelings follow the same stages as other emotions—charge (arousal), tension (hold), discharge (orgasm), relaxation, and flexibility.[11] There can be a problem in any stage if the person is unable to charge or discharge in a way that brings satisfaction to both the individual and his or her partner. The reason that this feeling is so important for hostage negotiators is that violence and threats of violence are often connected to frustrated sexual feelings in the form of jealousy, rage, loss of potency, and so on. There is a high correlation between abuse of children and parents with sexual dissatisfaction.

All these emotions—fear, anger, sadness, joy and love, and sexual feelings—can be linked back to the bonding process. When our bodies, intellects, emotions, and spirits are in full flow, there is an exchange of energy that goes back and forth within ourselves, and between people, pets, homes, goals, or any other attachment.

Opening ourselves to the possibilities of life allows us to accept what comes to us in full flow of all emotions. Trying to live life without the experience and expression of all emotions does not work. Hostage negotiators learn this approach, as do emotionally intelligent leaders.

Unfortunately, many people are not able to open themselves to what life has to offer. According to Daniel Goleman, people who do not want to feel emotion will probably stay locked into a state of detachment.[12] These people are the most likely to be taken hostage by whatever comes into their lives, regardless of what it might be. Now that we have looked at the stages of emotion, and the types of emotion, it is necessary to understand three ways to experience emotions.

1. *Reactive emotion.* This is the ideal. It is when someone gives an appropriate emotional response to the actual situation. The degree and type of emotion are fitting.

Cheryl asked Jean, her assistant, if Jean would tidy her desk, because it had become too messy. In response, Jean expressed anger that her boss was overcontrolling her and that, in fact, her "messy desk" was not out of line or affecting other employees, customers, or her performance. Her boss had an immediate reaction of anger at the pushback and then realized that she was being a perfectionist and, after a further discussion, the two reached a level of compromise about the order of the materials kept on the desk. Cheryl's anger was quickly brought back to an appropriate degree.

Reactive emotions form the basis of positive interpersonal transactions. However, a nonreactive emotion happens when someone gives an inappropriate response to the stimulus.

2. *Rubberband emotion.* This way of experiencing emotion can be a problem. It occurs when a present stimulus reminds the person of something else from the past.[13] People can go into their memory banks and pull out experiences associated with this or that type of situation or stimulus. They are then taken hostage by the past experience, and they project it onto the present. This has profound consequences, as a discussion or negotiation can suddenly be cast in a negative light just because of the use of one word, one sentence, or one stimulus unknown to the hostage negotiator. If a person grew up with an abusive father who screamed and used physical pain, then, with the stimulus of a loud voice or strong male voice, the person may recall the emotion of the beating from the past, associate it with the present situation, and charge and discharge an emotion from the past onto the immediate person or situation. It comes out as too much and inappropriate to the present context.

A woman was paying for some bread and milk at a supermarket checkout counter. The charge was small—$2.95. In paying, she handed over $2.70. The checkout lady pointed out the woman was twenty-five cents short. The woman immediately went into a rage, screamed that the cashier was calling her a thief, and threw the groceries on the floor.

When I arrived with the police and spoke to the woman, I learned her sad story. Four years earlier, she had lost her husband, and now she was about to lose her home, her last secure base. When she was a young girl, her father had been abusive, often accusing her of stealing cookies, money, or fruit, and frequently beating her. Therefore, she regularly felt as if she had to defend herself. With the loss of a final secure base, the woman's amygdala went into overdrive. Consequently, though the checkout lady had politely questioned her, the woman's unconscious mind immediately recalled painful events, and she proceeded to discharge the unresolved grief caused by the abuse of her father, the death of her husband, and the anticipated loss of her house onto the checkout lady.

Negative rubberbands are almost always outside conscious awareness. The rubberband phenomenon also has a positive side.

A present stimulus can activate a positive memory. You are walking down the street and you smell freshly baked bread. You immediately remember the times when your grandmother baked fresh bread when you were a child. You may even recall the specific memory of her kitchen and the act of spreading the butter and jelly on the warm bread. You can feel all the pleasant emotions of being there with her unless, of course, you still have grief over her death, in which case the memory will evoke crying or make you feel sad. It is called a rubberband because it propels us from the present to the past like the snap of a rubber band. It can also be known from a negative perspective as "pushing someone's buttons" or "triggers" that then set people off. To never be a hostage means to know and control our rubberband emotions.

3. *Substitute emotion.* This is when the person substitutes one emotion for another. For example, someone may be angry and instead starts crying. Or, rather than being appropriately frightened, the person may start laughing. Many boys are taught not to show tears as they grow up, and they may then substitute anger for sadness or fear. Girls, conversely, are often taught not to be angry, and so they substitute crying in place of anger. Family, culture, and group norms all may contribute to which emotions people can experience and show. Remember that emotions are energy, so just substituting them does not work for an effective discharge. We can never discharge enough of an emotion if it is covering for another deeper emotion.[14]

At her annual assessment, Shelley felt that her boss was treating her unfairly by giving her a low rating and criticizing the quality of her work. She became very angry and burst into tears.

Her boss, a man, did not know how to deal with a "crying woman," so he told her she was too emotional and suggested she go back to her office until she had calmed down. She left as a hostage, feeling sad, disengaged, and victimized.

What Shelley could have done was stay in her boss's office, turn to him, and explain that she was feeling angry because of the way he was treating her. He, of course, was blocking any dialogue by remaining aloof and detached, which is another form of substitution for compassion. Shelley actually had many options to stay engaged and to influence her boss into another mind-set. This would mean she was no longer a hostage to him or to herself.

MOTIVATION

Motivation is the driving force behind all human action. It is an internal state that energizes and directs goal-oriented behavior. It is based on emotions, specifically on the avoidance of negative emotional experiences and the search for positive ones. How positive and negative are defined is very individual and influenced by social norms. Motivation is important because it is involved in all performance.

At a more simple level, every action humans take basically is linked to the desire to avoid pain, the desire to gain pleasure, or a combination of both. When we motivate or inspire ourselves, one aspect is to link pain to what we do not want to do and pleasure to what we want to do. This, of course, is easier said than done. How strong does the pain have to be before we choose to abandon the original goal and do something else, and what happens if we learn in our brain to enjoy the pain? If you want to influence a person's behavior, attach pain to the direction in which you do not want them to go and attach pleasure to the direction in which you want them to go.

I remember the story of a man who wanted to stop smoking. He tried often, but each time he soon started again. He couldn't remember the pain associated with smoking. Then one day his ten-year-old daughter came to him in tears. She sat crying in his lap and told him her class had been taught about what happens to the health of people who smoke. She feared her father would die and not see her in her wedding dress when she married. That thought was too excruciating for him. He immediately put out his half-finished cigarette, hugged his daughter, and reassured her he would stop smoking and be there on her wedding day. Whenever he then felt the impulse to have a cigarette, he recalled his daughter's tears. Fifteen years later, he not only was at his daughter's wedding but also had never smoked again.

There is a strong connection between motivation, emotions, and desire.

To be motivated, one must be able to activate strong, positive emotions toward a benefit or purposeful goal. Daniel Goleman referred to self-discipline as "the bedrock of character," and continued, "A related keystone of character is being able to motivate and guide oneself, whether in doing homework, finishing a job or getting up in the morning. And, as we have seen, the ability to defer gratification and to control and channel one's urges to act is a basic emotional skill, one that in a former day was called will."[15]

To achieve excellent results, we will be required to hold the benefit in our mind's eye even during periods of pain and frustration. For some people, this is a habit wired in their brain and it seems natural. For others, it is an ongoing struggle to be successful. The question for those people is to look at their lives and see what secure bases they had and what they might have learned from them. The classic example is the sports world, in which athletes endure great pain and frustration for days, weeks, months, or even years, with the focus on the benefit or goal at the end. They always have models in mind and coaches to help.

The ability to control oneself to delay immediate gratification is one factor in determining success in life.

Stanford University psychology researcher Walter Mischel demonstrated how important self-discipline (the ability to delay immediate gratification in exchange for long-term goal achievement) is to lifelong success. In a longitudinal study that began in the 1960s, he offered hungry four-year-olds a marshmallow, but told them that if they could wait for the experimenter to return after running an errand, they could have two marshmallows.

The test was designed so that those who could wait the twenty minutes for the experimenter to return would be demonstrating the ability to delay gratification and control impulse.

The result was that two thirds of the children could not wait for the delayed gratification. About one third of the children grabbed the single marshmallow right away while the second third resisted a little longer, but ate the marshmallow before the researcher returned. Only one third could endure the frustration of waiting for the delayed reward. They covered their eyes so they would not have to stare at temptation, or rested their

*heads in their arms, talked to themselves, sang, played games with their
hands and feet, and even tried to go to sleep.*

*Years later when the children graduated from high school, the differences
between the two groups were dramatic: the resistors were more positive,
self-motivating, persistent in the face of difficulties, and able to delay
gratification in pursuit of their goals. They had the habits of successful
people, who tend to experience more successful marriages, higher incomes,
greater career satisfaction, better health, and more fulfilling lives than
most of the population.*

*Those having grabbed the marshmallow were more troubled, stubborn
and indecisive, mistrustful, less self-confident, and still could not put
off gratification. They had trouble subordinating immediate impulses to
achieve long-range goals. When it was time to study for the big test, they
tended to get distracted into doing activities that brought instant gratification. This impulse followed them throughout their lives.[16]*

Psychiatrist M. Scott Peck writes, "Delaying gratification is a
process of scheduling the pain and pleasure of life in such a way
as to enhance the pleasure by meeting and experiencing the pain
first and getting it over with. It is the only decent way to live."[17]

People can be motivated by fear, such as fear of failure. For
example, if people are told that their jobs are at risk if they do not
improve, that feedback may stimulate them into greater action. To
avoid the pain, their fear can move and motivate them to change
their behavior. Alternatively, people who are afraid of success may
demotivate themselves by anticipating the grief that will come
when they reach their goal.

THE VALUE OF EMOTIONAL
INTELLIGENCE IN BUSINESS

We may understand the importance of managing emotions in our
personal lives, but what about the applicability in business life?
After all, business is about business and rational, logical information, right? Wrong! Many studies show that companies that focus
on emotional intelligence outperform those that dismiss the "soft
skills" to focus only on "the hard facts and numbers."

A compilation of studies called *The Business Case for Emotional Intelligence,* by Rutgers University researcher Cary Cherniss, found repeated evidence that possession of such emotional competencies as cooperation, accurate self-assessment, optimism, and the ability to handle stress led to greater productivity, job satisfaction, or worker retention.[18]

Research that studied two thousand supervisors and managers shows that fourteen of the sixteen abilities that distinguished the high performers were directly related to emotional intelligence.[19]

From the work of E. L. Thorndike on social intelligence in the 1920s to the pioneering work of Daniel Goleman on emotional intelligence, the business world has seen evidence that emotions drive motivation, which in turn drives engagement of employees, which leads to quality and customer service.[20] In the end, without positive emotions within an organization, there is no way it will sustain high performance and success.

Goleman defines emotional intelligence as "the capacity for recognizing our own feelings and those of others, for motivating ourselves, for managing emotions well in ourselves and also in our relationships."[21]

Four competencies are vital for emotional intelligence:

1. *Self-awareness.* This refers to knowing our own emotions and the effect they have on ourselves and others, as well as being confident in our abilities while knowing our limits. This includes awareness of how we charge and discharge emotions and knowing how we act under stress and in conflict situations.

2. *Self-management.* This involves knowing how to manage our emotions, recognizing our own triggers or "hot buttons," and learning how to control disruptive impulses, as well as acting to manage our stress and handling of conflict.

3. *Social skills.* This relates to our ability to listen, to influence and be persuasive, to engage in dialogue, to collaborate, and to nurture relationships, as well as using our own states to influence the emotions of others.

4. *Empathy.* This refers to the ability to be sensitive to other people's needs, wants, and interests and to being able to sense or read how others are feeling. Empathy also includes showing compassion.

THE IMPACT OF EMOTIONS ON MOOD

Emotional states and physical states are deeply connected. One way to change our emotions is to change our physiological states, adopting a "look out, look up" mentality, as coined by James Lynch.[22] Take a deep breath. If you are locked into a state of denial or detachment, one easy technique to change it is to move your body. When a person is in a psychological position he or she may not be able to change—a "mind-state lock"—it is often accompanied by a fixed physical position. It is important to stand up and move around to keep energy flowing.

A recent study by Brian Meier, North Dakota State University, found that depressed people tend to look down, while more optimistic people tend to look up. It is possible that posture can reinforce moods, and "it may be possible to relieve some depression in certain people by persuading them to break their habits and move their gaze upwards." According to Phillip Hodson, a fellow of the British Association for Counseling and Psychotherapy, "If you feel down, you look down. It is a psychological as well as physical function. Soccer players drop their heads when they miss a penalty as their muscles go limp and they feel deflated, even falling to the ground. If they score, they get a shot of adrenalin and they breathe more deeply, and stand taller." Both are examples of charge and discharge of emotions.[23]

We can also influence someone else's emotions by what we say. If they are told that they look really tired, this can change their state and actually make them more tired. Similarly, if they are told they look really vibrant, this can change their state for a more positive outcome. The secret to having this impact is authenticity. As we saw in Chapter Six, the words we use and the dialogues we have can seriously affect the health of ourselves and others, for better or for worse.

DEALING WITH EMOTIONS

About eight o'clock one evening as I arrived at an international hotel in London, I noticed the gentleman in the taxi ahead of me jump out of the car, hastily give money to the driver, and rush into the hotel. I observed that he was clearly overcharged and seemed to be looking for a fight.

I paid my taxi fare and followed the man into the hotel. When I got to the reception desk, I heard the conversation between the man and the hotel desk clerk. He threw his credit card onto the counter and ordered the young woman to "Give me my room!" Fearful, she politely asked him for his name.

"It's on the card!"

Detached and unbonded, the man further intimidated the woman by his attitude and his block to dialogue. She looked into her computer monitor and said, "Sir, I can't find your reservation. Can you tell me who made it and when?"

This response escalated him even more, and he began to shout. "What sort of hotel is this? Why does it matter who made my reservation? One was made and that's all that matters!" Here he used another block to dialogue and more escalation.

Soon, the assistant manager came to the desk to help the clerk look through papers and the computer to try to find the reservation. Finally, the manager heard the noise and joined them as well.

The "guest" was still shouting and becoming increasingly agitated while the three employees tried to defend the hotel, saying they were doing their best to find his reservation.

At that point, deciding to practice my negotiation skills, I gently tapped him on the shoulder, stepped to the side, gave him enough space, looked right into his eyes, and warmly said, "Sir, excuse me. Did you ask them if they have a room?"

Now, he was so overcharged his response burned itself into my mind.

"Oh. Oh. Oh," he uttered, as his anger slightly decreased. The three employees stayed in their states and stared at him, waiting for the next attack. Instead, he immediately turned and asked the clerk, "Do you have a room?"

The clerk responded affirmatively. The assistant manager offered to give him a room, and the manager urged, "Give him a junior suite."

After receiving the room assignment, he turned to me with a smile and happily said, "Hey, thanks."

The point of this story is that both parties could have handled the episode very differently. The hotel guest could have engaged in more effective bonding at the outset and then moved into a dia-logue and negotiation. The hotel employees could have handled it differently by recognizing the real issue—rather than question-ing whether there had been a reservation mix-up. They could have focused on whether they had a room available for the man. If they had not had a room, all good service organizations know to then make every effort to find alternative accommodation and do every-thing in their power to build and keep that bond. At the point that he was escalating his anger, the man may have been on the verge of threatening violence or picking up his suitcase and leaving the hotel in a rage: the fight-or-flight mechanism in full action. Why did I tap him on the shoulder and, at the same time, move to one side, give him space, look in his eyes, and, with a warm expression, ask a question? The answer is that I wanted to respect his own power to ask for a room, take into account his personal space, encourage him to see me as an ally as opposed to an enemy, and, through bonding with him, invite him to bond with me. Con-versely, if I had stayed behind him and said, "Ask if they have a room," or if I had intervened and talked directly to the desk clerk and said, "Do you have a room for this guy?" I would have opened up the possibility for him to attack me verbally—"Hey buddy, mind your own business"—or possibly even physically. So it is a delicate process as we enter a conflict in the role of a secure base and keep the bond with the person. The goal in this example was to shift the focus from the previous reservation to that of providing a room. How many times have we been taken hostage by our emotions when we lost our focus on the real goal?

As difficult as it may seem at times, it is important to be objec-tive. If we overreact emotionally to a problem or conflict, we tend to adopt the role of the "victim": we then tend to define the prob-lem in terms of an injustice done to us and the solution in terms of how we will extract a pound of flesh from the other person. Such a solution implies that the other party generally must expe-rience some degree of humiliation or lose face in the process.

Emotion-driven exchanges result in the making of extreme demands, which push people apart. Once extreme demands are made, one or both sides feel obligated to defend them. The more time and effort spent justifying these extreme positions, the harder it becomes for either party to put aside their egos and take a problem-solving, win-win approach. Both sides get locked into their positions and their demands, feeling that they cannot afford to look weak by seeking compromise. Often the extreme demands are escalated, and all parties are driven further apart.

When you are aware that you may be overreacting emotionally to certain issues, do the following:

- Acknowledge your emotional involvement. Understand what is causing your emotional reaction.
- Restate the situation as objectively as possible. Consider the most important facts, not your feelings.
- Focus on the goal and a positive solution.
- Identify what you and the other person need to reach a win-win solution.
- Express your feelings in a nonaccusatory, factual manner.
- Listen objectively. Put yourself in other people's shoes to determine how they perceive the situation and what their real needs are (not just their expressed needs).

If you deal with people who overreact emotionally to you, do the following:

- Communicate your understanding of their emotion.
- Avoid making them rationalize or justify their demands.
- Encourage them to communicate their feelings and solutions to the situation by asking questions.
- Empathize with them in an authentic way.

THREE SIMPLE TOOLS TO DEESCALATE EMOTIONS

Three simple tools for deescalating emotional situations are to give choice, provide perspective, and take a time out.

1. *Give choice.* A powerful tool to use when you are asking someone to change their mind is to give them a choice. People sometimes feel that being seen to change their mind is a sign of weakness. They have given in, you have won. However, if you switch the focus from changing their mind to having a choice or

giving an option, it then enables the person to make a decision, based on additional information, that feels rational but is actually emotional.

Sarah was having a problem with her five-year-old daughter, Beth. Every morning, Beth would refuse to get dressed. Stressed due to the time pressure of getting the children to school on time and herself to work, Sarah yelled at Beth, "Get dressed now!"

Beth refused.

Sarah yelled more loudly, "Beth, stop being a spoiled brat and get dressed now. You're going to make us late for school and work!"

Beth still refused.

Sarah grabbed Beth and tried to dress her, physically forcing the clothes onto the child. Beth was now crying and screaming; Sarah was frustrated and furious with Beth.

How could Sarah have handled the situation differently? The answer is through providing choice. Giving choice provides options to a person and removes the focus on a one-position stance.

"Beth, would you like to wear the pink dress or the blue dress today? Do you want to get dressed before breakfast or after breakfast? Would you like me to help you get dressed today or do you want to do it?"

Give choice in one form or another. There is always a way to give choice. When people are given enough choice, they think it is a rational analytical process, although actually people usually change their minds for emotional reasons.

2. *Provide perspective.* How we deal with overescalated emotions depends on how our mind's eye is focused. When people are overwhelmed, usually one of three things is happening.

- They feel the situation is permanent (in time, it will last for eternity). Your response may be a question, such as, How much will this matter in fifty years?
- They feel the situation is overcritical (too important, losing sight of meaning). Your response may be to ask, What really is the worst thing that can happen as a result?

- They feel the situation is all pervasive (all they see and think about). Your response may be to ask, What is really the most important thing in your life?

The goal is to help people refocus and see the situation from another perspective to help deescalate their emotions.

3. *Take a time out.* When you are in a high emotional state and you perceive that you are overwhelmed, take a time out or a pause. In stepping back, you have power and are not likely to be taken hostage. This is also a good suggestion to make to someone else if you can see that they are highly overcharged and need a break before continuing. If it is with a work colleague, suggest going to get a coffee. If it is with a friend, take a walk. If it is with your child, move from one room to another or step outside.

Dealing with emotions, our own or others', can be challenging. As we have seen, our emotions are a natural response to protect us. By recognizing what is happening within us and around us, we have a far greater chance of being able to manage the emotion in a way that is constructive and positive.

THE AMYGDALA HIJACK

Professor Nigel Nicholson, author of *Executive Instinct,* talks about how we use emotions, not reason, as the first screen for all information received.[24] We avoid risky situations when we feel relatively secure but we fight frantically when we feel threatened.[25] This is when the amygdala comes into play.

The amygdala is part of the human brain. It is an almond-shaped cluster of interconnected structures perched above the brain stem near the bottom of the limbic ring. The amygdala is an expert on emotional matters. In many ways, it is a hostage-taker, a terrorist, able to hijack the brain and take it hostage, causing it to flood the body with stress hormones and activating the fight-or-flight mechanism in our reptilian brain. The process of being hijacked by our amygdala has been beautifully described and depicted by Joshua Freedman (see Figure 8.2).

Normally a sensation—such as a visual cue—is routed to the thalamus. The thalamus acts as an "air traffic controller" to keep

FIGURE 8.2. THE AMYGDALA HIJACK

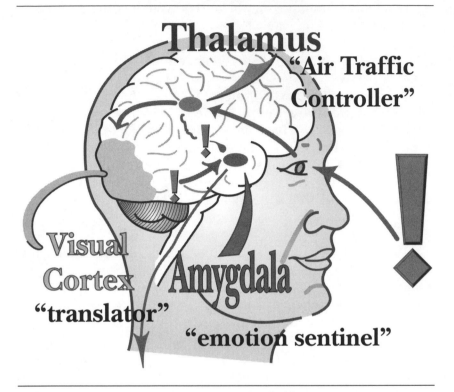

Source: Joshua Freedman, *EQ Today,* "Hijacking of the Amygdala: This is what happens in your brain when you get really mad—or really *anything!*" Available at www.eqtoday.com/archive/hijack.html.

the signals moving. In a typical situation, the thalamus directs the impulse to the cortex—in this case the visual cortex—for processing. The cortex "thinks" about the impulse and makes sense of it. "Aha," it says, "this is an exclamation mark! It means I should get excited." That signal is then sent to the amygdala, where a flood of peptides and hormones are released to create emotion and action.

In what Daniel Goleman labeled "The Hijacking of the Amygdala," the thalamus has a different reaction.[26] Like any skilled air traffic controller, the thalamus can quickly react to potential threat. In that case, it bypasses the cortex—the thinking brain—and the signal goes straight to the amygdala. Now, what makes this more interesting is that the amygdala can only react based on previously stored patterns. Sometimes this kind of reaction can save our lives. More frequently, it leads us to say something harmful or to escalate the situation. In some cases, it can even lead to violence. To minimize the damage from an amygdala hijack, it is important to practice behavior that leads to deescalation.

From that hijacked state, that condition when our brain is flooded with electro-chemicals, we still have options. We do not need to stay hijacked—we still can choose actions. After all, the chemicals do not persist—they will dissipate in three to six seconds.[27]

We can see the amygdala hijack in action in a number of daily situations. A car spins out of control and hurtles toward a crowd. Some people react immediately and throw themselves out of the way. Others may literally "freeze" at the sight of the oncoming car, and, in fact, they may be rooted to the spot by a sudden surge of adrenalin.

Paul had been on a business trip all week and was looking forward to getting home. When he got to the airport for his Friday evening flight, he was told it had been cancelled. Unable to adjust his mind's eye away from his desire to be home, Paul began to yell at the check-in clerk, angrily demanding to see the manager. He could hardly contain his frustration and anger and immediately took himself hostage with rage.

What Paul could have done is recognize his grief at not going home and focus on other options to get home or spend the evening. His rage gave no helpful options to solve the problem. He would have been better served to bond with the agent and engage that person's help in solving the problem.

Learning to recognize when our amygdala is stimulated will help us to avoid becoming hostages to either ourselves or others.

SUMMARY

Research shows that decisions are highly influenced by emotion. Therefore, for both our personal and professional lives, it is vitally important that we understand how our own emotions have an impact on the decisions we are making.

Successful people are able to self-regulate their emotions and manage the benefits that come from using emotions effectively. In a conversation I had with Daniel Goleman, he said, "Personal competence is the mastering of one's own emotions, and social competence is learning to master and influence other people's emotions."

Emotions go through five stages: charge, tension, discharge, relaxation, and flexibility. There are many opinions about the various types of emotion; however, some core emotions are fear, sadness, anger, joy and love, and sexual feeling. Whenever we experience an emotion, the goal is to allow it to move through the stages. When an emotion gets blocked, it will manifest itself in many forms such as sickness, anger, or frustration. How we manage our emotions affects how well we are able to bond.

Motivation is vital in determining success through providing the energy, emotion, and focus to achieve a specific goal or outcome. Motivation is inextricably linked to the desire to avoid pain or seek pleasure, or a combination of both. The expression "no pain, no gain" is intended to motivate people through the suffering of an experience to the enjoyment of the end goal.

It is increasingly recognized that emotional intelligence is a far greater measure of the likelihood of success than is IQ. Companies that focus on emotional intelligence also report greater employee engagement, leading to increased productivity and levels of customer satisfaction. Research also shows that both our mental health and physical health are affected by our emotions.

When dealing with our emotions, we can apply three simple tools: give choice, provide perspective, and take a time out. Our emotions are often a natural response based on a survival instinct, and we should learn to listen to and trust our intuition.

The amygdala is a part of our brain that can hijack us, causing us to act in extreme ways in tense situations. Bypassing the thinking brain, the thalamus will send a signal straight to the amygdala, which in turn will immediately flood our bodies with chemicals and put us into fight-or-flight mode.

By understanding our emotions and how and why they work as they do, we can maintain power over ourselves. Also, when we understand the triggers that may be caused by experiences from the past, we can better manage emotions to avoid becoming hostages and, equally, to avoid taking others hostage.

Key Points to Remember

1. Emotions are energy, and when energy is created, it must go somewhere. Use emotions for creating inspiration in yourself and others. You can change emotions by changing states, and you can change states by physically moving your body or changing focus in your mind's eye.

2. To master our emotions and avoid being taken hostage by them, we need to understand how we are feeling so we can self-regulate.

3. Just because we cannot explain a feeling does not mean we should ignore it. Our intuitions can provide us with valuable information that could even save our lives.

4. To motivate yourself toward a goal, try associating pain with what you do not want to happen and associate pleasure with the outcome you seek.

Chapter Nine

Living with a Hostage-Free State of Mind

Olympic gold medalist Wilma Rudolph was the twentieth of twenty-two children. Her parents, Ed and Blanche Rudolph, were honest but very poor people. Mr. Rudolph worked as a railroad porter and handyman; Mrs. Rudolph did cooking, laundry, and housecleaning for wealthy white families.

A premature baby, Wilma weighed only 4.5 pounds at birth. During the first few years of the child's life, Wilma's mother nursed her through one illness after another: measles, mumps, scarlet fever, chicken pox, and double pneumonia. When Wilma was four, her parents took her to the doctor after they discovered that her left leg and foot were becoming weak and deformed. She had had polio, a crippling disease with no cure.

The doctor told Mrs. Rudolph that Wilma would never walk. However, Mrs. Rudolph refused to give up on her daughter. She learned that Wilma could be treated at Meharry Hospital, the black medical college of Nashville's Fisk University.

Even though it was fifty miles away, Wilma's mother took her there twice a week for two years, until Wilma was able to walk with the aid of a metal leg brace. Then the doctors taught Mrs. Rudolph how to do the physical therapy exercises at home.

All of Wilma's brothers and sisters helped, too, rubbing her legs four times a day. By eight, she could walk with a leg brace. After that, she used a high-topped shoe to support her foot and played basketball with her brothers every day.

Three years later, her mother came home to find her practicing basketball barefoot. By twelve, Wilma could walk normally—without crutches, brace, or corrective shoes.

In high school, Rudolph became a basketball star, setting state records for scoring and leading her team to a state championship. A track coach encouraged her to start running.

She ran so well that during her senior year in high school she qualified for the 1956 Olympics in Melbourne, Australia. At sixteen, Wilma Rudolph won a bronze medal in the women's 400-meter relay.

In 1959, she qualified for the 1960 Olympic Games in Rome by setting a world record in the 200-meter race. At the Olympics that year, she won two individual gold medals, in the 100-meter and the 200-meter races.

She then sprained her ankle but ignored the pain to help her team win a gold medal for the 100-meter relay. With this victory, Wilma became the first American woman to earn three gold medals in the Olympics.

This achievement led to her becoming one of the most celebrated female athletes of all time. In addition, her celebrity caused gender barriers to be broken in previously all-male track and field events.

Retiring from running when she was twenty-two, she went on to coach women's track teams and encourage young people.

Wilma thought God had a greater purpose for her than winning three gold medals. She served as a track coach, an athletic consultant, and the assistant director of athletics for the Mayor's Youth Foundation in Chicago. She also started the Wilma Rudolph Foundation to help children learn about discipline and hard work. A noted goodwill ambassador, Rudolph was also a talk show hostess who became active on the lecture circuit.

Though Wilma Rudolph died of brain cancer in 1994, her influence lives on in the lives of many young people who look up to her.[1]

The remarkable story of Wilma Rudolph provides us with many examples of concepts described in this book. First, there was the focus and strength in the mind's eye of her mother. When told Wilma would never walk, her mother did everything in her power to make sure her daughter did walk. The secure base of the mother and the bonding experience with the whole family, who took turns massaging Wilma's legs over an extended period of time, all contributed to her success. Then there was the determination, will, and belief within Wilma's mind's eye to focus only on the possibilities in her life. She did not allow herself to be a hostage or be limited by her potential handicap. Even with a leg brace, she was out playing basketball with her brothers every day. All of them, especially Wilma, were willing to pay the price to succeed.

Through the encouragement of a sports coach, another secure base, she started running and broke records at every level. When on the way to becoming the first woman to win three gold medals in track at an Olympic Games, she managed to suppress the pain from a sprained ankle and, with her goal firmly fixed in her mind's eye, ran the relay.

Wilma's life indicates that she was bonded to both people and goals; this enabled her to have high self-esteem and a real belief in herself and what she could achieve. Her mother could have been taken hostage by the doctor who told her that her daughter would never walk, and yet she did not listen or succumb to an authority figure. Wilma could have been taken hostage by the fact that she could not walk properly, and yet she did not give up. The mother, the family, and Wilma all chose another option—the option of possibility. There is no doubt that both Wilma and her mother had to sacrifice a great deal and suffer a lot of pain, frustration, and discomfort. However, the end benefit—the pleasure of being able to walk and run—outweighed the years of work and commitment required.

Leaders can learn a great deal from Wilma's story. First, do they see possibility rather than limitations? Second, can they make sacrifices and endure pain for the end benefit? Third, do they have secure bases that can support them in achieving their goals?

Working to win a major contract with a customer can require long hours; weekends at the office; working dinners; and long, often heated negotiations and discussions with the customer. However, all efforts are considered worthwhile once that contract is signed and the win celebrated. Similarly, a company's appearance at a major exhibition involves substantial work behind the scenes and months of preparation. Yet, when the actual event happens and is deemed a "success," again, the previous work is considered worthwhile. Many business leaders put themselves through executive education programs while still being fully responsible for their jobs, resulting in increased stress and having an impact on the short-term work-life balance. However, successful completion of the course lifts the spirits; increases knowledge, learning, and confidence; and can improve long-term job prospects. The sacrifice made to complete the course is seen as necessary to gain the end benefit.

Whether it is in the personal or professional parts of our lives, each one of us must remember that actions determine outcome. Powerlessness and passivity go hand in hand. If we take no action, then we indeed become "trapped" and therefore hostages. For example, wherever elephants are kept in circuses, they can be seen chained by one foot to a pole. Now, that full-grown elephant is strong enough to pull over the pole and go exactly where it pleases, but it does not. As a baby elephant, it learned that trying to escape produced no result, and it retains that memory of "learned helplessness" into adulthood.

Ultimately, we must be willing to bear responsibility for the attitudes and outcomes we create in life. If we allow ourselves to be taken hostage by others or by ourselves, we are, in fact, making a choice to give up power. This is a life dilemma: What can we control, what can we not control, and what will our attitude be?

HIGH SELF-ESTEEM

Self-esteem is the opinion we have of ourselves. It is normal for moods to fluctuate based on daily experiences. However, these fluctuations will be less frequent and more temporary in someone with high self-esteem. For people with low self-esteem, these fluctuations can be exaggerated and can easily take them hostage. A sign of high self-esteem is the ability to face the toughest challenge while remaining true to oneself.

As we saw in Chapter Four, secure bases with both people and goals, be they historical or present day, are essential to develop high self-esteem. Self-esteem develops and evolves throughout our lives, based on lifelong learning. Childhood experiences; relationships with family members, teachers, peers, coaches, and other authority figures; and experiences with performance hardwire the brain on how to approach people, goals, and achievement. What is important to remember is that self-esteem is always maturing.

Self-esteem can be positive (high) or negative (low), resulting in a self-fulfilling prophecy of success or failure. Self-esteem is connected to every aspect of life, including work, the way we think, the way we think others see us, our purposes in life, our ability to act and be independent, our achievements, and, fundamentally, how much we "value" ourselves.

High self-esteem is based on the ability to accurately know ourselves and still be able to accept and value ourselves. People with high self-esteem are able to acknowledge both their strengths and their limitations while maintaining their self-respect and a feeling of being worthwhile. People who have high self-esteem are not set back by failure, negative feedback, or criticism, or if they are, they bounce back quickly. If a person has experienced healthy bonding to secure bases as a child and incorporated internal mental models about how to deal with failure and frustration, then that person is more likely to have high self-esteem. When this occurs, we can be a secure base to ourselves by being clear in our emotional states and even through constructive self-talk. However, regardless of how strong a secure base we are to ourselves, the need for external secure bases will always remain.[2]

As discussed in Chapter Four, people who have high self-esteem will display a joyful attitude and a general happiness to be alive. They are able to balance between giving and taking and are able to give and receive positive compliments. They search for opportunities and exhibit spontaneity, flexibility, and playfulness in life. They have creative reactions to problems and gain satisfaction from experiences. They can be intimate with other people. They consider others important, and they possess an openness to life and to others. They have a sense of ease with themselves and their place in the world. They retain perspective about their place in the universe and exhibit a grateful attitude toward life.

LOW SELF-ESTEEM

Low self-esteem is the opposite of all the things said in the previous section about high self-esteem. People who lack self-esteem often can feel like they are floating without an anchor or a secure base, like a ship drifting across the ocean at the mercy of the wind and water. People with low self-esteem overcriticize themselves to the point of perfectionism. They may need constant reassurance and external approval to counteract their negative and critical inner dialogues with themselves. Reassurances are never enough because these are persons with low self-esteem and, in fact, not a secure base to themselves. Author Michael Hebron observed that "humans are the only species on earth with the ability to interfere with their own performance." He remarked that "self-interference is a learned skill; we are not born with it."[3]

People with low self-esteem also suffer from poor self-images. They are reluctant to take risks and often function with a fear of rejection. Fundamentally, they do not believe they are worthy or good enough and must prove both worth and value. Their inner voice keeps telling them that they are not good enough, criticizing what they are doing and how they are performing. This is directly related to a failure to incorporate a positive working model from a secure base network in their lives.

For people with low self-esteem, positive feelings are temporarily connected mostly to external events such as passing an exam or getting a promotion. These people may appear happy to the outside world, but inside they are terrified of failure and live in continuous fear of being "found out." They may live with constant anger blocking their flow of emotions. As a result, they may rebel against or overadapt to authority figures, blame others for their misfortunes, or even appear arrogant and aloof. They may feel unable to cope with the world and have an air of self-pity about them, the victim waiting to be rescued by someone else. Clearly, low self-esteem is part of feeling, thinking, and acting like a hostage. The good news is that it is always possible to rewire the brain and build high self-esteem.

BOOSTING SELF-ESTEEM

Former first lady Eleanor Roosevelt once remarked that "no one can make you feel inferior without your consent."[4] There are five simple steps you can follow to boost your self-esteem.

1. *Cultivate self-awareness.* Know just where you stand today in terms of self-esteem. Be honest with yourself. Look at how you respond to the challenges and the people in your life. Think back

to your childhood. Who were your secure bases? Who were the positive and negative authority figures? What successes and what failures stand out in your mind? Who cared if you succeeded or not? Who celebrated your successes with you? Did you grow up in an encouraging constructive environment or a negative, destructive one? How has that influenced you today? What did you learn from your secure bases? From this information, you can gain an understanding of the foundations of your self-esteem. For example, do you work better under pressure or when you have plenty of time? The more you can learn about yourself, the more you can build your self-esteem.

2. *Accept what you cannot change.* We cannot change some things in life, or at least it is difficult to do so, and we must learn to accept ourselves as we are. For example, we cannot change our parents, the country we were born in, our height, our complexion and skin color, our basic body shape, and so on. Also, if we have faced loss, we have to accept those losses in order to be able to move on. Are there losses in your life that you have not said goodbye to properly? Learning to grieve, as discussed in Chapter Three, is essential to finding joy in yourself, around you and in life. Acceptance of who you are is vital in the composition of your self-esteem.

3. *Make friends with your inner voice.* Practice listening to what you tell yourself. Catch what you are saying in your mind. Is it positive, constructive, and helpful, or is it negative, destructive, and unhelpful? After a presentation, do you focus on the fact that people congratulated you and said it went well, or do you focus on the message you forgot to give or the section where you went backward with the slides instead of forward? When people compliment you, do you tell yourself that they are right, or do you question it and think they were just "being nice?" Let yourself off the hook. No one is perfect. Do not expect perfection in yourself or anyone else—if you do, you are bound to be disappointed. Borrow from secure bases in your life who are models of high self-esteem and say the same things they say to you.

4. *Celebrate yourself.* If you bought an expensive car, you would make sure that you looked after it. You would put the right gas in the tank, keep it clean, and make sure it was serviced regularly. Treat yourself in the same way. After all, a car may last a decade. Your body and mind have to last your whole life. Make sure that you get enough sleep, you exercise regularly, you keep good hygiene,

and you eat reasonably well. Do things you enjoy doing, no matter how simple or small. Reward yourself for small accomplishments or compliment yourself when you have done something well. Enjoy that relaxing bath, glass of wine, or book. Leave a voicemail message wishing yourself a nice day.

5. *Get help from others.* Humans are social animals, and all the research shows that we generally feel more positive when we have a strong social network. If you are more introverted, it is important to create the bonding you need to recharge your energy. Having the courage to ask those around you for help is a key way to improve your self-esteem. Ask someone who is a secure base for you what he or she would do if they were in your shoes. Write down positive things people have said and keep them posted on your refrigerator or on your desk. Find friends to just sit and listen while you confide your feelings and offload your frustrations. Ask for a hug, a handshake, a physical touch. Go to a class or read up on self-esteem through books or on the Internet. If the situation warrants it, seek professional help.

Leaders often ask me the question, "Don't you have to be arrogant to succeed, and isn't arrogance a sign of high self-esteem?" The answer is a resounding no! Actually, humility is almost always a sign of high self-esteem.

EMPOWERED HUMILITY

Humility is modesty, meekness, and simplicity in attitude. It is a lack of vanity, pretentiousness, and self-importance. People can easily be taken hostage by their own vanity or ego. There is a significant difference between humility and arrogance. Arrogance is when one is filled with conceit, insolence, and loftiness, in order to make others feel lower. Everyone aspires to be somebody. The humble person finds a sense of being "somebody" with a clear meaning and purpose. From the depth of our souls, there is a persistent cry to find significance.[5] The search for meaning manifests itself in many ways, from self-seeking to self-sacrifice. We do many things to prove that our lives matter, are worthwhile, and have significance. When frustrated with the process of feeling that one is worthwhile, or when having strong feelings of inferiority, some people go to the other extreme of arrogance. These people are taken hostage by their display of an arrogant attitude to the world that actually masks an underlying feeling of inferiority and lack of self-worth. They often remain unbonded and isolated emotionally. The search for meaning and significance should not be confused with personal ambitions for success.

Personal humility is a trait that has been recognized as an important aspect of high performance. In research to find what distinguished great companies from good ones, one of the surprise findings by Jim Collins was that all the CEOs of those excellently performing companies displayed humility. As part of what Collins termed "Level 5 Leadership" in his bestseller *Good to Great*, there are a number of characteristics that demonstrate whether someone has humility: such people have a compelling modesty, shun public adulation, and are never boastful. They act with a quiet, calm determination, relying principally on inspired standards, not inspiring charisma, to motivate. They channel ambition into the company, not the self, setting up successors for even more greatness in the next generation. These people also look in the mirror (accepting responsibility themselves), not out of the window, to apportion responsibility for poor results, never blaming other people, external factors, or bad luck. Level 5 leaders display this kind of humility along with a strong professional will. When pressed to talk about themselves, they say things like, "I hope I'm not sounding like a big shot," or "I don't think I can take much credit for what happened. We were blessed with marvelous people." Says Collins, "Level 5 leaders are a study in duality: modest and willful, shy and fearless."[6]

According to Dr. Paul Wong, humility can yield many benefits.[7] It is beneficial to mental health, social relationships, leadership, and human progress. For instance, a humble person is more likely to be happy and content than is an arrogant person. A humble approach contributes to better relationships because that makes it easier to create and maintain bonds. Developing humility provides all-round benefits to individuals, families, organizations, and society as a whole.

Pat Tillman was an Arizona Cardinals football player who turned down a three-year, $3.6 million contract to enlist in the army in May 2000.

"My great grandfather was at Pearl Harbor, and a lot of my family has gone and fought in wars, and I haven't done a damn thing as far as

laying myself on the line like that," Tillman told NBC News in an interview the day after the 9/11 attacks. Later, posted in Afghanistan with the army's Special Forces, Tillman was killed in action during a firefight with anticoalition militia forces (sadly, a victim of friendly fire). He was twenty-seven.

Former Cardinals head coach Dave McGinnis said he felt both an overwhelming sorrow and a tremendous pride in Tillman, who "represented all that was good in sports." "Pat knew his purpose in life," McGinnis believed. "He proudly walked away from a career in football to a greater calling."

"In sports, we tend to overuse terms like courage, bravery and heroes," said Cardinals Vice President Michael Bidwell, "and then someone like Pat Tillman comes along and reminds us what those terms really mean."

NFL Commissioner Paul Tagliabue insisted, "He was an achiever and leader, on many levels, who always put his team, his community, and his country ahead of his personal interests."

Tillman could have chosen a path that involved wealth and fame. Instead, he chose a route in which his contribution to society came before his contribution to self.[8]

Humility is not about low self-regard, self-deprecation, or a low sense of self. It is having an accurate sense of who you are, what you are, and why you do what you do while recognizing the right of others to do the same. People with high self-esteem are indeed humble and modest. True humility is a rich, multifaceted concept characterized by an accurate sense of one's own abilities, a sense of one's own limitations, and forgetting the self. Clearly, it is a rare moment when a humble person resorts to feeling or acting like a hostage.

HELPING OURSELVES AND OTHERS THROUGH CONTINUOUS LIFELONG LEARNING

In nature, if something is not growing, it is atrophying. We are either developing or decaying. There is no interim stage. This is also true for our minds. When we are learning, we are growing and, literally, creating huge numbers of new brain cells. If we are stagnating, we are actually killing large numbers of brain cells. Therefore, by constantly seeking to learn, developing ourselves and others, we make our lives more vibrant. When people concentrate on developing others, they often find that they develop themselves in the process.

Following are three areas that you can focus on to enhance life-long learning.

1. *Overcome fears.* Fears that are based on irrational beliefs about an object, event, person, or feeling will result in negative, disastrous, disturbing, unsettling, or even life-threatening consequences for you. Our fears can take us hostage so quickly and easily. Fear prevents and blocks us from living a powerfully bonded life because of the negative state created. How can we feel positive if we are focused on our fears? Knowing that our brain is hardwired to look for danger and pain through fear, we must actively direct the mind to look for the benefit. So what can we do about fears that can easily take us hostage? The first step is to identify the fear. What is it? Write it down, look at it again, and "put the fish on the table" with yourself. Ask yourself the question, "Why do I have this fear?" Look into your mind's eye and reflect on what aspects of your past may be contributing to the fear. Understanding our fears is the first step toward conquering them. Then search in your mind for the secure bases in your life who would put a hand on your shoulder and, with great advice, walk with you through your fear. There is an old Senoi Indian technique, as mentioned in Chapter Two, of teaching children and adults to use a known secure base to turn an enemy into an ally, and fear into courage. If you have no secure base, then find one from your social network, or a positive one from a book or from the movies. Use visualization techniques to see yourself as someone who is not frightened and able to cope. Then act, act, and act.

Any soldier or police officer will tell you that there is a very short distance between fear and courage. The distance is covered by action. The most fearful people can become the most courageous. Eliminating fear is not the goal, as there may be occasions when that fear is based on an objective reality. The aim is to train your mind's eye to focus on a positive goal with the support of the best secure bases you can find and then to act bravely. You can view overcoming your fear as learning and developing courage. By facing fears and learning to act, you give yourself the power to live with a hostage-free state of mind and, as a result, find freedom.

2. *Learn to do new things.* Risk taking is about learning to open up to change, to what is possible, and even to what is uncomfortable. It is being unafraid to expose ourselves, to "stick our necks out." It involves accepting the need for change and then taking the steps necessary to make the change. Risk taking requires us to weigh up the positives and negatives of a situation and then to make a choice to take a required action. We are then able to act, completely aware of the possible risks without being taken hostage. One challenge in risk taking is to know what is important for us and to take action without needing the approval of others. Secure bases give support and encourage autonomy, which is very different from the dependency of wanting approval.

Secure bases are important in providing an environment in which we feel able to take risks. They provide the security that allows us to explore new ideas and new possibilities knowing that, irrespective of the result, we will be loved and worthy of love. Borrowing from those secure bases is part of the process to "not avoid risks."

If you are facing a problem or challenge, ask yourself what is stopping you from solving it. What prevents you from taking necessary actions? What holds you back? You may discover it is fear, for example, fear of failure, or fear of rejection, or fear of humiliation. At this point, you must train your brain to attach a pleasure and a benefit to the outcome that outweigh the potential pain or loss. Ask yourself not only what the consequences are of taking the risk but also what the consequences are of not taking the risk. Again, think about the worst-case scenario. Visualize taking the risk and succeeding. One of the best ways to develop our ability to become less averse to risk and change is to do something different every day, preferably something new and uncomfortable, to learn something new. The neurons in our brain expand with learning, and the best learning for our minds occurs outside our comfort zones.

Risk taking is another opportunity to live with a hostage-free state of mind.

3. *Learn to let go.* As we read in Chapter Three, the bonding cycle is a fundamental process that all humans must repeatedly go

through. Many people are unable to attach and bond effectively because they have not been able to accept the separation and grieving stages. If we have not truly been able to let go of something or someone in our lives, it can block us from going forward. Learning to let go is vital in empowering ourselves to live with a hostage-free state of mind. Letting go may involve making a decision to take an action that will result in a significant change in our lives. Letting go can release us, and others, from a perceived or real feeling of guilt or sadness. Letting go frees us to make new attachments and new bonds or to renew attachments and bonds in another way. Letting go allows the opportunity to self-regulate and take responsibility. For many years, I had the great fortune to study with Elisabeth Kübler-Ross, the Swiss-American pioneer who did research into death and dying. Three of her most powerful messages to me were the following:

1. You must say goodbye before you can say hello. You cannot say hello until you say goodbye.
2. Grieving is a social experience. You cannot grieve alone. You must do it with significant others, that is, family, clan, or tribe.
3. You cannot live until you are willing to die. Fear of death stops one from fully living.[9]

There are many things that we must "let go." They can be guilt, grief, dependency, fear, anger, denial, and, ultimately, being able to let go through death itself. What stops us from letting go? Many of the obstacles come from our past experiences that have shaped our mind's eye and the view of how we feel about a certain type of loss. We may view letting go as being too vulnerable, too frightening, too painful, too dangerous.

How can we help ourselves let go and move forward? First, identify the type of letting go you need to do. Is it related to a loss, fear, anger, sadness, denial, over-responsibility, or over-dependence? Once you have identified what it is, act to go through it. What is the person, place, or event in your past or present that you need to let go? Why have you not been able to let it go? Become clear in your mind about the goal you have in letting go and saying goodbye. Attach a benefit to the end goal, asking what the hello will be, to help you continue as you go through the pain associated with letting go. Come to terms with the feelings you have and let yourself experience and grieve them. Then let yourself find a renewed joy in life. When you can do this, you will be able to move on, reattach and rebond, and experience life at its fullest. Only then can you live with a hostage-free state of mind. Today, several years after the 9/11 attacks, there are many stories of people who experienced that great tragedy and yet have gone on to find the joy of life again.

FINDING FREEDOM THROUGH CHOICE

In the book The Paradox of Choice, *author Barry Schwartz tells the story of when he went to The Gap to buy a pair of jeans. He went into the store and told the salesperson that he wanted a pair of jeans—size 32-28. "Do you want them slim fit, easy fit, relaxed fit, baggy, or extra baggy?" she asked. "Do you want them stonewashed, acid-washed, or distressed? Do you want them button fly or zipper fly? Do you want them faded or regular?" He managed to splutter out something like, "I just want regular jeans. You know the kind that used to be the only kind."*

He wrote that the trouble was, with all these options available to him, he was no longer sure that "regular" jeans were what he wanted. He decided to try them all, convinced that one of the options must be "right" for him. He was determined to figure it out, but he could not. In the end, he settled for easy fit because relaxed fit might imply he was "getting soft in the middle" and needed to cover up! The jeans he chose turned out fine, but it occurred to him that buying a pair of pants should not be a day-long project.[10]

Sometimes there is so much choice that we become paralyzed or, in other words, we become hostages to choosing or our failure to choose. How many times have you sat in front of the television, flicked through the fifty or more channels, and concluded, "There's nothing on"? Take a walk down the cereal aisle of any supermarket and count the number of choices you have with respect to what kind of cereal you can eat for your breakfast. What happens when we have too much choice? In order to cope, some people tend to stick with what they know; others spend endless time trying to decide, while others just give up all choice by letting someone else decide. Even when we know what we want, the array of options or changing circumstances may confuse us. In some ways, life may appear simpler when we have no choice, so some people give responsibility for their lives to someone else. Then they do not have to make a choice, but they have become hostages.

When we are clear about what we want, it is easier to make a choice because we also know what we do not want. A dilemma emerges when we become too rigid in our thinking about who we are and what we want, so we do not open ourselves up to new possibilities. It is a challenge to be clear about what we want and yet, at the same time, keep ourselves open to new possibilities.

Choice is the mental process of judging the merits of multiple options and selecting action. It can range from what kind of behavior to engage in to what route to take when driving across the country. When we feel empowered to choose, we are less likely to be taken hostage because we have some control over our destinies and the ability to decide what we do.

People who make choices based on immediate gratification become hostages and will always be limited in their success. We achieve more when we make choices based on long-term goals. For that reason, we need to get our bodies to follow our minds. Our mind's eye needs to focus beyond the clutter, frustration, and pain to understand the benefits, knowing that the "price to pay" is a continual choice. In this sense, "no pain, no gain" is a true statement. High performers view the pain as a necessary path to the benefit. Musicians who practice every day learn to "enjoy" it. Motivation ultimately becomes hardwired in their brain so that when they get out of bed it is a habit to practice. However, behind every habit there lies a choice that has been made.

When people forget that there is always choice, they can become hostages to their own passivity. To live with a hostage-free state of mind, we need to remember to act on our personal power by recognizing the choices being made. Behind all behavior is some choice or potential choice. At the end of the day, based on our inner worlds, our mind's eye, and our secure bases, it comes down to what we choose to do. Even if that choice is to say to someone who is a secure base, "I need help."

Philosopher Isaiah Berlin distinguished between negative liberty (freedom from things such as constraint or being told what to do) and positive liberty (the freedom to do things, to be the author of our lives, and to make them meaningful and significant).[11] If people want "freedom from" constraints that are appropriate (for example, having to stop at a red light), they are still being held hostage by their own rebellion. There are people who, in the need for freedom, make destructive choices. That is why, if we have not made peace with the authority figures in our youth, we can maintain an ongoing rebellious attitude toward all authority. Healthy rebellion is about seeking constructive and valuable goals. Negative rebellion is always to "go against" authority regardless. In the end, fear of making attachments and creating secure bonds does not constitute freedom; instead, it results in becoming a hostage to loneliness. Conversely, attachment and bonding to people and goals bring freedom.

Schwartz's research about choice provides a number of valuable lessons, some counterintuitive:

1. We would be better off if we embraced certain voluntary constraints on our freedom of choice, instead of rebelling against them.
2. We would be better off seeking what is "good enough" instead of seeking the best.
3. We would be better off if we lowered our expectations about the results of decisions.
4. We would be better off if the decisions we made were nonreversible.
5. We would be better off if we paid less attention to what others around us were doing.[12]

LIVING IN FLOW

Psychologist Mihaly Csikszentmihalyi wrote, "When we sit by a river and watch the water pass by, we can see the beauty of flow in action. The water is flowing and moving naturally, sure in its direction. It has an energy, a power, and a certainty about it, a combination that exudes a sense of calm and oneness with the world. The best moments usually occur when a person's body or mind is stretched to its limits in a voluntary effort to accomplish something difficult and worthwhile."[13]

Many people lose freedom and become hostages because they do not enjoy the things they have to do. Sports figures, musicians, great leaders—all of them have to do things that they may not like but train themselves to enjoy doing what is necessary to achieve the end goal. When researching different professions, Csikszentmihalyi discovered that when people were engaged in optimal or peak performance, they forgot themselves, the time, and their problems. He cautions that many people misinterpret this flow as a kind of "spacing out" and then seek it in passive leisure activities. "Most people so much look forward to being home, relaxing. Then they get home and do not know what to do. They aren't challenged, so they sit in front of the TV, depressed."

Brazilian soccer legend Pele described days when everything was going right and he felt "a strange calmness I hadn't experienced in any of the other games. It was a type of euphoria. I felt I could run all day without tiring, that I could dribble through any of their teams or all of them, that I could pass through them physically. I felt I could not be hurt."[14]

Flow occurs when our bodies, intellects, emotions, and spirits all combine in a natural way and hold us in a "zone." When working in a zone, we find ourselves in a meditative state and have greater energy, concentration, and power than when we are normally working on something. Flow helps us find enjoyment in the most routine of activities, as in repeated practice or in fine-tuning skills.

You can recognize flow and work toward creating it in eight ways:[15]

1. *Have clear goals.* Know in your mind's eye what you want and need to do. The merging of action and awareness then becomes automatic, relaxing the conscious mind.
2. *Receive immediate feedback.* Know at every moment how you are doing and if you are getting closer to your goal. Trust your intuition and use knowledge from internal and external secure bases to guide you.
3. *Match challenges with the skills of the person.* The challenge should be neither too low nor too high and should provide a sense of continuous learning. The activity should be at your skill level or slightly above. Then raise the bar continuously as performance improves.

4. *Focus and concentrate.* Have a single focus and attention on what you are doing without splitting attention or becoming distracted by internal mental clutter or external activities.
5. *Operate in the moment with clarity of mind.* Remove everyday frustrations and intrusions. Learn to use "tunnel vision" to tune out those factors over which you have no control.
6. *Have a sense of control.* Have a feeling of being in charge of yourself, your actions, and the environment. It is the sense of lack of worry and concern about failure.
7. *Lose self-consciousness.* Focus on the activity by transcending the self, forgetting the self and cutting out criticism of yourself. You become one with the activity. Concerns about self disappear, including physical and emotional worries.
8. *Realize when your sense of time is transformed.* Time adapts itself to your experience by being in the rhythm of the activity and not the external time of day. Time may slow down, speed up or stand still.

The sense of flow is a sign of freedom and always an antidote to being a hostage. Yet flow is not a conscious act but more a state of mind in which we allow it to happen. Our conscious mind may actually interfere with flow. However, we can remove obstacles and recognize the signs when it does occur. Being present in the moment is always necessary. If we are living in the past, or in the future, we will not experience the enjoyment of the activity. Learn to love the present, say yes to whatever is, and appreciate the beauty of life wherever you are.

SUMMARY

The option to live with a hostage-free state of mind is one we can take right now. Even if we may be taken hostage physically, we can ensure that psychologically, we retain our own power. Similarly, when we are not a physical hostage yet face a difficult predicament at work or home, we can still retain personal power and train our mind's eye to focus on the goal we want to achieve. We never have to feel like hostages.

Positive self-esteem is important in helping us to manage ourselves to achieve what we want from life. Using our mind's eye to focus on what is truly important for us will help us then make the right choices in our lives.

Retaining a sense of empowered humility is a sign that someone has positive self-esteem and is self-aware. Humble people understand their position in life and have a healthy perspective on how they fit into the total universe.

When we help others, we also help ourselves. By overcoming our fears, becoming risk takers and learning to let go of past losses, we can free ourselves from that which may be holding us back. Accepting responsibility for our lives, our thoughts, and our feelings is fundamental to living with a hostage-free state of mind.

Living in the present, in the moment, and having an appreciation and a gratitude for life will help us to be in the flow—those moments when everything comes together in an interconnected fashion. We operate with a sense of Zen-like calm, and we have a strength, wisdom, and power that exudes from our bodies, intellects, emotions, and spirits. When we are in flow, we are fulfilled and at one with our being.

Being happy is about choice. Happiness is a state of mind, a level of consciousness, and a degree of acceptance. As we have seen, our mind's eye can choose to remember or project events in either a positive or a negative way. Our brain is hardwired for danger in order to ensure our survival. However, we can override this natural drift toward the negative and choose to be positive. We have to learn that happiness is not dependent on external factors, things outside our control. Happiness is a choice we can make today, no matter what the circumstance or situation.

Recognizing what we have to be grateful for is one way of maintaining a state of humility and happiness. We can be happy simply because we are alive. Ultimately, happiness is a choice, and it is good for us. Relationships can work for and against us in terms of health and happiness. Married people live longer. People with pets are happier and tend to live longer. There is a positive correlation between stress and heart disease. People who have an optimistic view of life live longer. People in good physical shape are better equipped to deal with stress. A full and rewarding personal life nourishes the body, mind, emotions, and spirit.

Take the time to reclaim yourself and decide to be who you want to be. Live life as an adventure, a journey, and view it as an opportunity to learn, to contribute, to grow every minute, every hour, every day. Accept the tremendous power that is within you, and, with humility, make the choices that you want in order to enable your life to be fulfilling with a hostage-free state of mind.

Key Points to Remember

1. Self-esteem evolves throughout our lives. There are ways to boost your self-esteem at any stage of life. Use your mind's eye to override pain for the benefit of the goal.

2. Continuous lifelong learning is a powerful strategy for expanding our minds and lives. Always seek challenge, do something that takes you out of your comfort zone, and learn something new so that you are constantly growing and developing.

3. The best way to achieve high goals is to seek a challenge that matches or slightly exceeds our skills. This allows us to reach a state of flow in which, through practice and discipline, the uncomfortable becomes the enjoyable.

4. We can help ourselves and others by using personal power, making choices, and maintaining a state of humility.

NOTES

Chapter One

1. Joseph Chilton Pearce, *Magical Child: Rediscovering Nature's Plan for Our Children* (New York: Dutton, 1977).
2. Paul MacLean, *The Triune Brain in Evolution* (New York: Plenum Press, 1990).
3. MacLean, *The Triune Brain in Evolution.*
4. Daniel Goleman, *Working with Emotional Intelligence* (New York: Bantam, 1998), pp. 375–376.
5. Robert W. Schrauf and Julia Sanchez, "The Preponderance of Negative Emotion Words in the Emotion Lexicon: A Cross-Generational and Cross-Linguistic Study." *Journal of Multilingual & Multicultural Development,* 2004, *25*(2/3).
6. Lao Tzu, *The Tao of Power,* trans. R. L. Wing (New York: Doubleday, 1985).
7. Martin Seligman, *Helplessness: On Depression, Development, and Death* (San Francisco: W. H. Freeman, 1975); and S. Sauter, J. Hurrell Jr., and C. Cooper (Eds.), *Job Control and Worker Health* (New York: Wiley, 1989).
8. Christopher Peterson, Steven F. Maier, Martin Seligman, *Learned Helplessness: A Theory for the Age of Personal Control* (Oxford: Oxford University Press, 1993).
9. I. I. Pavlov, *Conditioned Reflexes,* trans. G. V. Anrep (London: Oxford University Press, 1927).
10. Seligman, *Helplessness,* p. 18.
11. Michael J. McMains and Wayman C. Mullins, *Crisis Negotiations: Managing Critical Incidents and Hostage Situations in Law Enforcement and Corrections,* 2nd ed. (Cincinnati: Anderson, 2001), pp. 165–183.
12. S. Karpman, "Fairy Tales and Script Drama Analysis," *Transactional Analysis Bulletin, 7*(26), 39–43.

13. Scott Parks, "Critics Target Tactics Used on Civilian Suspects," *The Dallas Morning News,* September 26, 1999.

14. Shaila Dewan and Laurie Goodstein, "Hostage's Past May Have Helped Win Captor's Trust," *The New York Times,* March 16, 2005; and CBS News, "Police Praise Atlanta Hostage," Atlanta, March 13, 2005, available at www.cbsnews.com/stories/2005/03/13/national/main 679802.shtml.

15. Fatima Meer, *Higher Than Hope: The Authorized Biography of Nelson Mandela* (New York: Harper & Row, 1988), pt. 4, ch. 30.

Chapter Two

1. Stephen Breen, "Swimmer's Charity Atlantic Crossing," *The Scotsman,* July 15, 1998.

2. Michael J. McMains and Wayman C. Mullins, *Crisis Negotiations: Managing Critical Incidents and Hostage Situations in Law Enforcement and Corrections,* 2nd ed. (Cincinnati: Anderson, 2001).

3. Eric Berne, *Transactional Analysis in Psychotherapy* (New York: Grove Press, 1961), p. 13.

4. Michael Specter, "The Long Ride: How Did Lance Armstrong Manage the Greatest Comeback in Sports History?" *The New Yorker,* July 15, 2002, pp. 48–58; and Lance Armstrong with Sally Jenkins, *It's Not About the Bike: My Journey Back to Life* (New York: Penguin Putnam, 2000), p. 88.

5. Associated Press, "Lottery Winner's Life Far from Idyllic," *The Billings Gazette,* December 14, 2004. Retrieved from www.billingsgazette.com/index .php?display=rednews/2004/12/14/build/nation/50-winners-life.inc.

6. Daniel Goleman, Richard Boyatzis, and Annie McKee, *Primal Leadership* (Boston: Harvard Business School Press, 2002), p. 30.

7. G. W. Domhoff, *Senoi Dream Theory: Myth, Scientific Method, and the Dreamwork Movement* (2003). Retrieved September 19, 2005, from www.dreamresearch.net/Library/senoi.html.

8. Goleman, Boyatzis, and McKee, *Primal Leadership.*

9. Aaron N. Sardell and Steven J. Trierweiler, "Disclosing the Cancer Diagnosis: Procedures That Influence Patient Hopefulness," *Cancer,* 1993, *72,* 3355–3365.

10. Hippocrates, *Works,* trans. W.H.S. Jones and others (Cambridge, Mass.: Harvard University Press, 1984), Precepts, p. 319.

11. Eric Berne, *What Do You Say After You Say Hello? The Psychology of Human Destiny* (New York: Grove Press, 1972).

12. Peter Senge, *The Fifth Discipline: The Art & Practice of the Learning Organization* (London: Random House, 1990), p. 9.

13. Warren Bennis, *On Becoming a Leader* (New York: Perseus Books, 1989), p. 3.

Chapter Three

1. Bill George, *Authentic Leadership: Rediscovering the Secrets to Creating Value* (San Francisco: Jossey-Bass, 2003), p. 23.
2. Joseph Chilton Pearce, *Magical Child: Rediscovering Nature's Plan for Our Children* (New York: Dutton, 1977), p. 72.
3. John Bowlby, *Attachment and Loss, Vol. 1: Attachment* (New York: Basic Books and Hogarth Press, 1969).
4. J. Cassidy and P. R. Shaver (eds.), *Handbook of Attachment: Theory, Research, and Clinical Applications* (New York: Guilford, 1999).
5. Inge Bretherton, "The Origins of Attachment Theory: John Bowlby and Mary Ainsworth," *Developmental Psychology*, 1992, *28*, 759–775.
6. Gallup Study, "Poll Reveals Germans Are Just Working to Live," January 21, 2004. Available at www.dw-world.de/dw/article/0,1564, 1094681,00.html.
7. Gallup Study, 2004.
8. Elisabeth Kübler-Ross, *On Death and Dying* (London: Tavistock, 1970); and Stephen Levine, *Healing into Life and Death: A Gradual Awakening* (New York: Doubleday, 1989).
9. James Lynch, *The Broken Heart: The Medical Consequences of Loneliness* (New York: Basic Books, 1977).
10. James Lynch, *A Cry Unheard: New Insights into the Medical Consequences of Loneliness* (Baltimore: Bancroft Press, 2000).
11. Silvano Arieti and Jules Bemporad, *Severe and Mild Depression: The Psychotherapeutic Approach* (New York: Basic Books, 1978).
12. Lynch, *A Cry Unheard*.
13. William Bridges, *Managing Transitions: Making the Most of Change*, 2nd ed. (Cambridge, MA: De Capo Press).

Chapter Four

1. Jamie Andrew, *Life and Limb: A True Story of Tragedy and Survival* (London: Portrait, 2003).
2. John Bowlby, *A Secure Base: Clinical Applications of Attachment Therapy* (London: Tavistock/Routledge, 1988), p. 11.
3. Bowlby, *A Secure Base*, p. 11.
4. John Bowlby, *The Making and Breaking of Affectional Bonds* (London: Tavistock Publications, 1979), p. 104.
5. Mortimer Feinberg and John J. Tarrant, *Why Smart People Do Dumb Things* (New York: Simon & Schuster, 1995).
6. John Bowlby, *Attachment and Loss, Vol. 2: Separation: Anxiety and Anger* (New York: Basic Books, 1973).
7. M. Ainsworth, M. C. Blehar, E. Waters, and S. Wall, *Patterns of Attachment: A Psychological Study of the Strange Situation* (Hillsdale, NJ: Erlbaum, 1978); Harry F. Harlow, "The Nature of Love," *The American*

Psychologist, 3, 673–685; and M. Mahler, *The Psychological Birth of the Infant* (New York: Basic Books, 1975).

8. Robert S. Weiss, "Attachment in Adult Life." In C. M. Parkes and J. Stevenson-Hinde (eds.), *The Place of Attachment in Human Behavior* (New York: Basic Books, 1982), pp. 171–184.

9. Weiss, "Attachment in Adult Life."

10. Bowlby, *A Secure Base.*

11. John Bowlby, *Attachment and Loss, Vol. 1: Attachment* (New York: Basic Books and Hogarth Press, 1969).

12. Joseph Chilton Pearce, *Magical Child: Rediscovering Nature's Plan for Our Children* (New York: Dutton, 1977).

13. Various versions of this saying are attributed to Einstein, although the exact wording and source are not known.

14. Bowlby, *The Making and Breaking of Affectional Bonds,* p. 104.

15. "How Attachment Discoveries Help in Marriage and Other Love Relationships." Available at www.helpguide.org/mental/love_relationship_advice_adult_attachment_help.htm.

16. Mukul Pandya, Robbie Shell, Susan Warner, Sandeep Junnarkar, and Jeffrey Brown, *Nightly Business Report Presents Lasting Leadership: What You Can Learn from the Top 25 Business People of our Times* (Upper Saddle River, NJ: Wharton School Publishing, 2005).

17. Diane L. Coutu, "Putting Leaders on the Couch: A Conversation with Manfred F.R. Kets de Vries," *Harvard Business Review, 82*(1): 64–71, 113.

18. Richard Branson, *Losing My Virginity. How I've Survived, Had Fun, and Made a Fortune Doing Business My Way* (London: Virgin, 1998).

19. James W. Prescott, "Affectional Bonding for the Prevention of Violent Behaviors: Neurobiological, Psychological and Religious/ Spiritual Determinants." In L. J. Hertzberg and others (eds.), *Violent Behavior Vol. I: Assessment and Intervention* (New York: PMA Publishing, 1990), pp. 110–142.

20. Bill George, *Authentic Leadership: Rediscovering the Secrets to Creating Value* (San Francisco: Jossey-Bass, 2003), p. 31.

21. For a good read on self-esteem, see Nathaniel Branden, *Self-Esteem at Work: How Confident People Make Powerful Companies* (San Francisco, Jossey-Bass, 1998.)

22. R. Gilligan, "Adversity, Resilience and Young People: The Protective Value of Positive School and Spare Time Experiences," *Children and Society, 2000, 14*(1), 37–47.

23. American Psychological Association, "The Road to Resilience: 10 Ways to Build Resilience," 2004. Available at www.apahelpcenter.org/featuredtopics/feature.php?id=6&ch=4.

24. Carl Brashear, U.S. Naval Institute oral history interview, conducted November 17, 1989, at the U.S. Naval Station, Norfolk, quoted at www.chasingthefrog.com/reelfaces/menofhonor.php.

25. American Psychological Association, "The Road to Resilience: 10 Ways to Build Resilience."

Chapter Five

1. Peter Senge, *The Fifth Discipline: The Art & Practice of the Learning Organization* (London: Random House, 1990), p. 249.

2. Salon, "Crazy Love: James Carville and Mary Matalin, America's Oddest Couple, Offer Their Reflections on Valentine's Day." Available at www.salon.com/feb97/carville970212.html.

3. Brother David Steindl-Rast, *Gratefulness, The Heart of Prayer: An Approach to Life in Fullness,* (Mahwah, NJ: Paulist Press, 1984).

4. Bob Bapes, "Coaching the Terrorist on Your Team." Available at www.presentation-pointers.com/showarticle.asp?articleid=222.

5. Dana Muriel, "Brave Teacher Stopped Gun Rampage." *CNN.com/ World.* April 27, 2002, Posted at 2:49 P.M. EDT. Available at http:// archives.cnn.com/2002/WORLD/europe/04/27/germany.shooting.

6. Hans Toch, *Violent Men: An Inquiry into the Psychology of Violence* (Chicago: Aldine, 1969).

7. Jim Collins, *Good to Great: Why Some Companies Make the Leap . . . and Others Don't* (London: Random House, 2001).

8. Carl. R. Rogers, "The Necessary and Sufficient Conditions of Therapeutic Change," *Journal of Consulting and Clininical Psychology,* 1957, *21,* 95–103.

9. Roger Fisher and Scott Brown, *Getting Together: Building Relationships as We Negotiate* (New York: Penguin, 1988).

10. W. Donohue and W. Kolt, *Managing Interpersonal Conflict* (Newbury Park, CA: Sage, 1992).

11. Eric Berne, *What Do You Say after You Say Hello?* (New York: Grove, 1972).

12. D. Balz, "Blair Meets with Sinn Fein at Belfast in Historic Talks." *Washington Post,* October 14, 1997.

Chapter Six

1. William Isaacs, *Dialogue and the Art of Thinking Together* (New York: Currency, 1999), p. 10.

2. Charles Fishman, "The Anarchist's Cookbook," *Fast Company,* 2004, (84), pp. 70–78.

3. James Lynch, *The Language of the Heart: The Human Body in Dialogue* (New York: Basic Books, 1985), p. 10.

4. John Kifner, Ex-Hostages on Kuwait Jet Tell of 6 Days of Sheer Hell, *New York Times,* Dec. 11, 1984.

5. Eric Berne, *Transactional Analysis in Psychotherapy* (New York: Grove Press, 1961).

6. Jacqui Schiff and others, *A Cathexis Reader* (New York: Harper & Row, 1975).

7. Ronald Laing, *The Self and Others* (London: Tavistock, 1961).

8. H. Paul Grice, "Logic and Conversation," in *Syntax and Semantics, Vol. 3, Speech Acts,* ed. Peter Cole and Jerry L. Morgan (New York: Academic Press, 1975), pp. 41–58; Lynch, *The Language of the Heart;* and William Isaacs, *Dialogue and the Art of Thinking Together.*

9. Nandula Wanasekara, "Exam-Oriented Education System Should Be Changed," *Daily News,* Wednesday, November 20, 2002.

10. James Lynch, *The Language of the Heart,* p. 77.

11. James Lynch, *The Language of the Heart.*

12. Y. E. Sokolov, *Perception and the Conditioned Reflex* (New York: MacMillan, 1963).

13. James Lynch, *A Cry Unheard: New Insights into the Medical Consequences of Loneliness* (Baltimore: Bancroft Press, 2000).

14. I. I. Pavlov, *Conditioned Reflexes,* trans. G. V. Anrep (London: Oxford University Press, 1927).

15. James Lynch, *A Cry Unheard,* pp. 198–205.

16. James Lynch, *The Language of the Heart.*

17. James Lynch, *The Language of the Heart,* pp. 140–145.

18. James Lynch, *A Cry Unheard,* p. 217.

19. James W. Pennebaker, *Opening Up: The Healing Power of Expressing Emotions,* revised edition (New York: Guilford Press, 1997).

20. James Lynch, *The Language of the Heart.*

21. John Bowlby, *Attachment and Loss, Vol. 3: Loss: Sadness and Depression* (London: Hogarth Press, 1980).

22. James Lynch, *The Language of the Heart,* pp. 230–240.

23. James Lynch, *The Language of the Heart,* p. 94.

Chapter Seven

1. Susan Dominius, "The Peacemaker of Flight 847." *The New York Times,* December 25, 2005.

2. Roger Fisher and William Ury, *Getting to Yes: Negotiating Agreement Without Giving In* (New York: Penguin, 1983).

3. Roger Fisher and William Ury, *Getting to Yes.*

4. Jean Baptiste Lamarck, *Zoological Philosophy,* trans. Hugh Eliot (New York: Hafner, 1963).

5. Roger Fisher and William Ury, *Getting to Yes.*

6. William Ury, *Getting Past No: Negotiating Your Way from Confrontation to Cooperation* (New York: Bantam, 1993).

7. Robert Cialdini, *Influence: The New Psychology of Modern Persuasion* (New York: Quill, 1984).

8. Napoleon Hill, *Think and Grow Rich Through Persuasion*, Rev. ed. (New York: New American Library, 1992).

9. Robert Cialdini, *Influence: Science and Practice* (Boston: Allyn & Bacon, 2000).

10. Robert Cialdini, *Influence.*

11. Rosabeth Moss Kanter, *Change Masters: Innovation and Entrepreneurship in the American Corporation* (New York: Simon & Schuster, 1985).

Chapter Eight

1. Joseph Chilton Pearce, *Magical Child: Rediscovering Nature's Plan for Our Children* (New York: Dutton, 1977).

2. Antonio Damasio, *The Feeling of What Happens: Body, Emotion and the Making of Consciousness* (Heinemann: London, 1999).

3. BBC Series, *The Human Mind,* presented by Robert Winston, 2004.

4. David Boadella, *Wilhelm Reich: The Evolution of His Work* (Chicago: Vision Press, 1973).

5. Personal conversations with Eva Reich.

6. Stephen M. Johnson, *Character Styles* (New York: W.W. Norton, 1994).

7. David Boadella, *Wilhelm Reich.*

8. William H. Frey, *Crying: The Mystery of Tears* (Minneapolis: Winston Press, 1985).

9. Elisabeth Kübler-Ross, *On Death and Dying* (London: Tavistock, 1970).

10. Personal conversations with Eva Reich.

11. David Boadella, *Wilhelm Reich.*

12. Personal conversation with Daniel Goleman.

13. D. Kupfer and M. Haimowitz, "Therapeutic Interventions, Part 1: Rubberbands Now," *Transactional Aanalysis Journal,* 1971, *1*(H2), 10–16.

14. Fanita English, "The Substitution Factor: Rackets and Real Feelings," *Transactional Analysis Journal,* 1972, *1*(1), Part II.

15. Daniel Goleman, *Emotional Intelligence: Why It Can Matter More Than IQ* (New York: Bantam, 1995), p. 328.

16. Yuichi Shoda, Walter Mischel, and Philip K. Peake, "Predicting Adolescent Cognitive and Self-Regulatory Competencies from Preschool Delay of Gratification," *Developmental Psychology,* 1990, *26*(6), pp. 978–986.

17. M. Scott Peck, *The Road Less Traveled: A New Psychology of Love, Traditional Values and Spiritual Growth* (New York: Simon & Schuster, 1978), p. 19.

18. Cary Cherniss, *The Business Case for Emotional Intelligence,* The Consortium for Research on Emotional Intelligence in Organizations, 2004. Available at www.eiconsortium.org/research/business_case_for_ei.htm.

19. R. Boyatzis, *The Competent Manager: A Model for Effective Performance* (New York: John Wiley, 1982).

20. Edward L. Thorndike, "Intelligence and Its Uses," *Harper's Magazine,* 1920, *140,* 227–235.

21. Daniel Goleman, *Working with Emotional Intelligence* (New York: Bantam, 1998), pp. 375–376.

22. James Lynch, *A Cry Unheard: New Insights into the Medical Consequences of Loneliness* (Baltimore: Bancroft Press, 2000).

23. Roger Dobson and Jonathon Carr-Brown, "Just Look Up to Find Happiness," *The Sunday Times—Britain,* July 24, 2005.

24. Nigel Nicholson, *Executive Instinct: Managing the Human Animal in the Information Age* (New York: Crown Business, 2000).

25. Nigel Nicholson, "How Hardwired Is Human Behavior?," *Harvard Business Review,* 1998, *76*(4), 134–147.

26. Daniel Goleman, *Emotional Intelligence,* pp. 15–32.

27. Daniel Goleman, *Emotional Intelligence;* and Joshua Freedman, *EQ Today,* "Hijacking of the Amygdala: This is what happens in your brain whem you get really mad—or really *anything!*" Available at www.eqtoday.com/archive/hijack.html.

Chapter Nine

1. "Wilma Rudolph (1940–1994)." Available at www.historychannel.com/exhibits/womenhist/?page=rudolph.

2. John Bowlby, *The Making and Breaking of Affectional Bonds* (London: Tavistock, 1979), pp. 103–118.

3. Michael Hebron, *Golf Swing Secrets and Lies: Six Timeless Lessons* (New York: Learning Golf, 1993), retrieved from www.buildfreedom.com/tl/tl04c.html.

4. Eleanor Roosevelt, *This Is My Story* (New York: Harper & Bros., 1937).

5. Viktor Frankl, *Man's Search for Meaning* (London: Hodder & Stoughton, 1959).

6. Jim Collins, *Good to Great: Why Some Companies Make the Leap . . . and Others Don't* (London: Random House, 2001), p. 22.

7. Paul T. P. Wong, "I'm Glad That I'm a Nobody: A Positive Psychology of Humility," International Network on Personal Meaning. Available at www.meaning.ca/articles/presidents_column/humility_nov03.htm.

8. "Ex-NFL Star Tillman Makes 'Ultimate Sacrifice'." Available at www.msnbc.msn.com/id/4815441.

9. Elisabeth Kübler-Ross, *On Death and Dying* (London: Tavistock, 1970).

10. Barry Schwartz, *The Paradox of Choice: How the Culture of Abundance Robs Us of Satisfaction* (New York: HarperCollins, 2004).

11. Isaiah Berlin, "Two Concepts of Liberty," in *Four Essays on Liberty* (London: Oxford University Press, 1969).

12. Barry Schwartz, *The Paradox of Choice.*

13. Mihaly Csikszentmihalyi, *Flow: The Psychology of Optimal Experience* (New York: Harper & Row, 1990).

14. Pele, with Robert L. Fish, *Pele: My Life and Beautiful Game* (New York: Doubleday, 1977).

15. Mihaly Csikszentmihalyi, *Flow.*

ACKNOWLEDGMENTS

Without significant contributions from many other people, this book would not have been written. I am especially grateful to Peter Lorange, IMD president, who gave invaluable support, encouragement, and creative ideas from his experience as a prolific writer. I am also deeply indebted to many faculty colleagues at IMD who offered feedback and suggestions when teaching together in executive education programs; especially Preston Bottger, Bala Chakravarthy, Jim Ellert, Kamran Kashani, Peter Killing, Jean-Francois Manzoni, Ulrich Steger, John Walsh, John Ward, and Jack Wood. Andy Boynton, now dean of the Carroll School of Management at Boston College, and Jim Dowd, now senior fellow for executive education at Harvard Business School, both helped me, through their friendship and as colleagues. Petri Lehtivaara, Beverley Lennox, Lindsay McTeague, and Inna Francis from the IMD research and development team made enormous contributions in too many ways to list. Gordon Adler, IMD director of public relations and communication, was always available for support and coaching. Lucie Jannin, my assistant at IMD, continuously offered her generous and competent assistance in many practical ways. My heartfelt thanks to all of you.

I am deeply grateful to the two members of my research and writing team, who helped gather and pull together the ideas presented here. Susan Goldsworthy, using her insight and the depth of her experience as a senior executive, helped write the material and contributed signficantly to this book. Frederic Wieder, over many years, helped research the topics covered in the book and provided great assistance in pulling together the research and ideas with patience and an attention to detail that I greatly admire.

Over the years, in many workshops and training programs, there have been innumerable contributions from organizers and participants alike. The IMD High Performance Leadership Program, an advanced executive development program on leadership for senior executives, provided ideas, examples, and stories that were immensely helpful in writing this book. In particular, I want to thank the coaches, who work side by side with me in delivering this world-class program, for all their input and suggestions: Olle Bovin, Sharon Busse, Duncan Coombe, Joyce Crouch, Susan Goldsworthy, Jean-Pierre Heiniger, Peter Meyers, and Andreas Neumann.

In addition, there have been many outstanding CEOs and senior leaders in organizations in which I have worked; as I conducted executive education it was never clear if I was learning more from them or they from me. Of special note are Joe Forehand, former CEO and now president of Accenture, and Gill Rider, chief executive officer for leadership at Accenture, who included me in the intense and engaging Accenture Leadership Development Program for all their partners. Nick Shreiber, former CEO of Tetra Pak, who spent countless hours leading programs with me for his senior global leaders, always had wonderful insights and suggestions for applications to the real world of business. They all deeply understood the ideas in this book.

This volume would not exist except for the wisdom and brilliance of Warren Bennis, whose personal commitment to this endeavor always inspired me. His knowledge of leaders and leadership seems limitless, and I am deeply grateful for his support and many suggestions as well as for all I have learned from him through his writing and the wonderful dialogues we have shared. I am honored to be a part of the Warren Bennis Book series. I also want to thank Daniel Goleman, William Ury, Peter Senge, and Bill George for their encouragement and their generous sharing of ideas and profound understanding of how to put knowledge into writing.

I also want to thank all my friends and colleagues in the worldwide transactional analysis community, especially the current president of the International Transactional Analysis Association, Jim Allen. Fanita English, Mary Goulding, Muriel James, Fritz Mautsch, Gianpiero Petriglieri, Denton Roberts, Claude Steiner, Alice Stevenson, Francisco Szekely, and Marijke Wusten all made an important contribution.

From many years of working as a police psychologist, I want to thank former Police Chief James Newby of the Dayton, Ohio, Police Department, Sheriff Gary Haines (deceased) of the Montgomery County Sheriff's Department, and former Police Chief Mike D'Amico of the Huber Heights, Ohio, Police Department. I also want to give special recognition to my longtime friend, colleague, and an outstanding hostage negotiator in his own right, Dave Michael (deceased) of the Dayton Police Department; he epitomized from the very beginning of hostage negotiation practice what it means to be a high-performing leader and hostage negotiator. From these gentlemen I learned more than they will ever know.

Lis Pringle, who has worked with me as a friend and colleague for some thirty years conducting workshops and training programs, also provided insight and ideas along the way. She is an outstanding psychologist, and our work together provided many opportunities for exploring ways to help people in the most dire circumstances find their way to a hostage-free state of mind. Tom Post, my lifelong friend, has been there for support and repeated encouragement. The man who knows more about gratitude than any human being I know, Brother David Steindl-Rast, deserves special recognition; I am deeply grateful to know him and to have benefited from his knowledge and encouragement. Without the support of my brother, Fred Kohlrieser, and my sister-in-law, Jan Kohlrieser, I simply could not maintain the level of international involvement that I do; their generosity seems endless. Claude Gaw, my secretary in Dayton, Ohio, and our family friends, Antonella Bruschi, Patty Kelmar, and Karolina Breitenmoser, all gave so much help. I feel endlessly fortunate to have all of these special people in my life.

I want to thank my editor at Jossey-Bass, Neal Maillet, for his constant support, availability, and patience in seeing this book to completion, and to the editing team led by Jeff Wyneken. I also want to express my special appreciation to Robin Fryer, who was my editor when I served as president of the International Transactional Analysis Association; she gave generously of her scholarly editing advice at various stages in the writing of this book. She does extraordinary work and over many years has helped me understand the power of writing and the special skill involved in organizing words well.

I am also grateful to all the hostage negotiators, peacemakers, and high-performing leaders who have participated in the programs I have conducted; their honest feedback and input helped create powerful learning experiences for us all.

Lastly, a very special thank you to my wife, Cinzia, for her love, patience, and willingness to endure the many hours dedicated to writing this book. She is the wind beneath my wings.

GEORGE KOHLRIESER

The Author

GEORGE KOHLRIESER is an organizational and clinical psychologist. He is also a police psychologist and hostage negotiator who focuses on aggression management, hostage negotiations, and leadership in crisis situations. In the course of his work, he has been taken hostage four times—once in a hospital emergency room and three times in homes during domestic violence disputes. Each time, using leadership skills, he successfully negotiated his way out.

He has worked with the police, the military, and humanitarian organizations in such hot spots as Israel, the Palestinian territories, and Croatia both before and after the war, as well as with police departments and police academies in the United States, the Netherlands, Germany, France, and India. In all, his work in leadership, conflict resolution management, and negotiation has spanned some eighty-five countries in North America, South America, eastern and western Europe, the Middle East, Asia, Africa, Australia, and New Zealand.

Kohlrieser is also a professor of leadership and organizational behavior at the International Institute for Management Development, one of the world's leading business schools, and director of its High Performance Leadership Program, a five-day intensive program especially designed for experienced senior executives.

In addition, Kohlrieser is associate clinical professor of psychology at Wright State University in Dayton, Ohio, and an adjunct faculty member at Zagreb University in Croatia.

His research, teaching, and consulting activities, which focus on high-performance leadership and teamwork, conflict management, change management, dialogue and negotiation, coaching, stress management, work-life balance, and personal and professional development, incorporate the lessons he has learned as a psychologist and hostage negotiator.

Kohlrieser is a consultant to global organizations around the world. Accenture, Alcan, Amer Sports, Barclay Global Investors, Cisco, Coca-Cola, Hewlett-Packard, IBM, IFC, Morgan Stanley, Motorola, Nestlé, Nokia, Roche, Sara Lee, Tetra Pak, and Toyota are some of his clients.

An engaging teacher and a highly sought-after motivational speaker for conferences and keynote addresses, Kohlrieser has been a guest on BBC, CNN, ABC, and CBS, as well as numerous radio programs. His work has been featured in the *Wall Street Journal* and other leading newspapers and magazines. "Matters of the Mind," his highly acclaimed radio call-in talk show in the United States, ran for over ten years. This program combined elements to offer help, give information, confront real-life issues, and provide entertainment.

George Kohlrieser completed his doctorate at Ohio State University, where he wrote his dissertation on cardiovascular recovery of law enforcement officials following high-stress situations. In this and other research, he has made significant contributions to our understanding of the roles that self-mastery and social dialogue play in helping leaders sustain high performance.

He is past president of the International Transactional Analysis Association, a nonprofit scientific organization established to investigate and promote the use of transactional analysis in psychotherapy, education, business, and other fields of human interaction.

The author is interested in your questions, comments, and actual or metaphorical hostage experiences. Please visit his Web site at www.hostageatthetable.com.

INDEX

A

Abstraction, 135–136
Abuse, 187, 188
Acceptance: mutual, 114–115; stage of grieving, 51–52, 210; of what cannot be changed, 210
Adams, G., 119
Addiction, 58–59
Adversity: benefits of, 172–174; secure bases and, 67, 88–90, 91; self-esteem and, 208
Afghanistan, 213
Agitation, 184
Agreement, 155, 164
Ahold, 72
Ainsworth, M., 75
Alcoholics Anonymous, 58
Alexithymia, 146
Alice in Wonderland (Carroll), 153
American Psychological Association (APA), 89–90
America's Most Wanted, 163
Amygdala hijack, 5–6, 199–201, 202
Andrew, J., 66–68
Anger: male socialization and, 82; nature of, 186; stage of grief, 49–50
Animal rights conflict, 125
Animal training, 164–165
Antidepressants, 59
Anxious attachment style, 90, 92–93
Apple, 34
Arafat, Y., 118
Arieti, S., 58
Arizona Cardinals, 212, 213
Armstrong, L., 25–26
Arrogance: authority versus, 171; nature of, 211–212; reward power and, 168; self-esteem and, 96, 209, 211–212; style of, 96
Atlantic Ocean swim, 19–20
Attachment: concepts of, 42, 44–47, 64–65; forming new, 52–53; grieving and, 47–56; to jobs, 45–46; loss of, 105; to people and goals, 63, 72–74, 79–87, 170; styles of, 91–96. *See also* Bonding; Bonding cycle; Detachment; Loss
Attachment and Loss (Bowlby), 75
Attachment avoidance, 49, 90
Attachment theory, 42, 69
Attacks, during negotiation, 160–164
Authentic Leadership (George), 41
Authenticity: in conflict management, 114, 121; in dialogue, 129, 131–132, 136; emotional influence and, 194; emotional intelligence and, 4; in negotiation, 8, 131–132, 172
Authority and authority figures: distrust of, 29–30; female, 80–81; influence and, 171; informal, 169–175; rebellion and, 219; as secure bases, 69, 70–71, 75, 80–81
Automatic influence, 178–179

B

Bargaining, 155
Benefits, focus on. *See* Mind's eye; Positive focus
Bennis, W., 35
Berlin, I., 218–219
Berne, E., 25, 32, 73, 117, 132
Best-case scenario, 95
Bidwell, M., 213
Blair, C., 38

Blair, T., 119

Blood pressure, 143, 144, 145, 146, 151, 183

Boadella, D., 180

Boarding school children, 49

Body movement, 194

Bonding: as antidote to powerlessness, 14–16, 17; assessment of, 65; change and, 63–64; concepts of attachment and, 44–47, 64–65; in conflict management, 116–119; defined, 42; in dialogue, 136; energy of, 46–47, 59; in hostage negotiation, 14–16, 43–44, 68–69, 128, 149–150; importance of, 40–42; leadership and, 15–16, 40–41, 62, 64; in negotiation process, 152, 162–163; organizational, 15–16, 61–62; reciprocity and, 165; styles of attachment and, 91–96. *See also* Attachment; Secure bases

Bonding, broken: conflict and, 60, 61–63, 90–91, 102–108, 110–112; manifestations of, 56–63; reasons for, 111–112; violence and, 43, 57–58, 103, 105–108. *See also* Detachment

Bonding cycle: assessment of, 65; breaks in, 56–63; change and, 63; concept of, 40–44; modeled in story, 37–39; overview of, 64–65; secure bases and, 68–69; stages of, 42–56. *See also* Attachment; Grieving; Secure bases; Separation

Boredom, 141

Boundary setting, 186

Bowlby, J., 42, 69, 71, 75, 76, 79, 146

Boyatzis, R., 27, 29

Brain wiring: amygdala hijack and, 5–6, 199–201, 202; attachment styles and, 79; danger orientation and, 28, 35, 70, 201, 222; dialogue and, 136; emotion and, 183; hostage mentality and, 4–6, 18; secure bases and, 79, 83; traumatic events and, 77–78. *See also* Physiology

Branch Davidians, 13–14

Branson, R., 81

Brashear, C., 88–89

Brevity, 139

Bridges, W., 63

British Association for Counseling and Psychotherapy, 194

Broken bonding. *See* Bonding, broken

Broken Heart, The (Lynch), 56

Bureau of Alcohol, Tobacco and Firearms (ATF), 13–14

Burnout, 59–60, 93–94

Burns, G., 52

Business Case for Emotional Intelligence, The (Cherniss), 193

Business leaders: attachment/bonding styles and, 91–96; bonding and, 15–16, 40–41, 62, 64, 83, 90–91; competitive nature of, 3–4; conflict management for, 119–121; humility in, 212; informal authority for, 169–175; listening and, 141–142; mother figures of, 81; as secure bases, 76, 90–91; self-expression by, 35; vision and, 34–35

Business settings. *See* Organizations

C

Cancer diagnosis disclosure, 30

Cardiac-orienting reflex, 143–144, 147, 182–183

Cardiovascular health, 142–146, 222

Caretakers, 93–94

Carroll, L., 153

Carville, J., 102–103

Celebration, 210–211

Challenge, 220

Change: bonding and, 63–64; resistance to, 111, 172–173; risk taking and, 215; selling, 172–174

Character, 191

Charge, emotional, 180–181, 184

Cherniss, C., 193

Chicago Mayor's Youth Foundation, 205

Child development: attachment behavior and, 44, 75–76, 79, 83; secure bases and, 80–85; self-esteem and, 207; separation and, 53

Children, as secure bases, 83–84

Choice: amygdala hijack and, 201; finding freedom through, 217–219, 222; giving people a, 197–198

Cialdini, R., 171–172

Classical conditioning, 9–10, 143

Coercion, 112, 114, 120

Collaboration and cooperation: law of reciprocity and, 165, 167–168; secure bases and, 70, 76, 79, 80–84; win-win attitude and, 101–102, 112

Collins, J., 109, 212

Comfort: attachment and, 44; despair and, 59; people as source of, 58–59, 79; secure bases as source of, 67, 69

Commitment, 61

Communication: in conflict management, 113–114; as source of conflict, 111, 112. See also Dialogue; Listening; Negotiation

Competence: emotional mastery and, 202; goal-related secure bases and, 74, 84–85, 87–88; high self-esteem and, 87–88

Competitiveness, 3–4

Complainers, 95–96

Complex relationships, 76

Compulsive caretaker style, 93–94

Computers, 76, 140

Concessions, 154, 159, 164–168, 174, 175

Conclusion, of negotiation, 155

Confession, 145–146

Conflict: benefits of confronting, 99–102, 122; broken bonding and, 60, 61–63, 90–91, 102–108; complexity-simplicity paradox of, 116; defined, 102; hostile dependent people in, 94; of interests versus needs, 115–116; loss and, 102–105; nature and roots of, 102–105, 122; organizational effectiveness and, 61–62; overview of, 121–122; secure bases and, 90–91; sources of, 110–112

Conflict avoidance, 95, 100, 101, 102, 107–108, 110

Conflict management: art of, 99–122; bonding in, 116–119; in business settings, 119–121; deescalating emotions in, 194–199; dialogue and, 123–148; international examples of, 118–119; overview of, 121–122; principles of, 116–119, 156–157; "putting the fish on the table" approach to, 108–110, 137; relationship dynamics in, 112–115. See also Hostage negotiation; Negotiation

Consensus, 158–159

Consistency, 171

Constraints, 219

Continuous learning, 213–217, 220

Contraction, 51, 182, 185

Contrast effect, 168

Control: loss of, 105; sense of, 221

Cortex, 5, 6, 200

Courage, 214–215

Creative leadership, 62

Credibility, 168

Crying, 50–51, 185–186, 189

Crying: The Mystery of Tears (Frey), 185–186

Csikszentmihalyi, M., 219–220

Cynicism, 4, 8, 91, 95

D

Damasio, A., 178

Danger orientation: brain physiology and, 28, 35, 199–201, 222; secure bases and, 70, 97. See also Fight-or-flight mechanism

Daughters: father relationship and, 82–85; mother relationship and, 81

Dayton Daily, 170

Death: fear of, 53, 216; grieving and, 47, 216; premature, 143, 146

Debating, 126

Deescalation of emotions, 197–199, 201

Defensiveness, 134, 196–197

Delayed gratification, 191–192

Demonizing, 103–104, 117

Denial: detachment and, 146; moving out of, 194; stage of grief, 49

Dependency, 93, 94

Depression: broken bonding and, 59; learned helplessness and, 10; violence and, 57–58, 107

Derickson, U., 149–150

Desire, 190–192

Despair, 48–49, 59

Detachment: burnout and, 59–60; despair and, 48–49; in dialogue, 129–130, 135–136; emotional, 187, 189–190; grief and, 51, 64–65; health and, 146; impact of, 40, 43, 45, 65–66; showing interest versus, 117–118; violence and, 106–107; in workplace, 45–46. *See also* Attachment; Bonding; Bonding, broken; Bonding cycle

Dial, R., 11

Dialogue: analysis of, 132–133; blocks to, 132–137, 147, 189–190, 194–195; bonding in, 136; focused, 154; internal and external, 129–132; nature of, 123–125; negotiation and, 7–9, 128, 130–132, 150–151, 154; organizational bonding and, 61–62; overview of, 146–148; physiological effects of, 142–146; principles of, 139–140; seeking greater truth through, 125–129; unblocking, 137–138, 147. *See also* Negotiation

Differences, types of, 111–112. *See also* Conflict

Direction: clarity of, in negotiation, 153; loss of, 60, 105, 136

Disabled American Veterans, 171–172

Discharge, emotional, 182, 189, 194

Discounting, 133–134, 137–138

Discovery, 125–129

Displacement, 186

Disrespect, 157

Dissociation, 129

Diversity initiative dialogue, 128

Divorce, 52–53

Donohue, W., 115

Dorothy Lane Market, 170

Dress code conflict, 172–173

E

Ego states, 25–27. *See also* Mind states

Einstein, A., 79

Emotion: awareness of, 129–132; cycle of, 180–184; dealing with, 194–197, 202; deescalation of, 197–199, 201; defined, 178; escalation of, 194–197; mood and, 194, 207; motivation and, 190–192, 202; nature of, 178–180; in needs conflicts, 116; overview of, 201–203; physiology of, 178, 180–190, 194, 199–201; rationality and, 112–113, 126–127, 178–179; stages of, 180–184, 202; types of, 184–187; ways of experiencing, 187–190

Emotional expression: bonding and, 44–45; in conflict management, 118; in dialogue, 129–132; in grieving, 50–51, 57; health and, 146; importance of, 183–184; overemphasis of, 135; patterns of, 187–190; verbal expression and, 126–127

Emotional intelligence (EQ): in business leaders, 3–4; business value of, 192–193, 202; competencies of, 193; defined, 193

Emotional management: father-daughter relationship and, 83; father-son relationship and, 82; mind-sets and, 176–178; secure bases and, 82, 83, 91; techniques of, 194–197

Emotional system, of the brain, 5–6

Empathy, 193

Enemies, transforming, 103–104, 117, 214

Enron, 72

Escalation and deescalation, 194–199, 201

Etzel, M., 106

Evaluating, as a listening skill, 141

Executive Instinct (Nicholson), 199

Expansion, 182

Expectations, 219

Exploratory behavior, 75–76, 90

F

Failure: fear of, 85–87, 91, 192, 209; self-esteem and, 208, 209

Family bonding and dialogue, 58, 140

Father figures, 82–85

Fear: awareness of, 129–130; bonding and, 47; of change, 63; in conflict avoidance, 108; of failure and success, 85–87, 91, 192, 209; focus on, 22; as motivator, 168–169, 192; nature of, 184–185; overcoming, 214–215; as persuasion tool, 168–169; secure bases and, 70; stage of grief, 51

Feedback, 220

Feinberg, M., 72

Female authority figures, 80–81

Fifth Discipline, The (Senge), 101

Fight-or-flight mechanism, 5–6, 70, 186, 196, 199–201. *See also* Danger orientation

Films, 76, 117

Firefighting, 179

"Fish on the table" approach to conflict management, 108–110, 137

Fisher, J., 66, 68

Fisher, R., 152

Fisk University, 204

Fitness-for-duty evaluations, 129–130

Flexibility, emotional, 183

Flow, 183, 219–221, 222

Ford, 34

Forgiveness stage of grief, 54

Four-sentence rule, 138

Frame of reference, 134

France, 2005 riots in, 77

Freedman, J., 199

Freedom: meaning of, 17, 218–219; through choice, 217–219

Freezing, 185, 201

Freud, S., 115

Frey, W. H., 185–186

From the Gut (Welch), 80

Future, loss of, 105

G

Gallup, 45

Gantt, J., 143–144, 146, 182

Gap, The, 217

Gender differences, 50–51, 57

General Electric, 80

Generalizing, 135

George, B., 41, 83–84

Gilligan, R., 88

Goal-corrected partnership, 76

Goals: differences in, 111; emotional motivation and, 190–192; flow and, 220; focus on, in conflict management, 103; focus on, in negotiation, 154, 155, 160; positions versus, 154; as secure bases, 63, 72–74, 84–87, 170. *See also* Mind's eye

Goleman, D., 5, 27, 29, 187, 191, 193, 200, 202

Good to Great (Collins), 109, 212

Gorbachev, M., 103–104

Gossip, 129

Gratification, delayed versus immediate, 191–192, 218

Gratitude: happiness and, 222; self-esteem and, 208; stage of grief, 54

Great Britain, 119

Grice, P., 139

Grief, anticipatory, 52–53, 93, 104–105

Grief, unresolved: in hostage takers, 43; impact of, 47–49, 54–55, 56, 64–65; violence and, 54, 56, 57–58, 68–69, 105–108. *See also* Loss

Grieving: change and, 63; defined, 42; in goal achievement, 85–87; letting go and, 215–217; nature of separation and, 47–49; sadness and, 50–51, 185–186; stages of, 49–56; in workplace, 55, 105. *See also* Loss; Separation

Guilt, 48, 63, 216

H

Happiness: choice and, 222; gratitude and, 54; mind's eye and, 22; self-esteem and, 208

Harlow, H. F., 75

Harvard Negotiation Project, 152

Harwell, J., 14

Health: dialogue and, 142–146; relationships and, 222. *See also* Psychosomatic illness

Hearst, P., 12

Hebron, M., 209

Heise, R., 106, 107

Hell's Angels, European, 123–124

Help, asking for, 211

High performers: flow of, 183; hostage-free mind-set of, 204–206; positive focus of, 19–22, 29, 35; positive state of mind of, 25–26, 29; visualization techniques of, 33, 34; willingness of, to endure pain, 191

Hill, N., 171

Hippocrates, 30

Hodson, P., 194

Honesty: in conflict management, 114; in dialogue, 136; in negotiation, 169. *See also* Authenticity

Hope, 90

Hormones, 44, 145–146, 183, 199

Hostage: defined, 4; emotional bonding of, 11–14

Hostage, being taken: blocked dialogue and, 137; brain physiology of, 4–6, 18, 199–201, 202; in business organizations, 3–4; conflict avoidance and, 100; by emotions, 5–6, 183–184, 188–189, 199–201; everyday examples of, 2–3; by fear of failure and success, 85–87; mind's eye and, 23–25; overview of, 17–18; powerlessness and, 6–10, 17

Hostage-free mentality: case of, 204–206; components of, 205–223; overview of, 221–223

Hostage mentality: escape mind-set and, 16; powerlessness and, 9–10, 17; Stockholm Syndrome and, 11–14

Hostage negotiation: bonding in, 14–16, 43–44, 68–69, 128, 149–150, 161–162; concession making in, 165, 167; dialogue in, 7–9, 128, 130–131, 140; emotional management in, 181, 182, 184, 187; mind's eye in, 24–25, 77, 103; process of, 152–155; secure base in, 77, 161–162. *See also* Conflict management; Negotiation

Hostage takers: bonding with, 11–14, 43–44, 68–69; burnout in, 60; understanding mind's eye of, 24–25

Hostile dependent style, 94

Hotel reservation conflict, 194–196

Humility, 171, 211–213, 222

Hunter, J., 142

Hypertension, 144, 145, 146

I

IBM, 34

Identity: bonding and, 51; conflict and, 111; loss of, 105

IMD, 70, 99

Immigrants, second- and third-generation, 77

Immune system, 183

Indecisive style, 96

Independent loners, 72, 93, 181, 184

Infant attachment, 44. *See also* Attachment

Influence, 168–174, 194

Informal authority, 169–175

Inner voice, 210

Insecurity: attachment style of, 90, 92–93; as source of conflict, 111

Intellectual intelligence (IQ), 3

Interest, showing, 117–118
Interests: conflict over, 112, 115–116; identifying, in negotiation, 153–154; needs versus, 115–116
Internal representation systems, 75. *See also* Mental models
Interpreting, as a listening skill, 141
Intuition, 179–180, 220
Isaacs, W., 124–125, 139
Israel, 118–119
It's Not About the Bike (Armstrong), 25–26

J

Jackson, S. L., 24
Japanese negotiation style, 158
Jeans, 217
Joy, 7, 59, 186, 208, 210, 220
Judgment, suspending, 103–104

K

Kets De Vries, M., 80–81
Killers, 106–107
Kirk, A., 179
Kolt, W., 115
Koresh, D., 13–14
Kübler-Ross, E., 49, 186, 216
Kuwaiti airline hijacking, 130–132

L

Laing, R. D., 134
Lamarck, J. B., 155
Language of the Heart, The (Lynch), 143
Lao Tzu, 9
Leaders. *See* Business leaders
Learned helplessness, 9–10, 18, 207
Lecomte, B., 19–20
Left brain, 5
Legion of Valor, Silver Cross medal, 150
Letting go, 215–217, 222. *See also* Bonding cycle; Grieving
Level 5 leaders, 212
Levine, S., 49
Life script, 32, 73

Lifelong learning, 213–217
Liking, 171
Limbic system, 5, 183
Listening: active, 140–142, 147, 164; components of, 141; in dialogue, 126, 140–142; exhaustion in, 134; physiological reactions to, 142, 144–145, 147. *See also* Dialogue
Logos, 124
London bombings of 2005, 76–77
Loneliness and isolation: detachment and, 45, 51; goal attachment and, 72; independent loner attachment style and, 72, 93; premature death and, 146; psychosomatic illness and, 56–57, 61; as stressor, 61; violence and, 57–58, 107
Loners, 72, 93, 181, 184
Loss: anticipatory, 52–53, 93, 104–105; conflict and, 102–105; despair and, 59; goal achievement as, 85–87; grief and, 43, 47–56; of job, 54; letting go and, 215–217, 222; of promotion, 55; of secure base, 50, 68–69, 70–71, 85–87, 98; as stressor, 60; of team, 55; types of, 104–105. *See also* Grief, unresolved; Grieving; Separation
Lottery winners, 26–27
Love, 186
Lynch, J., 56, 60, 127, 132, 139, 143, 144, 145, 146, 182, 194

M

Mackey, J., 125
MacLean, P., 4
Magical Child (Pearce), 2, 42, 78
Mahler, M., 75
Malaysian Indians, 28, 214
Mandela, N., 16, 81
Marathon running, 20–21
Maslow, A., 115
Matalin, M., 102–103
McGinnis, D., 213
McKee, A., 27, 29
Meaning, loss of, 105

Mediterranean fishermen, 108
Medtronic, 83
Meerkats, 165
Meetings, 136–137, 138, 166–167
Meier, B., 194
Mellor, K., 134
Memories: emotional, 178–179, 188–189, 200–201; of secure bases, 69, 77–78, 79, 97; self-fulfilling prophecies and, 30–31
Men: bonding and, 57, 93, 146; detachment of, 146; father relationship and, 82; grieving and, 50–51; independent loner style and, 93; mother relationship and, 80–81
Men of Honor, 89
Mental imagery, 32–35
Mental models: feminine, 80–81; masculine, 82–84; secure bases and, 75, 77, 80–84
Mentors, 69, 70–71, 75
Mergers and acquisitions, 64
Middle East conflict, 118–119
Military training, detachment in, 107
Mind-body connection, 78–79, 178, 194. *See also* Brain wiring; Emotion; Physiology; Psychosomatic illness
Mind maps. *See* Mental models
Mind-set: in conflict management, 103–104, 116, 117; in dialogue, 124, 125–129; emotional management and, 176–178; of escape, 16; in negotiation, 152, 155–164; positive, 18; power of, 17; of powerlessness, 7–10, 17
Mind states: influencing, 27–29; power of, 25–27; switching, 27
Mind's eye: in conflict management, 103–104; dynamics of, 21–22; emotional memories and, 178; in emotional overwhelm, 198–199; focusing with, 22–24, 191, 214–215, 221; of high performers, 19–22; influencing others', 27–29, 77; overview of, 35–36; power of,

25–27, 35–36; secure bases and, 77–79; self-fulfilling prophecy and, 29–32; understanding others', 24–25, 161–162; visualizing with, 32–35. *See also* Goals
Mind-state lock, 194
Mischel, W., 191–192
Moloney, D., 15
Monkeys, 165
Mood, 194, 207
Mother figures, 80–81, 205–206
Motivation: choice and, 218; emotion and, 190–192, 202; fear as, 168–169, 192
Mountaineers, 66–68
Mulcahy, A., 140
Murphy (escaped convict), 163

N
Native American pow-wows, 139–140
NBC News, 213
Needs, conflict of interests versus, 115–116
Negative focus: burnout and, 59–60; of complainers, 95–96; mind's eye and, 22–23, 28, 59; self-fulfilling prophecies and, 29–32, 45
Negative secure bases, 76
Negative self-talk, 6–7, 209
Negotiation: bonding in, 152, 162–163; breakthrough, 163–164; defined, 131, 150–151; dialogue and, 7–9, 128, 130–132, 150–151, 154; overview of, 174–175; positive approach to, 155–164; principles of, 155–174; steps in, 152–155, 163–164. *See also* Conflict management; Dialogue; Hostage negotiation
Negotiator, The, 24
Neocortex, 5, 6
New York Times, 149
New Yorker, 25
Newbury (escaped convict), 163
Nichols, B., 14–15, 24
Nichols, C., 25
Nicholson, N., 199

Nonverbal communication, 46–47, 160
North Dakota State University, 194
Northern Ireland conflict, 119

O

Obstacles, focusing on, 22–23
Olympic gold medalist, 204–206
On Becoming a Leader (Bennis), 35
Options generation, 154
Organizational change, 63–64
Organizational effectiveness, 61–62, 101–102
Organizations: attachment/bonding styles in, 91–96; bonding in, 15–16, 61–62; conflict management in, 119–121; failed, 72; ineffective dialogue in, 136–137; loss and grief in, 55, 105; secure bases in, 90–91
Ornelas, L., 125
Oslo peace accord, 118–119
Ostrich effect, 63–64
Overcompliant people, 95
Over-detailing, 134
Over-generalizing, 135
Overwhelm, emotional, 181, 198–199

P

Pain: desire to avoid, 190, 202; focus on, 22, 35; persuasion with, 168–169; willingness to endure, 172–174, 191–192, 206–207, 218
Palestine, 118–119
Paradox of Choice, The (Schwartz), 217
Parker, B., 11
Parmalat, 72
Passivity, 133, 141, 207, 218
Patience, 159–160, 161
Pavlov, I., 9, 143
Pearce, J. C., 2, 41–42, 78
Peck, M. S., 192
Pele, 220
Pennebaker, J. W., 145–146
People attachments, 63, 72–74, 79–84, 170
Perfectionism, 209

Performance pressure, 183
Person effect, 143–146, 171
Personal care, 90, 210–211
Personal needs, as source of conflict, 112
Personalizing, 16, 117
Perspective, providing, 198–199
Persuasion, in conflict management, 114, 168–174
Pet-a-Pet programs, 146
Pets, 43, 44, 48, 68, 146, 186, 222
Physiology: of dialogue, 142–146; of emotions, 5–6, 178, 180–190, 194, 199–201. *See also* Brain wiring; Psychosomatic illness
Playfulness, 74
Pleasure seeking, 168, 190, 202
Polaroid, 34
Police officers: detachment in, 107; fear in, 129–130
Positions, 154, 196–197
Positive focus: of high performers, 19–22, 35; with mind's eye, 20–24, 191, 214–215; in negotiation, 155–164; self-fulfilling prophesies and, 29–32
Postal, going, 6
Posttraumatic stress disorders, 51
Posture, 147, 194
Powerlessness: bonding as antidote to, 14–16, 17; passivity and, 207; poison of, 6–10, 17; violence and, 57–58, 107
Premature death, 143, 146
Presentations, over-detailing in, 134
Primal Leadership (Goleman, Boyatzis, and McKee), 27, 29
Pringle, L., 170
Procrastination, 96
Promotion: fear of, 85–86; loss of, 55
Protest and anger stage of grief, 49–50
Proximity seeking, 42, 44, 75
Psychosomatic illness: broken bonding and, 56–57, 60; emotional tension and, 181; verbal expression and, 126. *See also* Health; Physiology

Punishment, 168–169
Purpose, loss of, 60, 105
Purpose-Driven Life, The (Warren), 15

Q

Quality and quantity, in dialogue, 139
Questioning: active listening and, 140–142; in hostage negotiation, 128, 140, 144–145, 151; in negotiation, 164; physiological reactions to, 144–145

R

Rabin, Y., 118
Rage, 6. *See also* Anger; Violence
Rationality: emotion and, 112–113, 126–127, 178–179; overemphasis on, 135
Reactive emotion, 187–188
Reagan, R., 103–104
Reason. *See* Rationality
Rebellion, 219
Reciprocity, 164–168, 171–172, 174, 175
Red card game, 137
Redefining, 134
Reich, E., 181, 182, 186
Reich, W., 180, 181
Rejection sensitivity, 93, 209
Relationships: attachment styles and, 92–96; in conflict management, 112–115; dynamics of, 112–115; in negotiation, 162–163; secure bases and, 70, 76, 79, 80–84, 91
Relaxation: in cycle of emotions, 182–183, 186; not same as flow, 220
Relevance, in dialogue, 139
Reliability, in conflict management, 114
Remarriage, 52–53
Reptilian brain, 5, 199
Resilience: building, 89–90; secure bases and, 67, 88–90; self-esteem and, 88
Respect: in conflict management, 101–102, 114–115; in negotiation, 156–157, 164, 174

Responding, as a listening skill, 141
Reward power, 168–169
Right brain, 5
Risk taking, 215, 222
Rivalry, 111
Rogers, C. R., 115
Role confusion, 111
Roosevelt, E., 209
Rubberband emotion, 188–189
Rudolph, B., 204
Rudolph, E., 204
Rudolph, W., 204–206
Rutgers University, 193

S

Sadness: nature of, 185–186; stage of grief, 50–51
St. George's Hospital, 142
Sardell, A. N., 30
Sauter, S., 9–10
Scarcity, 172
Schiff, J., 134
Schrauf, R. W., 7
Schwartz, B., 217, 219
Scott, H., 66
Secure attachment style, 92
Secure bases: assessment of, 97; attachment/bonding styles and, 91–96; business leaders as, 76, 90–91; children as, 83–84; defined, 69; father figures as, 82–85; forms of, 68, 69–70, 75; goals as, 63, 72–74, 84–87, 170; importance of, 66–77; internalization of, 75; lack of, 79, 90–91; loss of, 50, 68–69, 70–71, 85–87, 98; mind states and, 28; mind's eye and, 77–79; mother figures as, 80–81, 205–206; negative, 76; in negotiation, 77, 161–162; overview of, 97–98; people as, 63, 72–74, 79–84, 170; resilience and, 67, 88–90; risk taking and, 215; self-esteem and, 72, 74–75, 87–88, 91. *See also* Bonding; Bonding cycle
Self-awareness: for building self-esteem, 209–210; competency of,

193; dialogue and, 129–132; of emotions, 183

Self-consciousness, 221

Self-discipline, 191–192

Self-disclosure, 91, 136, 145–146

Self-esteem: arrogance and, 96, 209, 211–212; and coping with change, 63; development of, 207, 209–211; high, 87–88, 207–208; humility and, 211, 213, 222; low, 207, 208–209; secure bases and, 72, 74–75, 87–88, 91

Self-expression, and leadership, 35

Self-fulfilling prophecy, 29–32, 45

Self-interference, 209

Self-management, 193

Self-regulation: in high-performance teams, 62, 170; of successful people, 201–202

Self-talk, 6–7, 208, 209, 210

Seligman, M., 9–10

Senge, P., 34, 101

Senoi Indians, 28, 214

Sensing, as a listening skill, 141

Sensory perception, 199–200

Separation: defined, 42; grieving and, 47–49, 53; letting go and, 215–217. See also Grieving; Loss

Separation protest, 76

September 11 terrorist attacks, 146, 213, 217

Sexual feelings, 186–187

Singer, E., 163

Sinn Fein, 119

Skin conductance, 146

Smith, A., 14–15, 24

Smith, D., 72–74

Social network, 211

Social proof, 172

Social skills, 193

Sokolov, Y. E., 143

Son: father relationship and, 82; mother relationship and, 80–81

Spacey, K., 24

Spouses: bonding of, 102–103; as secure bases, 83, 93

Stanford University, 191

Steinhauser, R., 106

Stetham, D., 150

Stockholm Syndrome, 11–14

Stress hormones, 145–146, 183, 199

Stressors, 60–61

Structure, loss of, 105

Substitute emotion, 189–190

Success, fear of, 85–87, 91. See also High performers

Suggs, C., 150

Suicide bombers, 76–77

Swiss hospital, violence management in, 123–124

Symbionese Liberation Army, 12

T

Tagliabue, P., 213

Talking, 126–129, 143–146. See also Dialogue

Tarrant, J. J., 72

Teams: bonding in, 15–16, 61–62, 170; conflict in, 101–102; negotiation in, 166–167

Television, 76, 140

Temper tantrums, 181

Tension, emotional, 181–182, 186

Territory, loss of, 105

Texas prison escapees, 163

Thalamus, 5–6, 199–200, 202

Teresa, Mother, 46

Thinking, 129

Thorndike, E. L., 193

Threats, 168–169

Tillman, P., 212–213

Time outs, 199

Time sense, 221

Timing, 159–160

Tour de France, 25–26

Transactional analysis: ego states in, 25; "I'm OK, you're OK" principle of, 117; life scripts in, 32, 73; technique of, 132–133

Trauma, secure bases and, 77–78. See also War trauma

Trierweiler, S. J., 30

Triggers, 189, 202
Trust: of authority, 29–30; climate of safety and, 119; conflict of needs and, 116; secure bases and, 91, 92–93
Tunnel vision, 221
TWA hijacking, 149–150
Tyco, 72
Type A personalities, 144

U

Uncertainty during periods of change, 63–64
Unconditioned positive regard, 115
Understanding: in conflict management, 113; of other's mind's eye, 24–25, 161–162
U.S. Army, 212–213
U.S. Naval Institute, 89
U.S. Navy, 89
Unlikely Angel (Smith), 14–15
Unresolved grief. *See* Grief, unresolved
Ury, W., 152, 163–164

V

Vacation planning negotiations, 157–158
Values, 111
Victim role, 196, 209
Video games, 76, 140
Violence: disrupted bonding and, 43, 57–58, 103; emotional charge and, 184; father-son relationship and, 82; listening and, 145; loss/grief and, 54, 56, 57–58, 68–69, 105–108; respect and, 156–157; sexual feelings and, 187
Vision, organizational, 34–35
Visual perception, 199–200

Visualization, 32–35, 214, 215
Viva! USA, 125
Voting, 158

W

Waco, Texas, 13–14
War trauma: grieving process and, 51; influencing mental states to prevent, 28
Warren, R., 15
Weiss, R., 75–76
Welch, J., 80, 81
Western culture: absence of bonding in, 58; grief aversion in, 58
Whittaker, J., 26
Whole Foods Market, 125
Why Smart People Do Dumb Things (Feinberg and Tarrant), 72
Wilma Rudolph Foundation, 205
Win-win attitude, 101–102, 112, 155, 157–159
Women: father relationship and, 82–85; mother relationship and, 81
Wong, P.T.P., 212
Wood, G., 45
Words, 126–127
Workaholics, 72–74
Worst-case scenario, 95, 215

X

Xerox, 140

Y

"Yes, but . . . ", 133, 137–138; game of, 138
Youth gang violence, 57

Z

Zone, being in the, 183, 220